Wanda Czełkowska

Wanda Czełkowska

Art Is Not Rest

edited by
Matylda Taszycka

SKIRA

Cover
Wanda Czełkowska,
Theme (*Temat*), 1970–1971,
black-and-white photograph.
Courtesy of the artist's estate

Design
Luigi Fiore

Editorial Coordination
Emma Cavazzini

Copy Editing
Carlotta Santuccio

Layout
Sara Marcon

Iconographical Research
Paola Lamanna

First published in Italy in 2023 by
Skira editore S.p.A.
Palazzo Casati Stampa
via Torino 61
20123 Milano, Italy
www.skira.net

Printed and bound in Italy. First edition

ISBN: 978-88-572-4995-7

Distributed in USA, Canada, Central & South America by ARTBOOK | D.A.P., 75 Broad Street, Suite 630, New York, NY 10004, USA.
Distributed elsewhere in the world by Thames and Hudson Ltd., 181A High Holborn, London WC1V 7QX, United Kingdom.

This book was published
on the occasion of the exhibition
Wanda Czełkowska: Art Is Not Rest
Muzeum Susch
15 July – 26 November 2023

Curated by
Matylda Taszycka

PUBLICATION

Editor
Matylda Taszycka

Managing Editor of the series
Agnieszka Sosnowska

Translations
Sara Noss for *Scriptum*, Rome
(from French into English: Matylda Taszycka and Émilie Bouvard's essays)
Anda McBride (from Polish into English: Antonina Gugała and Agnieszka Tarasiuk's essays)

MUZEUM SUSCH / ART STATIONS FOUNDATION CH

Founder of Muzeum Susch and Chairwoman of Art Stations Foundation CH Board
Grażyna Kulczyk

Chief Financial Officer
Małgorzata Dobak

Curator
Tanja Warring

Curator of Acziun Susch
Joanna Leśnierowska

Curator of Disputaziuns Susch
Agnieszka Sosnowska

Curator of Instituto Susch
Marika Kuźmicz

Advisor
Maciej Chorążak

Producer
Magdalena Adameczek

Creative Content Producer
Helena Lachowicz

Technician
Jan Steffen

Assistant & Receptionist
Brigitte Janikowski

Invigilator
Carlos Goncalves

MUZEUM SUSCH
Surpunt 78
CH-7542 Susch

www.muzeumsusch.ch
info@muzeumsusch.ch

Acknowledgements

Muzeum Susch and the curator would like to thank the following individuals without whom the exhibition and the accompanying publication would not have been possible: Andrzej Szczerski (Director of the National Museum in Kraków) and Ona Winogrodzka (from the artist's estate), lenders to the exhibition, as well as Eléonore Besse, Richard Demarco, Dorota Grubba-Thiede, Antonina Gugała, Maria Hussakowska, Anna Kłosowska (National Museum in Kraków), Tamara Książek, Jagna Lewandowska (Museum of Modern Art in Warsaw), Adam Lockhart (Demarco European Art Foundation), Agata Małodobry (National Museum in Kraków), Kirstie Meehan (National Galleries of Scotland), Jan Michalski (Galeria Zderzak), Terry Ann Newman (Demarco European Art Foundation), Szarota Nowak, Ewa Opałka, Jarosław Pajek (Centre of Polish Sculpture in Orońsko), Maria Pajek (Centre of Polish Sculpture in Orońsko), Tadeusz Rolke, Daria Semegen, Paulina Staszkiewicz, Jan Maria Stokłosa, Agnieszka Tarasiuk, Józef Robakowski, Szymon Rogiński, Monika Sosnowska, Ewa Ziembińska (Królikarnia – Xawery Dunikowski Museum of Sculpture, a division of the National Museum in Warsaw) for their support and help in the research.

Contents

Preface

Wanda Czełkowska was a key figure of the Polish avant-garde whose work has remained unnoticed by art history for much too long. One need only mention that her first extensive retrospective exhibition in her home country was held when the artist was 86 years old. Like many women artists of her generation, she rejected the label "woman artist". By referring to herself as a professional sculptor (not sculptress), she demanded to be treated equally to male artists in a period when structural inequality was significant.

Czełkowska was born in 1930 and graduated as a sculptor from the Academy of Fine Arts in Kraków, where she studied in Jerzy Bandura's studio. The period of her studies (1949–1954) coincided with the years of introduction of the doctrine of socialist realism into art by the communist regime. She was a member of the Second Kraków Group, along with Tadeusz Kantor, Maria Jarema, Erna Rosenstein or Tadeusz Brzozowski, even though she never actively engaged in it. She kept a somewhat distanced and separate position which is emblematic of her entire creative path. In Polish we refer to Czełkowska as *artystka osobna* – an individual artist. Despite the fact that the greater part of her artistic career falls under the communist regime, she believed in the unconditional autonomy of art and always maintained a critical stance towards the political engagement of art.

Her interest in the figurative is evident from her early works. Over time, her approach to sculpture became more conceptual, constantly pushing the boundaries of the traditional notion of sculpture up to its absolute elimination, as in her monumental work *Absolute Elimination of Sculpture as a Notion of Shape* (*Bezwzględne wyeliminowanie rzeźby jako pojęcia kształtu*, 1972).

I am proud and honoured to present at Muzeum Susch the first retrospective of Wanda Czełkowska outside Poland, which provides a comprehensive overview of her artistic career and a thought-provoking narrative highlighting her original contribution to the development of post-war sculpture in Europe. The monograph is yet another chapter in the series initiated by Muzeum Susch dedicated to the rediscovery of women artists who have been neglected by the main discourses and canons of art history.

I would like to thank the exhibition curator and editor of this monograph, Matylda Taszycka, for her research and curatorial investigation in the archive of the artist, and for her efforts to present Czełkowska's oeuvre to an international audience from a fresh perspective. I would like to extend my special thanks to Antonina Gugała, assistant curator of the exhibition, whose queries in the artist's archive and studio allowed us to obtain previously unpublished material.

I would like to express my gratitude to Ona Winogrodzka, the relative of Wanda Czełkowska and representative of her estate, for her valuable support of the project and her determination to preserve and take care of the artist's oeuvre, as well as to create the conditions for curators and researchers to study her work.

I would like to extend special thanks to all private and institutional lenders: the artist's estate and National Museum in Kraków.

I am grateful to all the prominent authors of this monograph for their invaluable voices and expert interpretations which enrich the reception of Czełkowska's work and contribute to greater recognition and understanding of her legacy: Émilie Bouvard, Mathieu Copeland, David Crowley, June Geddes, Amelia Jones, Charlotte Matter, Abigail Solomon-Godeau, Agnieszka Tarasiuk and Sarah Wilson.

Finally, I would like to thank my team – the team of Muzeum Susch – for their commitment in the realization of this complex exhibition project throughout its extended preparation period.

Grażyna Kulczyk
Founder and Chairwoman of the Board of Art Stations Foundation CH

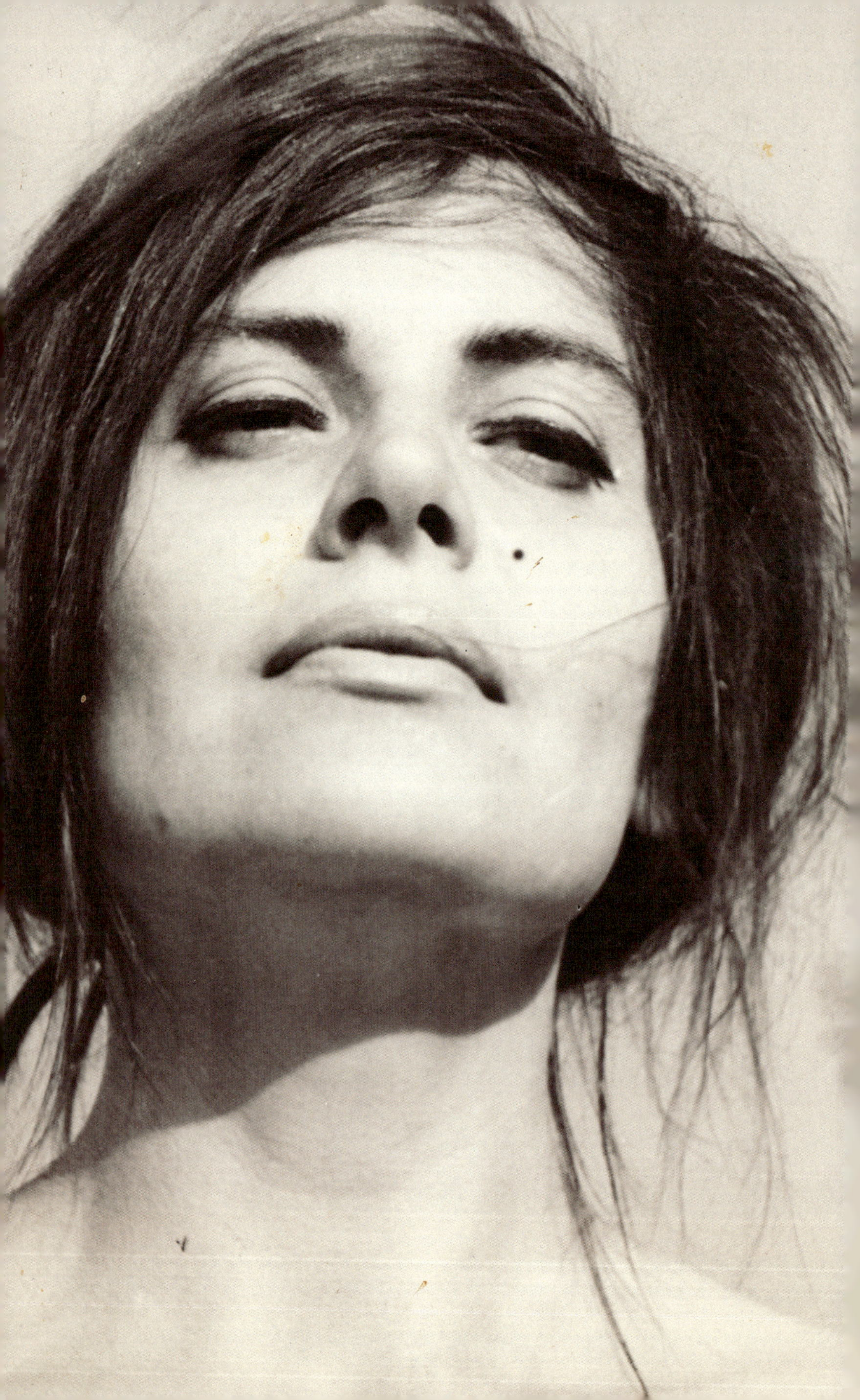

Wanda Czełkowska: Life in Images

Antonina Gugała

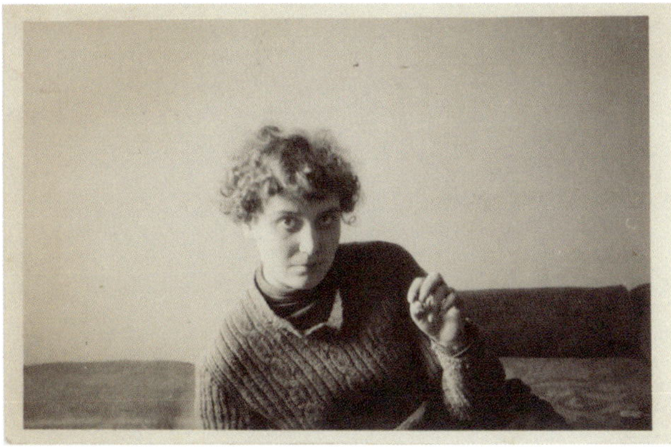

Wanda Czełkowska as a student, 1949–1954

Wanda Czełkowska was born on 28 November 1930 in Brześć nad Bugiem, Poland (since 1945, in Belarus). From an early age she was interested in mathematics and philosophy. While in high school in Olsztyn, she met the renowned artist and charismatic professor Xawery Dunikowski (1875–1964) who made her appreciate art's potential for being a form of studying and expressing one's concepts and reflections, and spurred her to pursue studies in sculpture. Soon afterwards she enrolled at the Academy of Fine Arts in Kraków, where she attended the class of Professor Jerzy Bandura (1915–1987).

▲

Wanda Czełkowska, c. 1970

◀

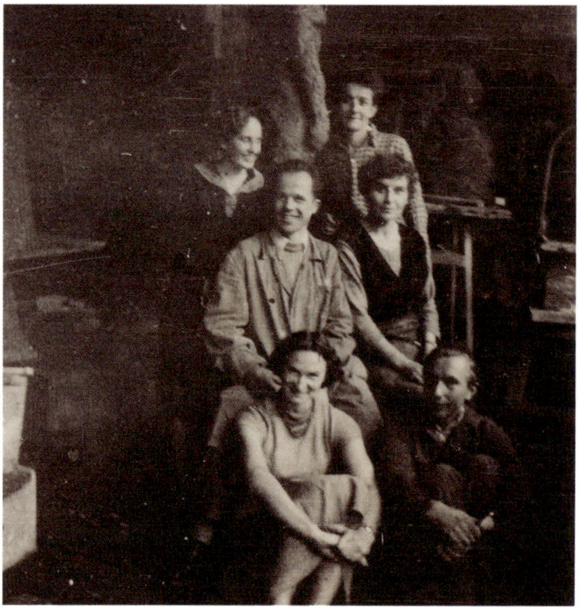

Wanda Czełkowska with fellow students from Professor Bandura's class, Sculpture Department at the Academy of Fine Arts in Kraków, 1949–1954. From top to bottom, left to right: Zofia Wojciechowska, Edward Gorol, Professor Jerzy Bandura, Wanda Czełkowska, Maria Potrzebowska, Marian Nowak

While a student at the Academy of Fine Arts, Czełkowska frequented local libraries and, in between classes, studied French thinkers as well as music theory. Even at this early stage, the artist showed a strikingly cerebral approach towards her practice as a sculptor. Her close social circle at the time included other artists, such as Tadeusz Sieklucki (1925–1994) from Xawery Dunikowski's class and Roman Cieślewicz (1930–1996) from the Faculty of Graphic Arts.

Wanda Czełkowska with her work *Man* (*Mężczyzna*), c. 1956

Czełkowska made this sculpture two years after graduating from the Academy of Fine Arts, in a year that proved critical in the history of the Polish People's Republic, which brought the momentous events of October 1956, or "the thaw". This was a turbulent time of dramatic political changes triggered by the death of Joseph Stalin in 1953, followed by sudden demise of the former Polish President Bolesław Bierut while on official visit in Moscow in March 1956, and the tragic events of the massive workers' revolt in Poznań in June. The year 1956 marked the end of the Stalinist era in Poland, and brought more freedom of expression for Polish artists. Czełkowska's sculpture is often viewed as the artist's ironic commentary on socialist realism as a creative method.

▸

Following pages:
Karmelicka Street in Kraków, 1955–1965
Photo: Marek Piasecki[1] © E. Jogałła, M. Smoczyńska, Courtesy of Archeology of Photography Foundation

"[W]hen I went out into the street I wondered at the human shapes, at the street. It seemed to me that the whole world looked like my sculpture."[2] Undated, from Czełkowska's personal notes.

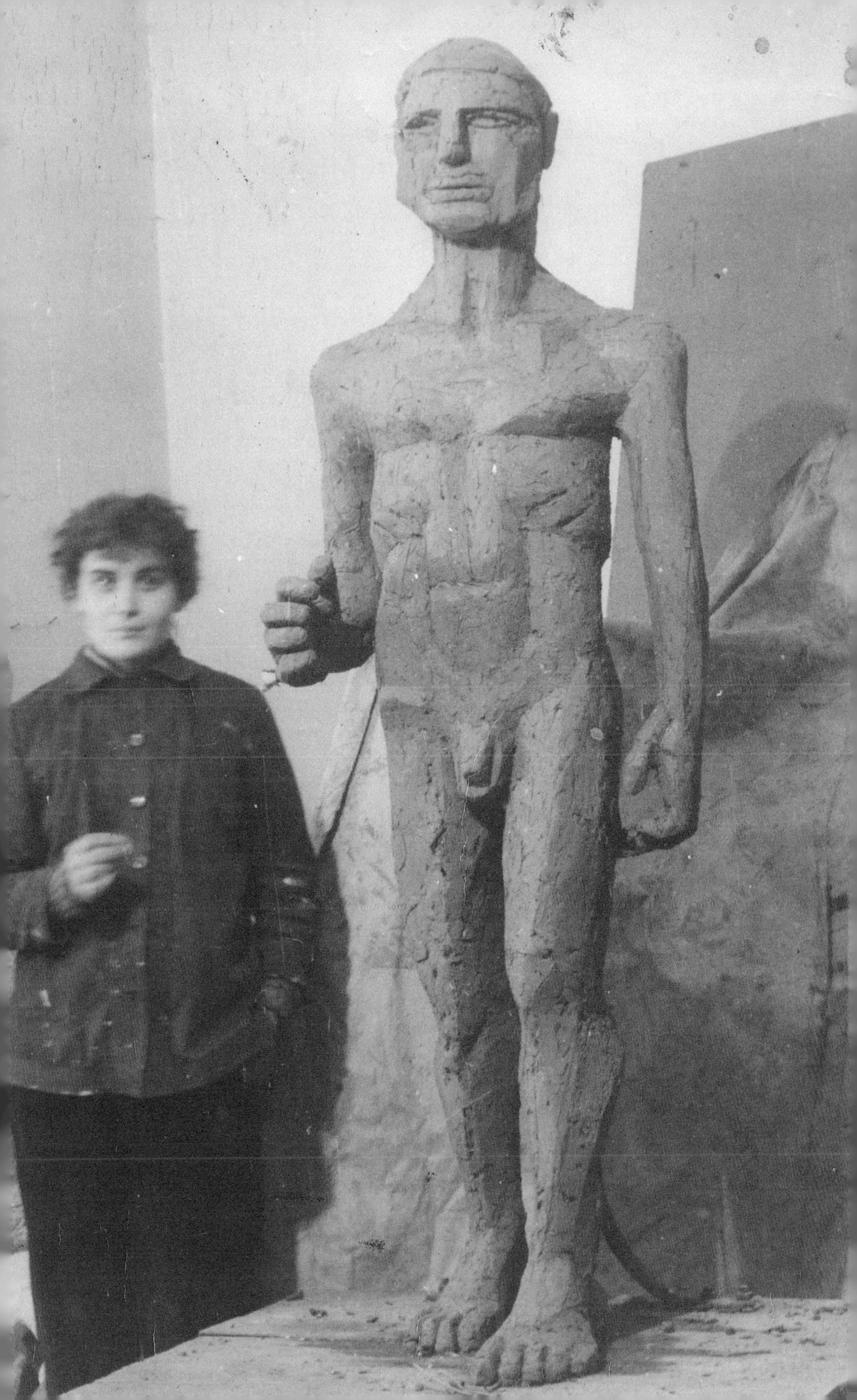

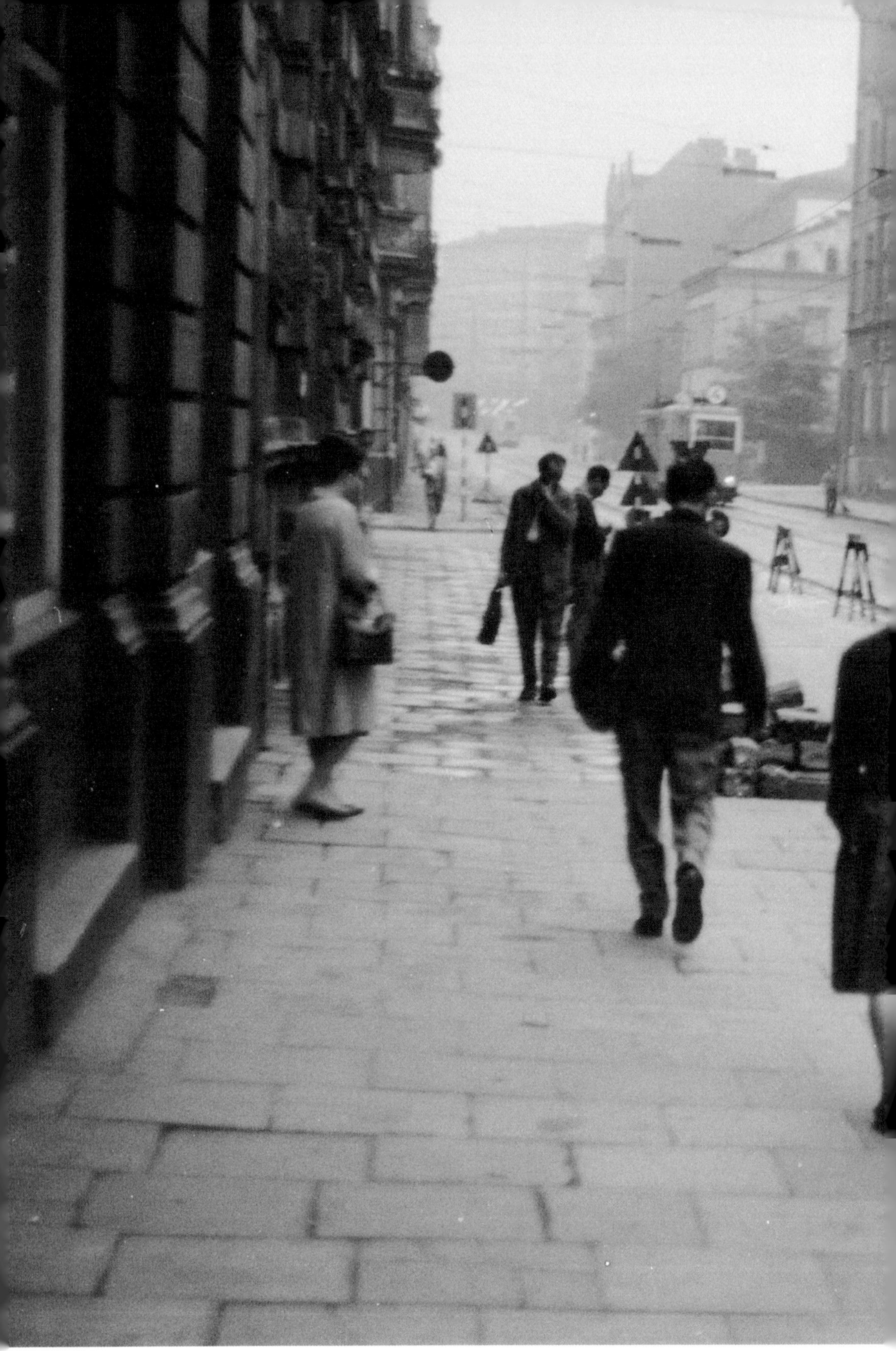

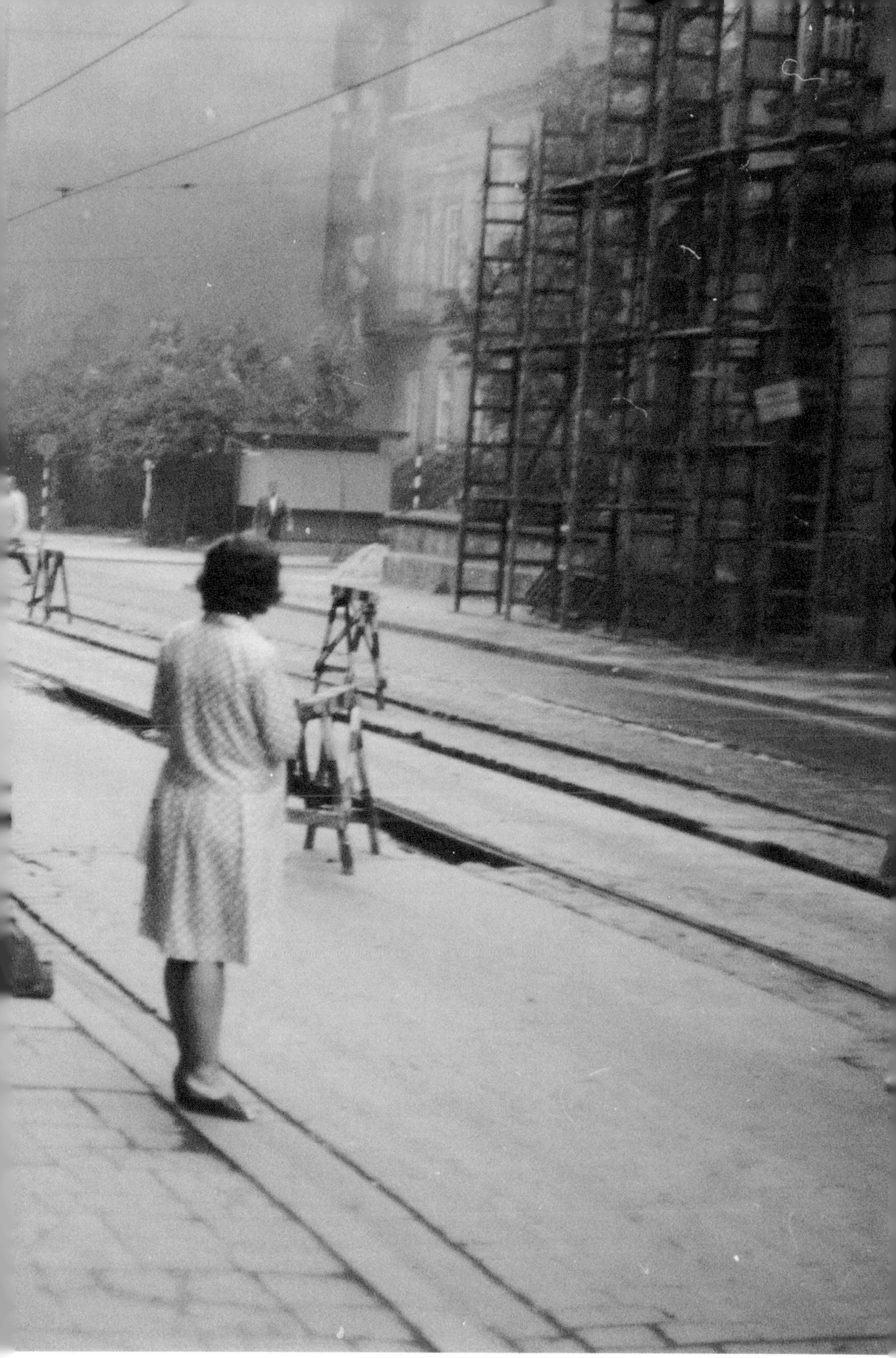

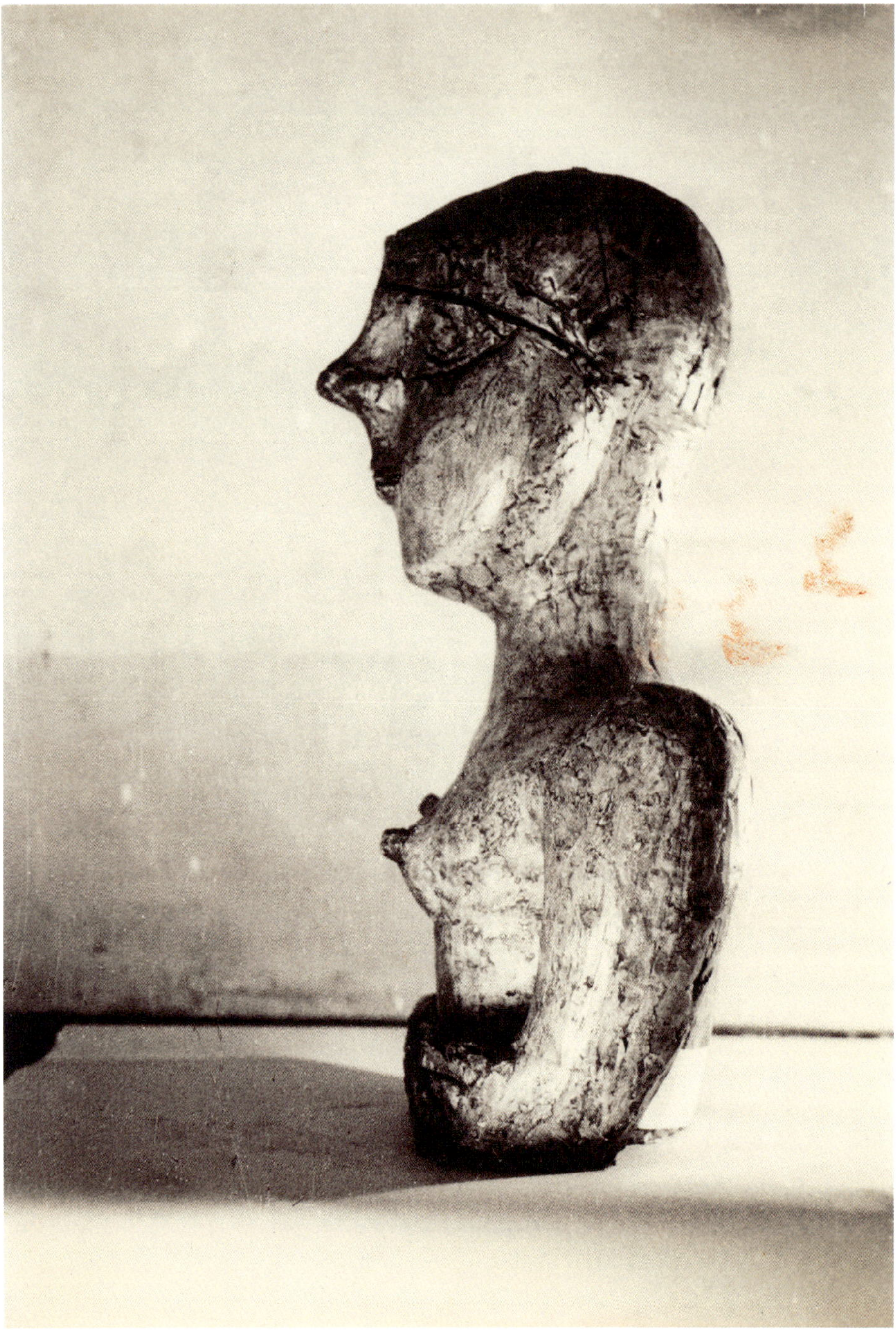

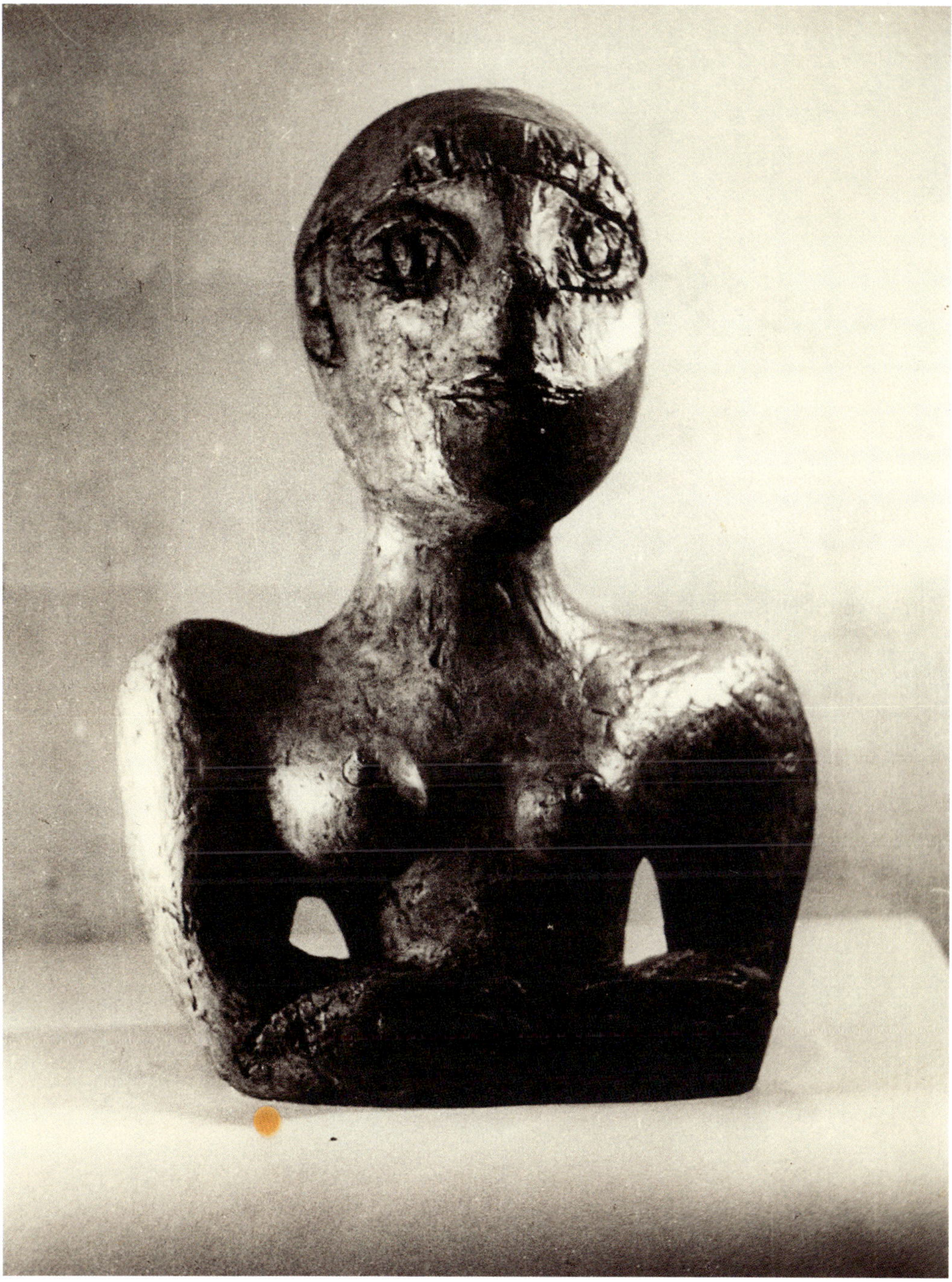

Wanda Czełkowska, *Self-Portrait* (*Autoportret*), 1959, sculpture. Photo: Andrzej Dąbrowski

A nude bust, which inspires a haptic response from the viewer. Etruscan and Minoan cultures are often pointed to as sources of inspiration for the artist's oeuvre of this period. As Czełkowska wrote in a letter to an editor in 1963: "Biographical note – date of birth not given. I was born when I made the first work that I liked. That was four years ago".[3] Today, a bronze cast of the work belongs to the collection of the National Museum in Kraków.

Wanda Czełkowska, *Players* (*Gracze*), 1960–1961.
Photo: c. 1961

First exhibited in 1961 at the National Museum in Warsaw, the large-scale work (193 × 123 × 85 cm) was awarded in two public art competitions. Nevertheless, it was never transformed into an outdoor sculpture. Today in the collection of the National Museum in Kraków, *Players* is also featured in Andrzej Wajda's iconic film *Man of Marble*, 1976.

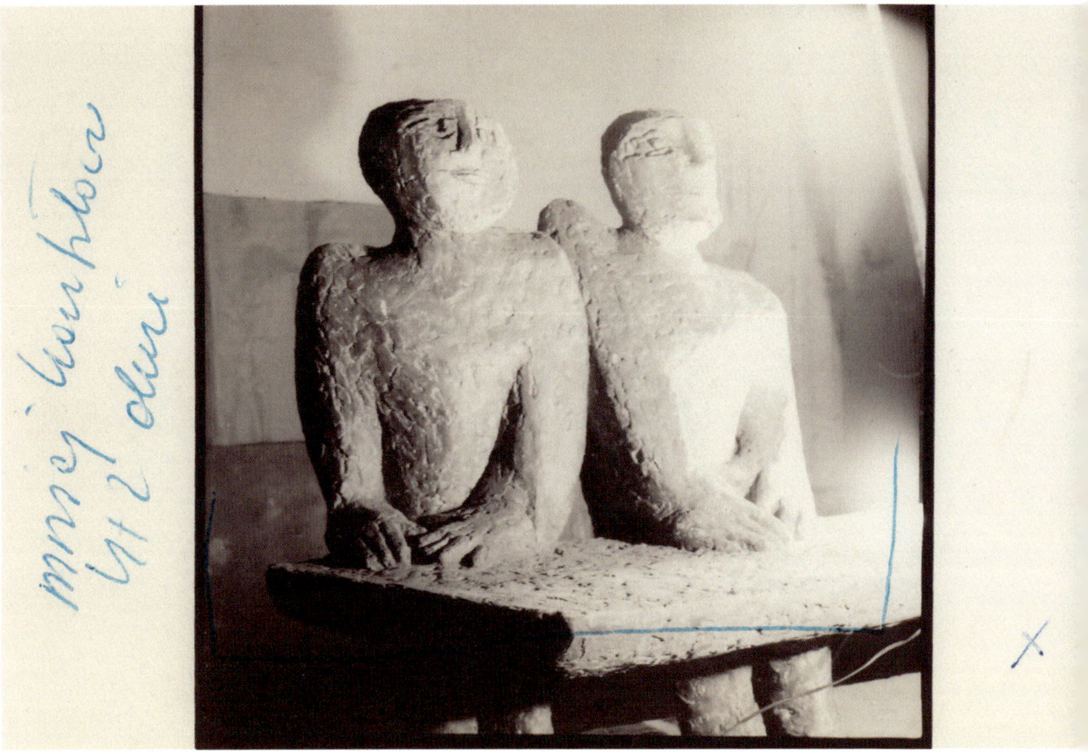

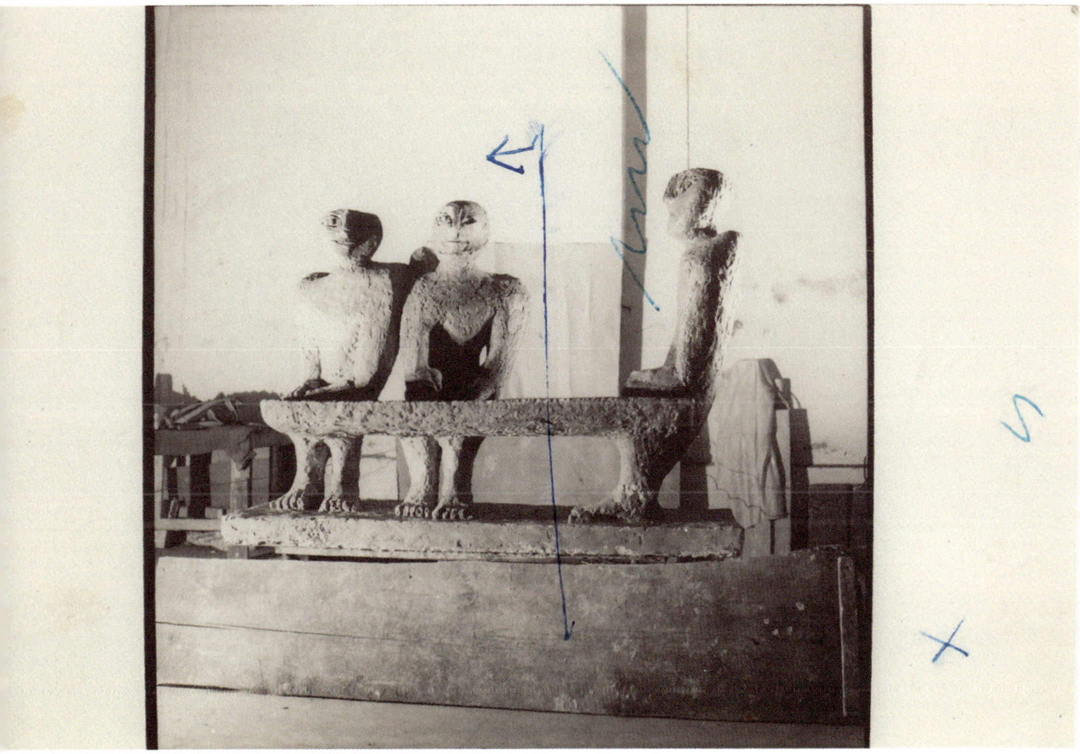

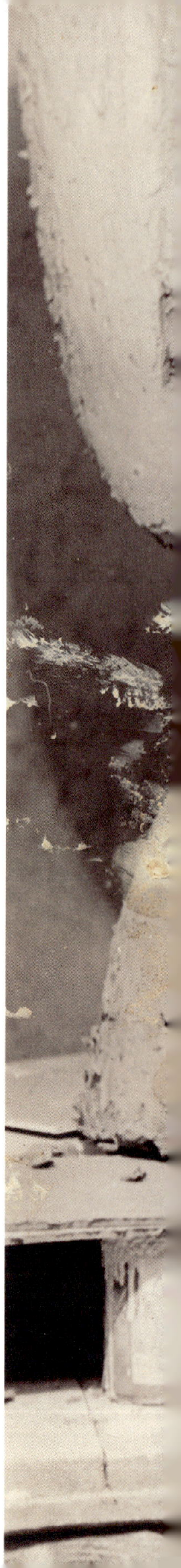

Wanda Czełkowska with *Project for the Monument for Those Who Were Shot Dead* (*Projekt Pomnika rozstrzelanych*), 1962–1963. Photo: c. 1963

Following pages:
Ty i Ja, no. 39, July 1963, 50–51

1963 was an important year for the artist. Czełkowska had her solo exhibition at the Krzysztofory Gallery in Kraków and her work was awarded Best Sculpture of the Year. The artist participated in a number of group shows in Poland and abroad, such as Contemporary Sculpture Exhibition at Madurodam Holland Festival in Hague and the 3rd Paris Biennale '63, where the sculpture *Self-Portrait* (1959) was shown alongside works by Christo, Niki de Saint Phalle, Daniel Spoerri, Peter Blake and David Hockney. On this occasion, Czełkowska was granted a government scholarship, which enabled her to travel to Paris, where she stayed with the artist couple Roman Cieślewicz (1930–1996) and Alina Szapocznikow (1926–1973).

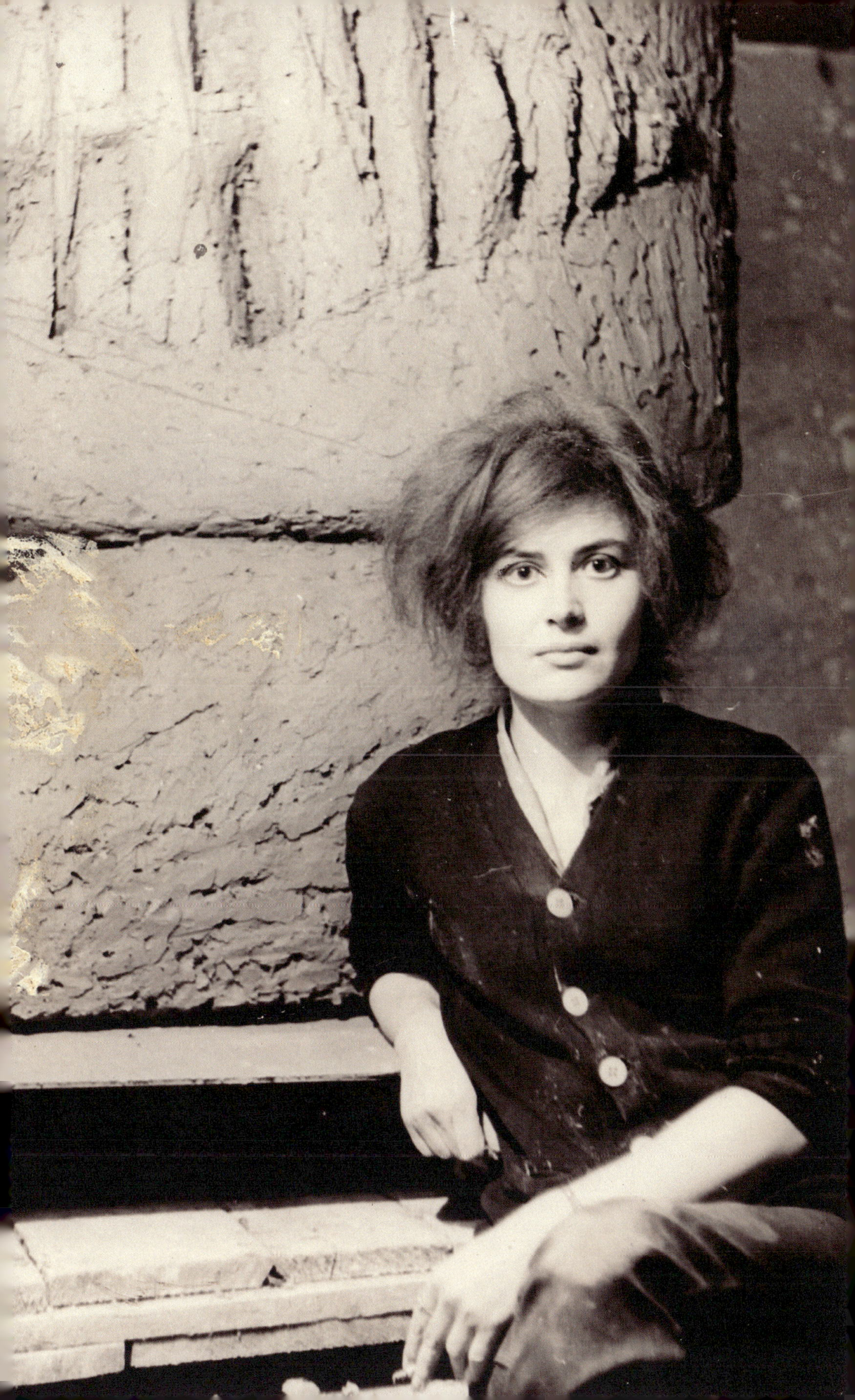

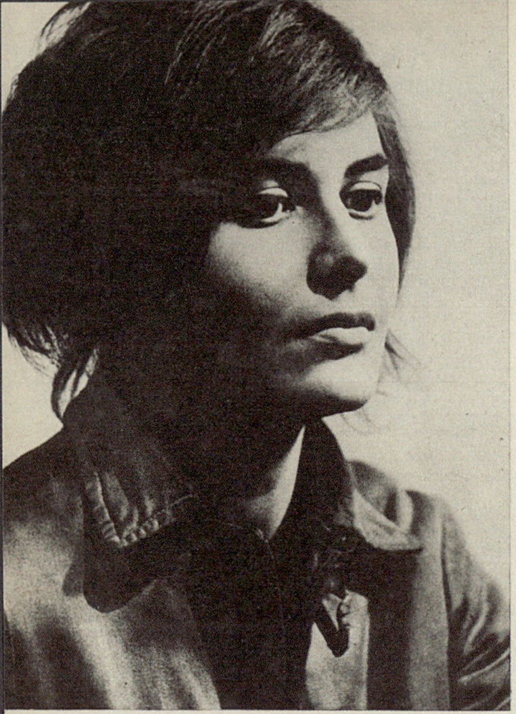

WANDA CZEŁKOWSKA

Daty urodzenia nie podaje. Ukończyła ASP w Krakowie w 1954 r. – absolutorium i dyplom u prof. J. Bandury. Od 1955 r. brała udział w licznych wystawach okręgowych i ogólnopolskich. Za granicą wystawiała w Norwegii w 1958 roku. Pierwsza nagroda i realizacja konkursu na medal 50-lecia ZPAP, 1961. Udział w wystawie Polskie Dzieło Plastyczne Piętnastolecia PRL, Warszawa – 1961/62. Pierwsze miejsce w konkursie na rzeźbę parkową dla Krakowa w 1962 roku (realizacja nie doszła do skutku). Prace w Muzeum Narodowym w Krakowie.

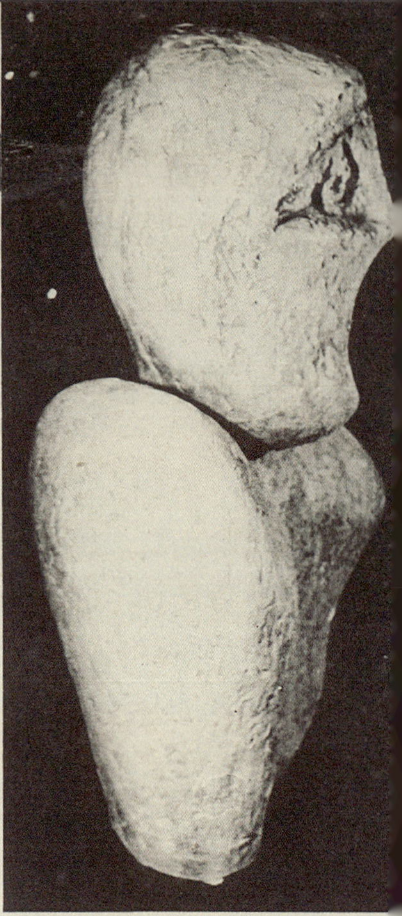

1962

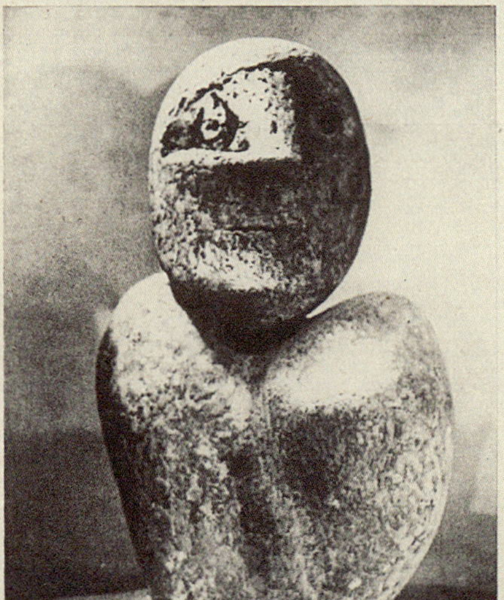

AUTOPORTRET, STYCZEŃ 1960

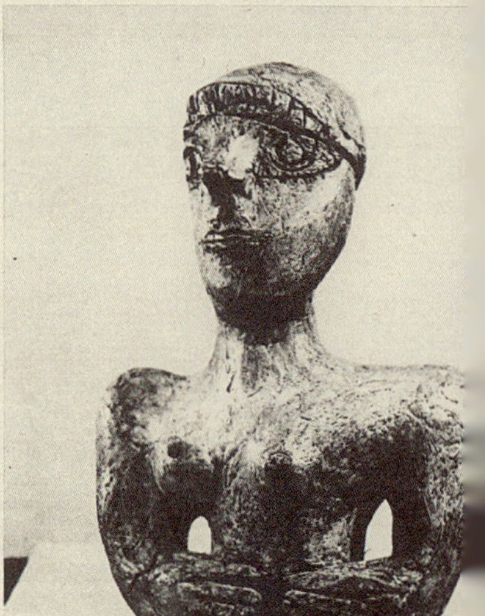

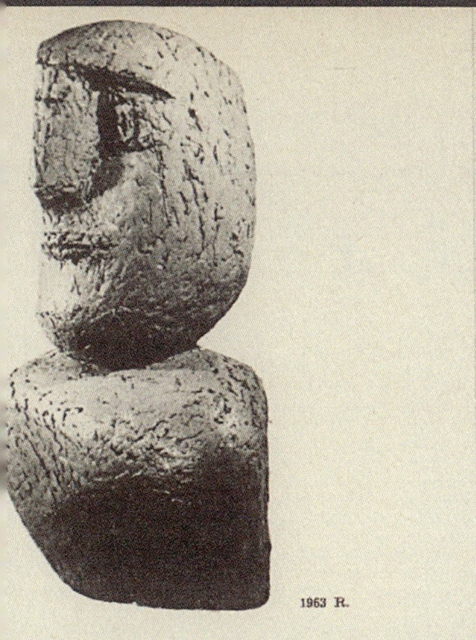

1963 R.

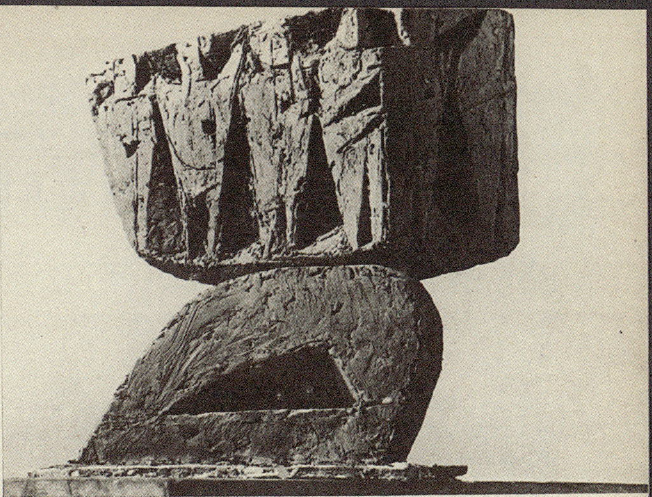

SZKIC DO POMNIKA ROZSTRZELANYCH

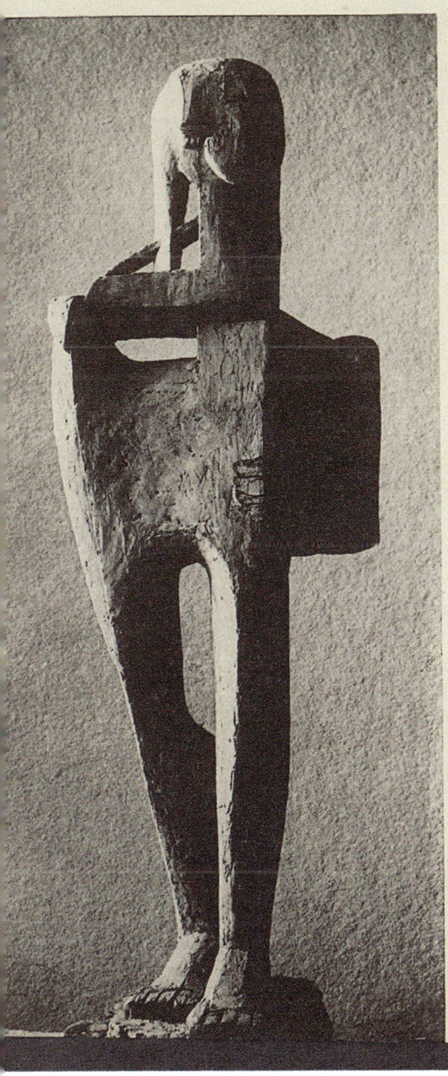

SZKIC DO POMNIKA ROZSTRZELANYCH

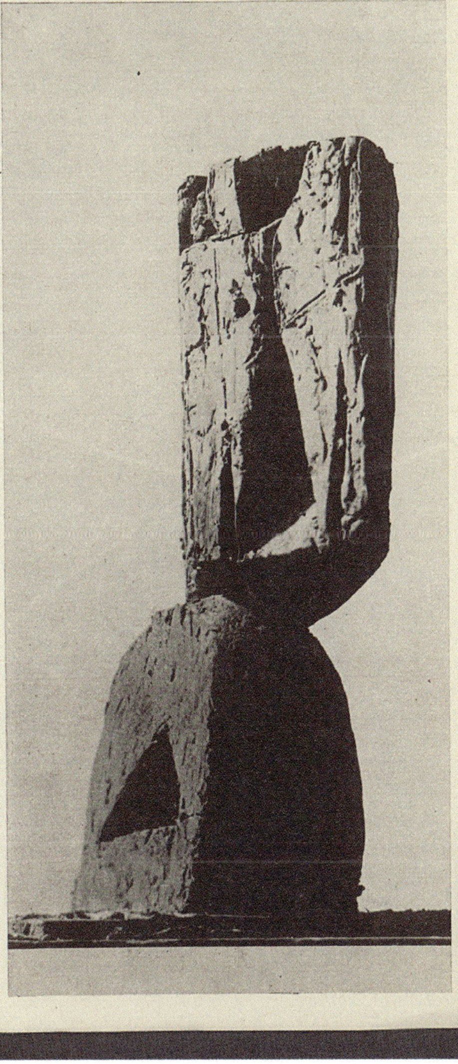

FOTOGRAFOWAŁ
ANDRZEJ DĄBROWSKI

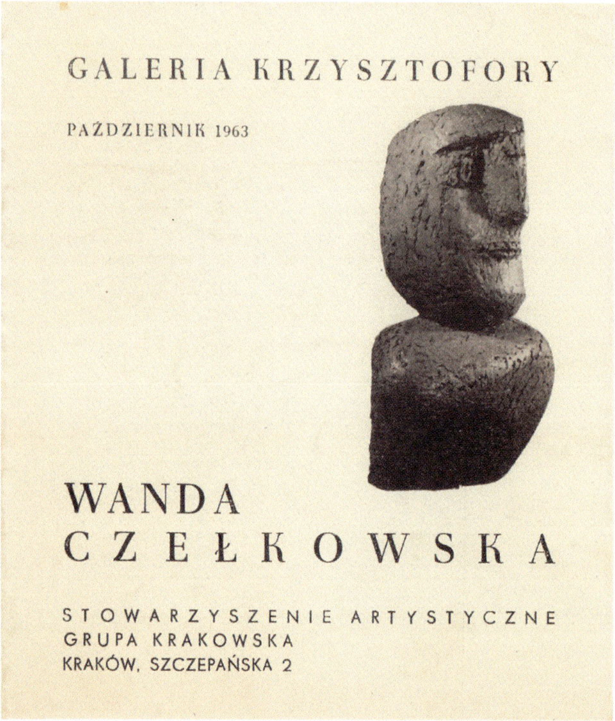

GALERIA KRZYSZTOFORY

PAŹDZIERNIK 1963

WANDA
CZEŁKOWSKA

STOWARZYSZENIE ARTYSTYCZNE
GRUPA KRAKOWSKA
KRAKÓW, SZCZEPAŃSKA 2

Catalogue of Wanda Czełkowska's solo exhibition at the Krzysztofory Gallery in Kraków, 1963

In his curatorial note for the show, art historian and important figure in the Second Kraków Group circle Piotr Krakowski (1925–1997) situates Czełkowska's oeuvre in the contemporary neo-expressionist genre and describes her practice in the following words: "Wanda Czełkowska's body of work is dominated by expression. She does not model clay for the purpose of creating a form in itself – she is interested in its meaning. Form plays merely an auxiliary role. With her sculptures, Czełkowska wants to express mental states and inner conflicts, which are both a central theme and the engine of her art".[4]

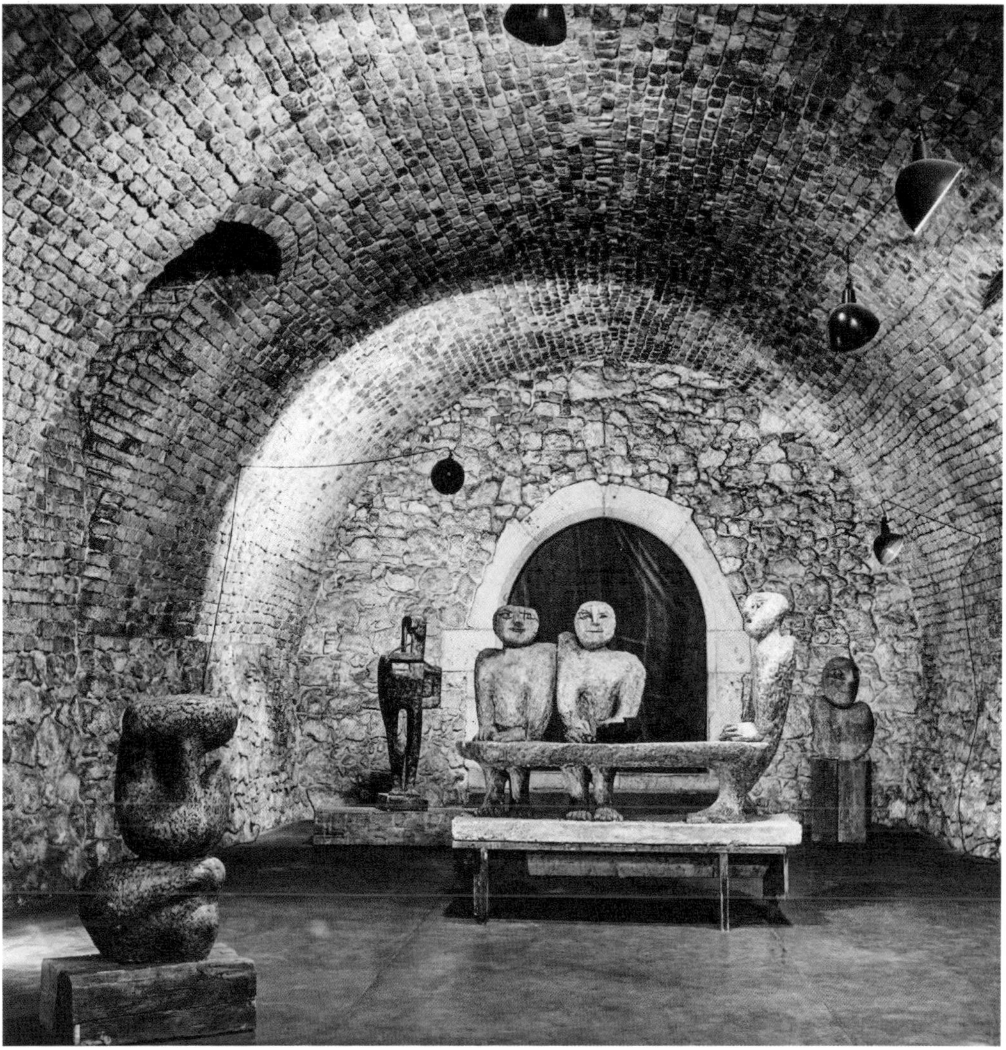

Sculptures at the Wanda Czełkowska solo exhibition at the Krzysztofory Gallery in Kraków, 1963. From left to right: *Head* (*Głowa*), 1962; *The 10th Study* (*Studium X-te*), 1957; *Players* (*Gracze*), 1960–1961; *Pink Head* (*Różowa Głowa*), 1962. Photo: Jacek Maria Stokłosa

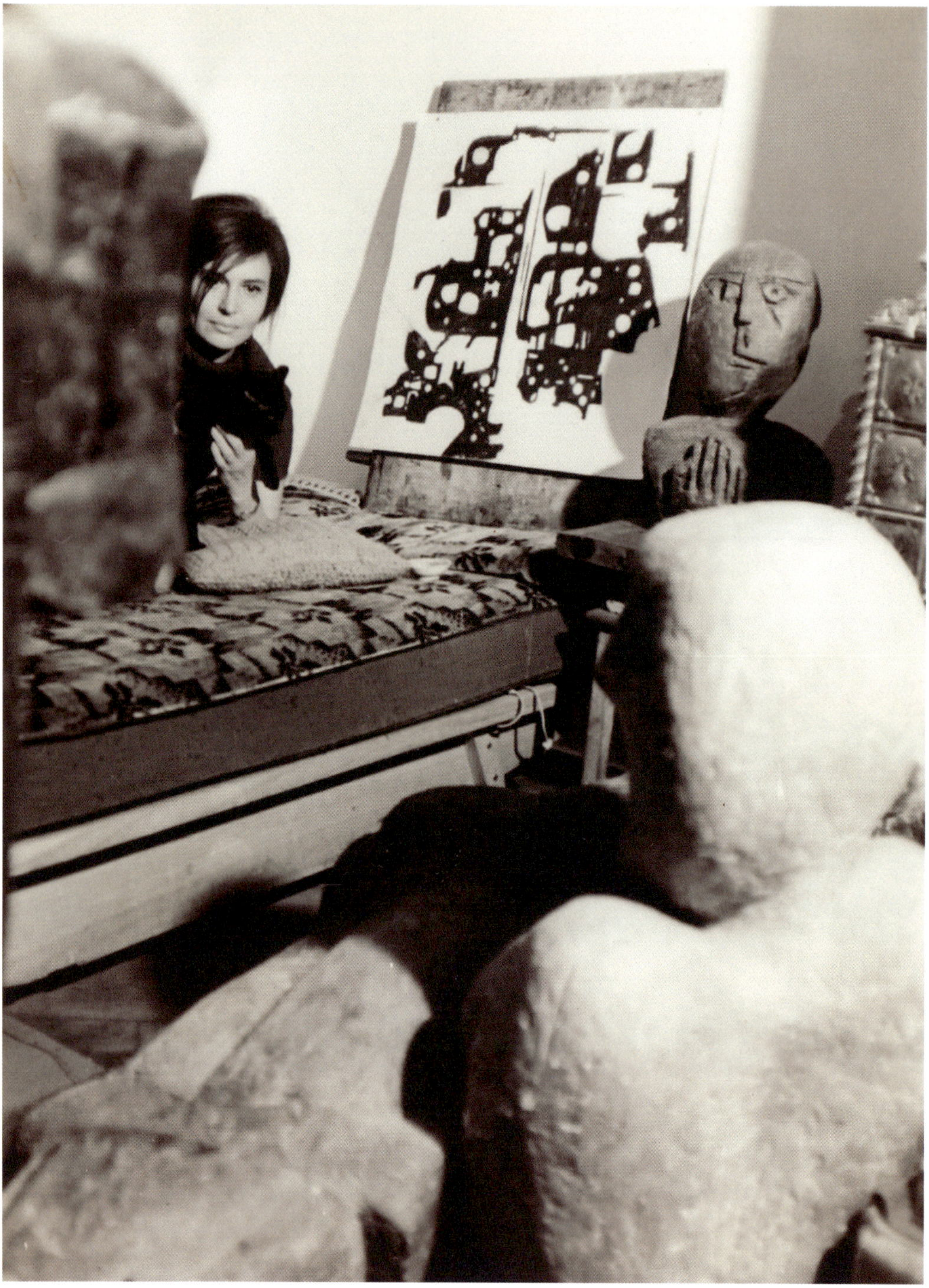

Wanda Czełkowska and her cat, Wacek, in her room at 27 Karmelicka Street in Kraków, c. 1967. Artworks featured in this image include, from left to right: charcoal drawing on filter paper from the series *Construction* (*Konstrukcja*), 1967; sculptures *Man's Head* (*Głowa mężczyzny*), 1957 and *Pink Head* (*Różowa głowa*), 1962. Photo: Wacław Nowak, courtesy of Szarota Nowak

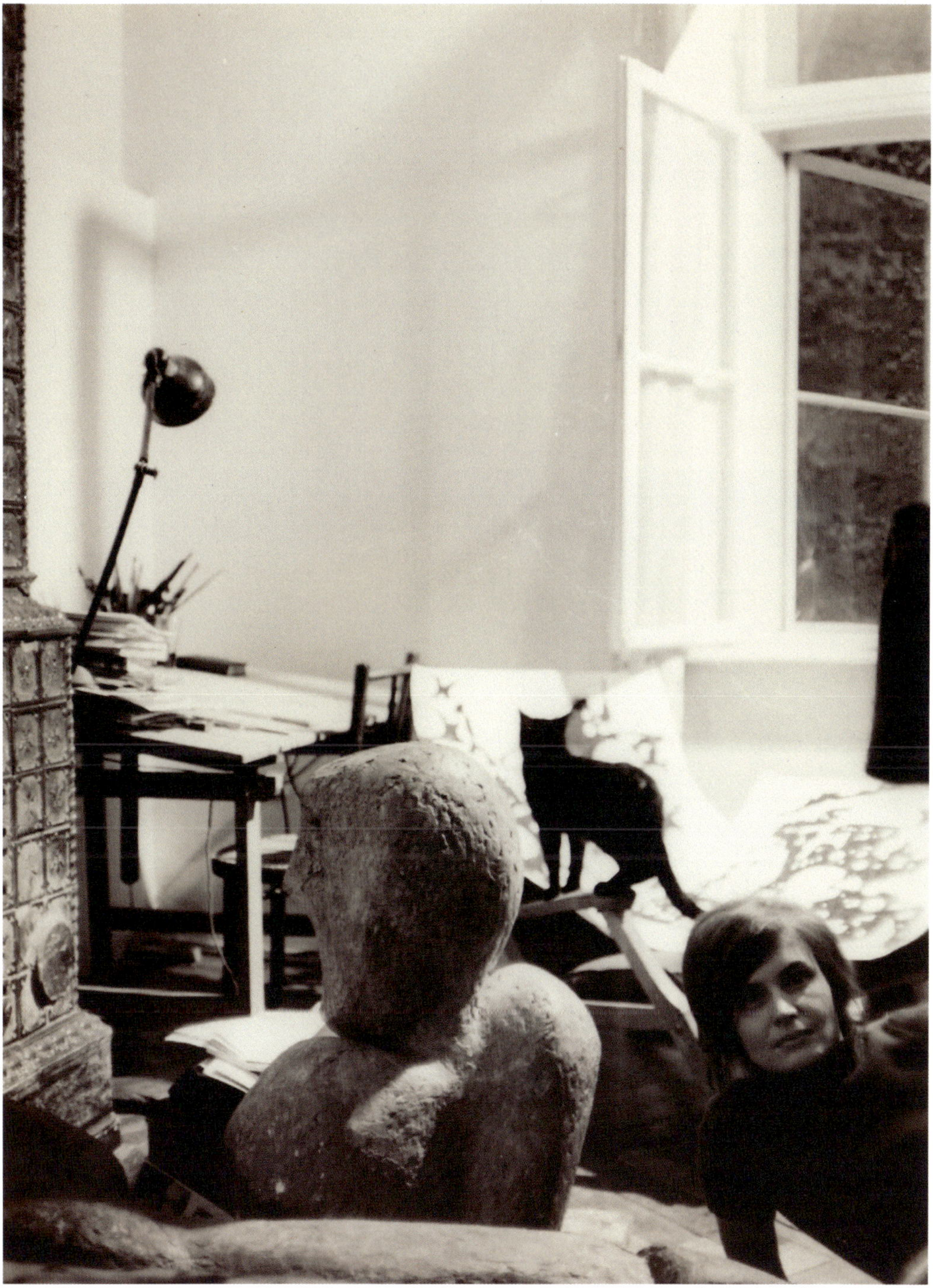

After Czełkowska graduated from the Academy of Fine Arts, she moved into Xawery Dunikowski's apartment on 27 Karmelicka Street. At that point, the renowned sculptor, who had already moved permanently to Warsaw, was persuaded by Czełkowska to transform his Kraków home into shared accommodation for young artists struggling to find a roof over their head after graduation. One of the rooms in the apartment became Czełkowska's home for the next fifty years.[5]

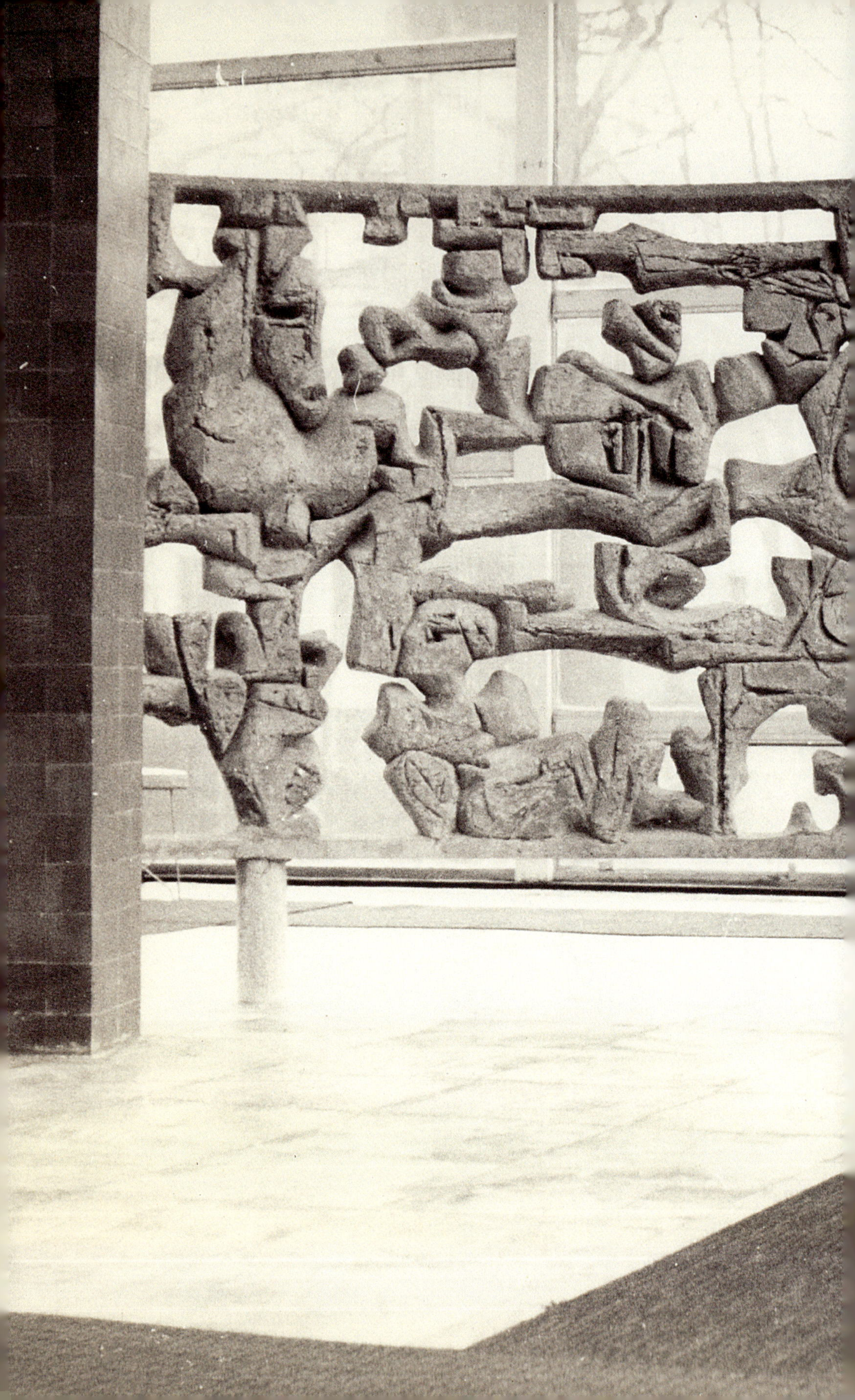

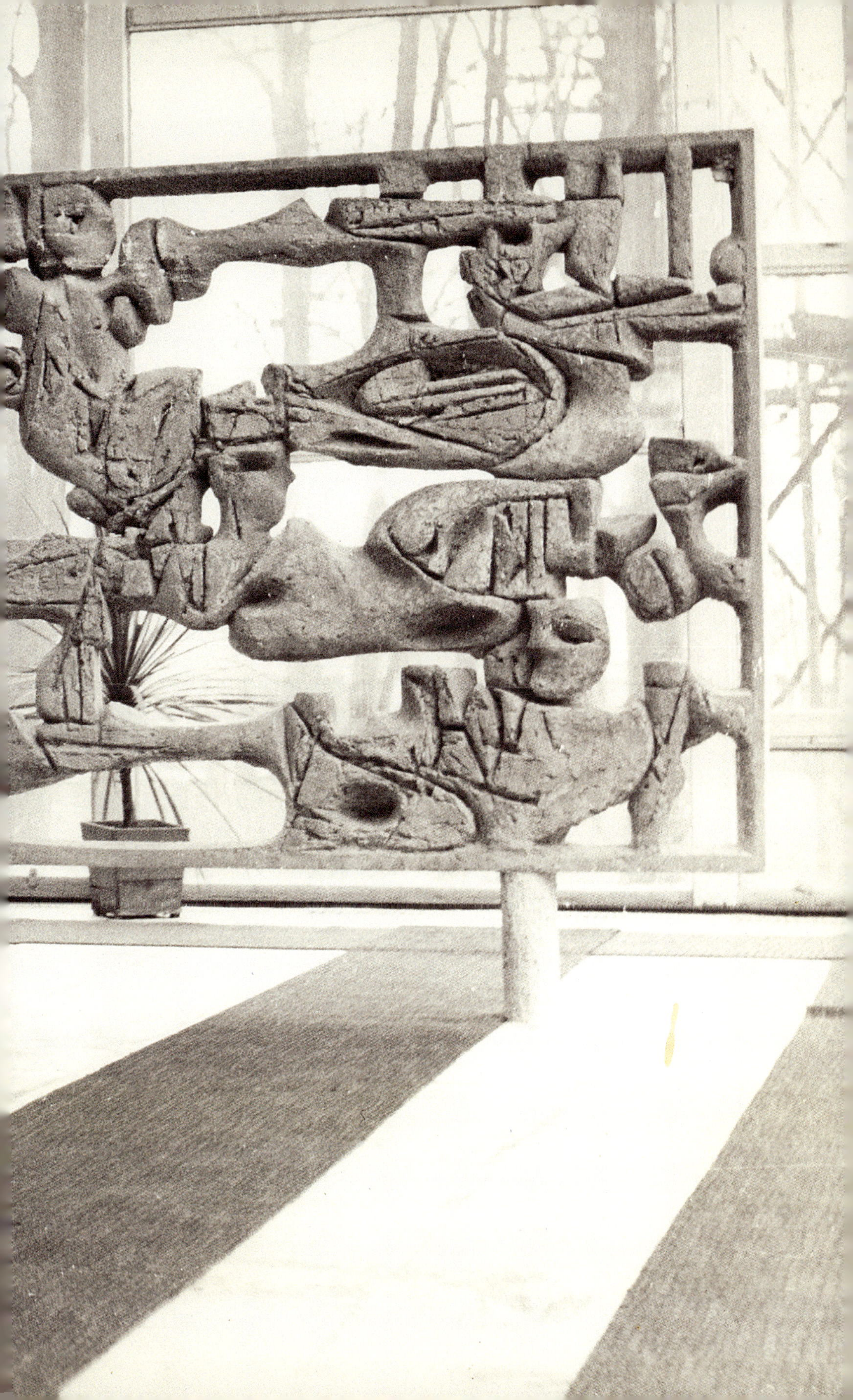

Previous pages:
Wanda Czełkowska, *Untitled*, 1964, 400 × 180 × 12 cm.
Photo: Wacław Nowak, courtesy of Szarota Nowak

Czełkowska made her modest living from art commissions. She dismissed the idea of monument commissions, the most popular type of work for sculptors at the time, and instead focused on designing medals and public sculptures. In 1964, Czełkowska produced a site-specific commission for the Rheumatology Institute in Goczałkowice-Zdrój, a natural health-resort near Kraków. The large-scale sculpture (400 × 180 × 12 cm) did not survive the renovation of the medical centre and today exists only in the form of photographic and written documentation.

Wanda Czełkowska, *Untitled*, 1966, charcoal and tempera on canvas, 90 × 121 cm. Photo: Paulina Staszkiewicz

In her artistic practice Czełkowska moved freely between sculpture, drawing, painting and photography, eventually making the transition to conceptual art, without losing a sense of her individual style, and constantly returning to a few selected motifs. The painting reproduced here is one of some eighty works on canvas remaining at the artist's studio today.

▸

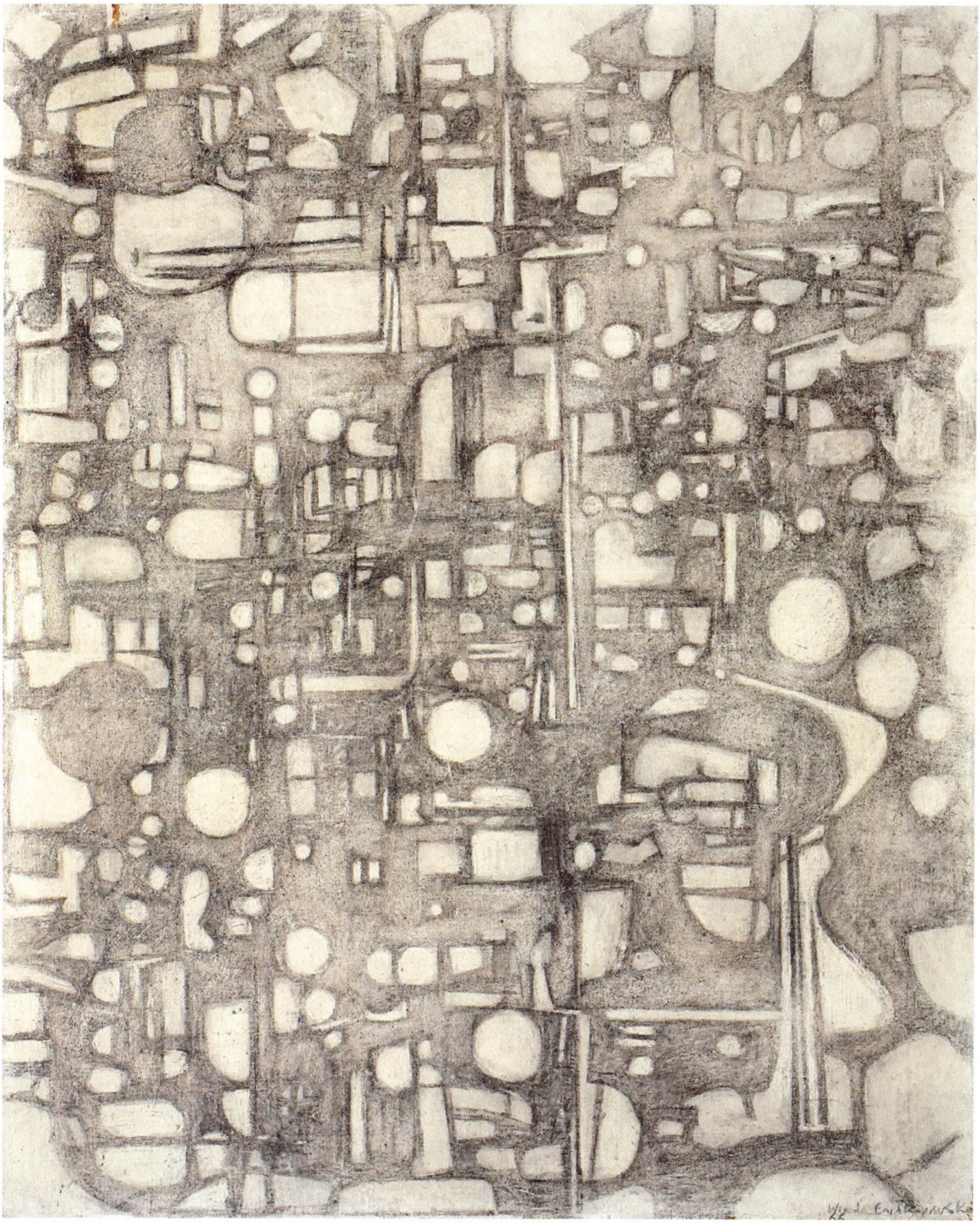

Wanda Czełkowska, *Theme* (*Temat*), 1970–1971, black-and-white photograph

Around 1968, Czełkowska begins to experiment with photography and self-portraiture, adding performance to her artistic toolbox. In this image the artist covers her head with a see-through fabric in a gesture resembling that of covering a clay sculpture with damp cloth in order to keep it from drying out. With this image Czełkowska seems to be suggesting that the head, or rather, the concept, is the true matter of her work. In her notes she comments: "I will not be returning to the figure. Arms and legs don't matter to me. It's all about the head, what's inside it".[6]

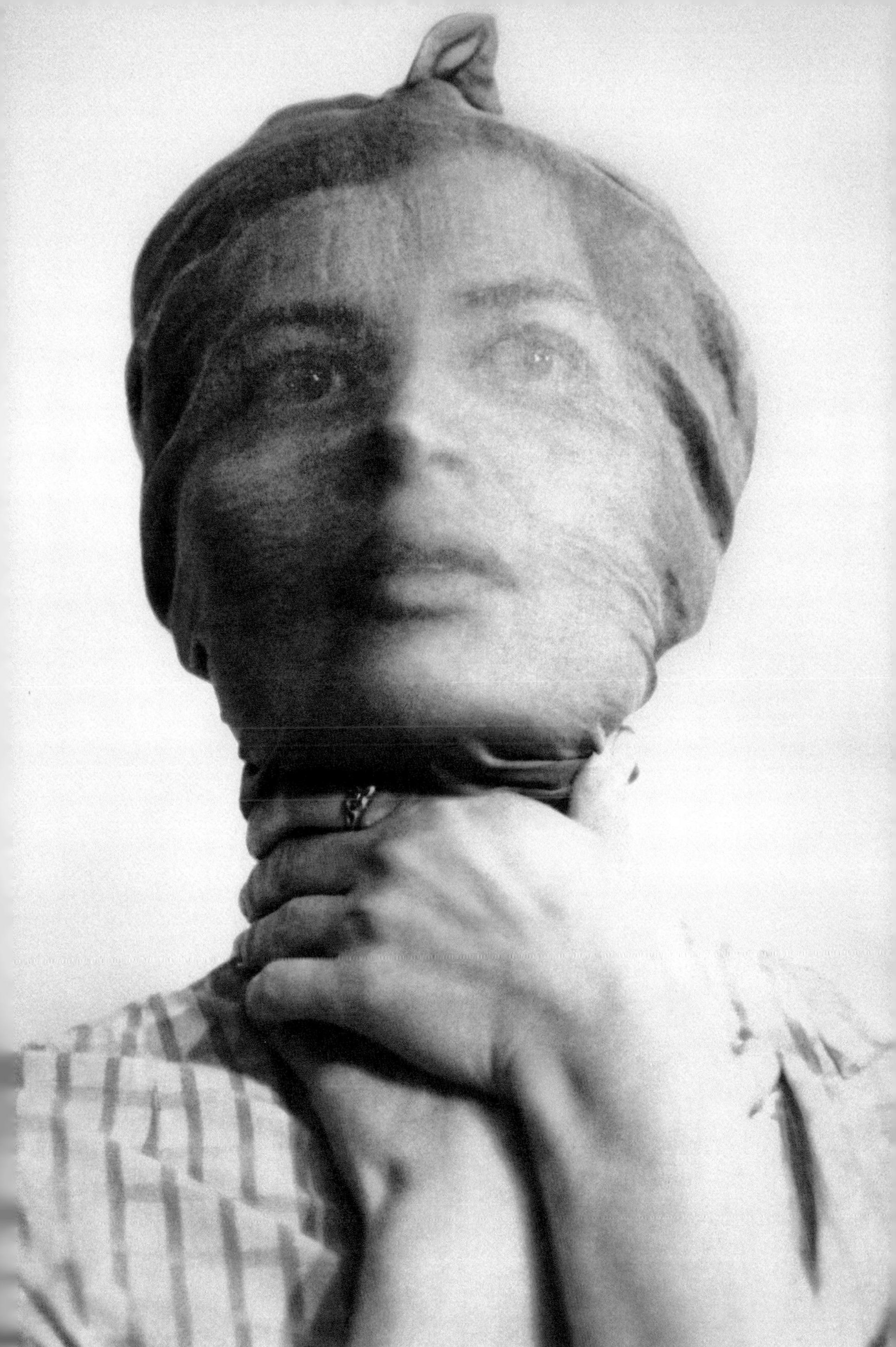

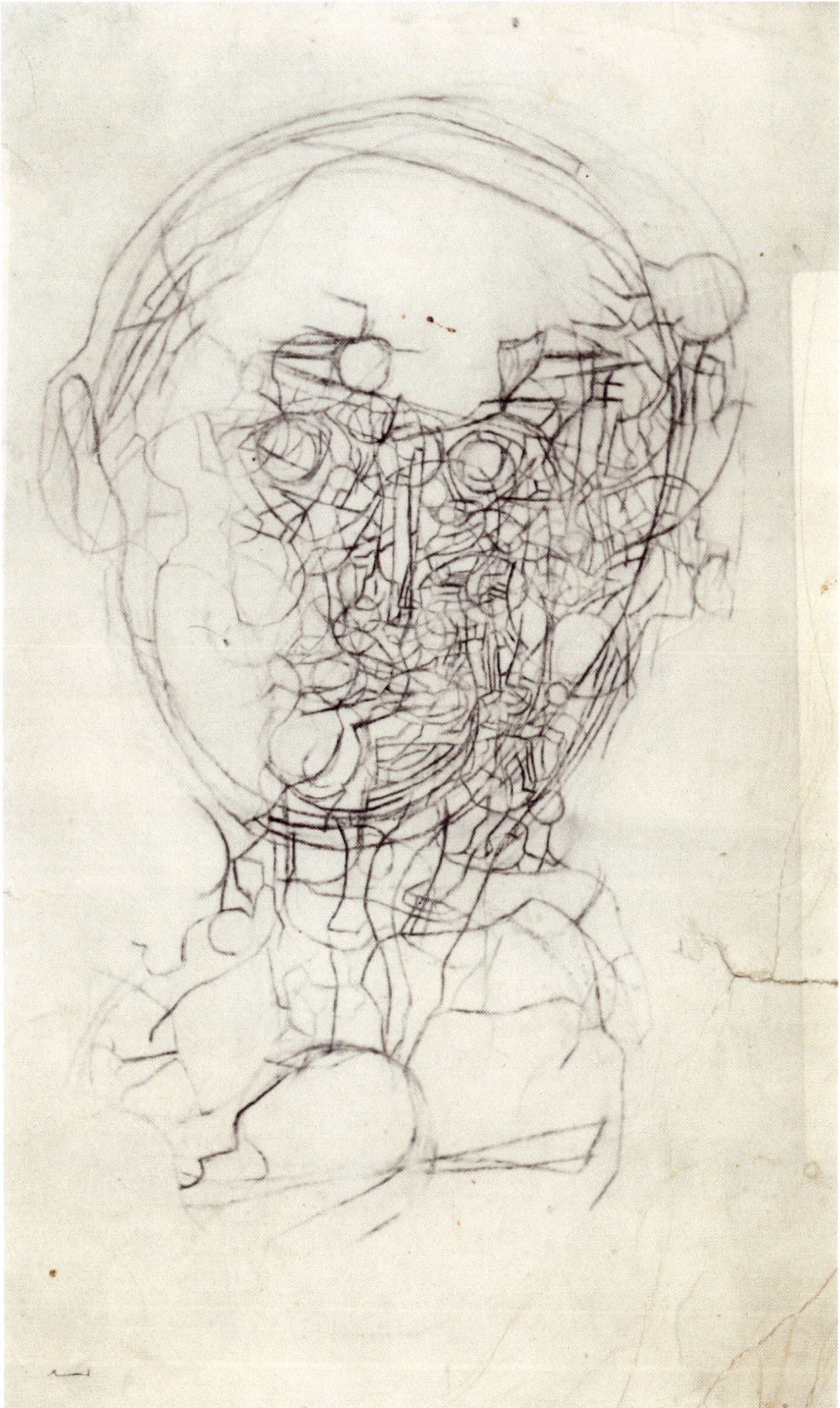

Wanda Czełkowska, *Portrait of Daria Semegen* (*Portret Darii Semegen*), 1969, drawing

Daria Semegen (b. 1946) is a contemporary American composer of classical music. In 1968, she came to Poland on a Fulbright scholarship to study the body of work of composer and conductor Witold Lutosławski (1913–1994). She met Wanda through mutual friends. The two artists quickly formed a close bond, spending a few months together in Kraków.
◄

From left to right: Wanda Czełkowska, Artur Sandauer (literary critic and author, 1913–1989), Barbara Zbrożyna (artist, 1923–1995) and Daria Semegen at the opening of the artist's 1969 solo exhibition at Współczesna Gallery in Warsaw, where Czełkowska presented the series *Head* (*Głowa*), 1969, consisting of 20 drawings

Towards the end of the 1960s, Czełkowska became a member of the Second Kraków Group, a collective of artists, authors, critics and composers gathered around Tadeusz Kantor and his experimental theatre. The group was formed as a direct successor of the avant-garde traditions of the pre-war Kraków Group (active 1933–1937). In 1957, the Second Kraków Group formally became an association, with its headquarters in the Krzysztofory Gallery. The artists Tadeusz Brzozowski, Maria Jarema, Tadeusz Kantor, Jadwiga Maziarska, Kazimierz Mikulski, Jerzy Nowosielski, Erna Rosenstein, Jerzy Skarżyński and Jonasz Stern were at the core of the newly formed group. With time, other members were invited to join their circle. From 1968 to 1981, Czełkowska participated in numerous exhibitions organized by the Kraków Group, beginning with the collective drawing exhibition (9th exhibition) at the Krzysztofory Gallery.
▼

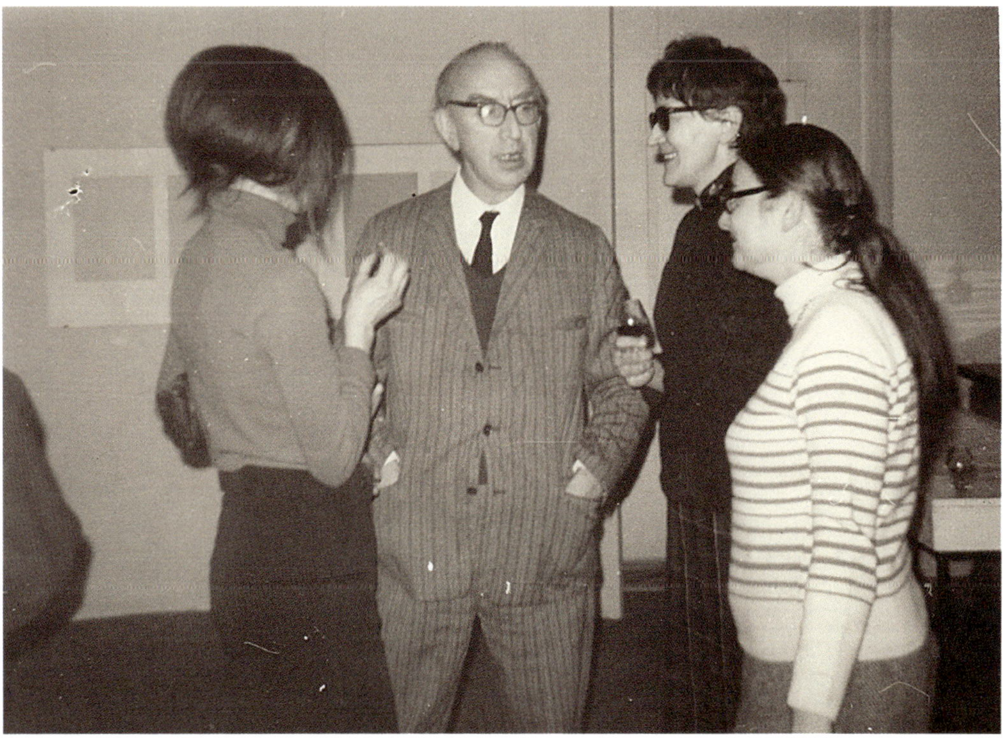

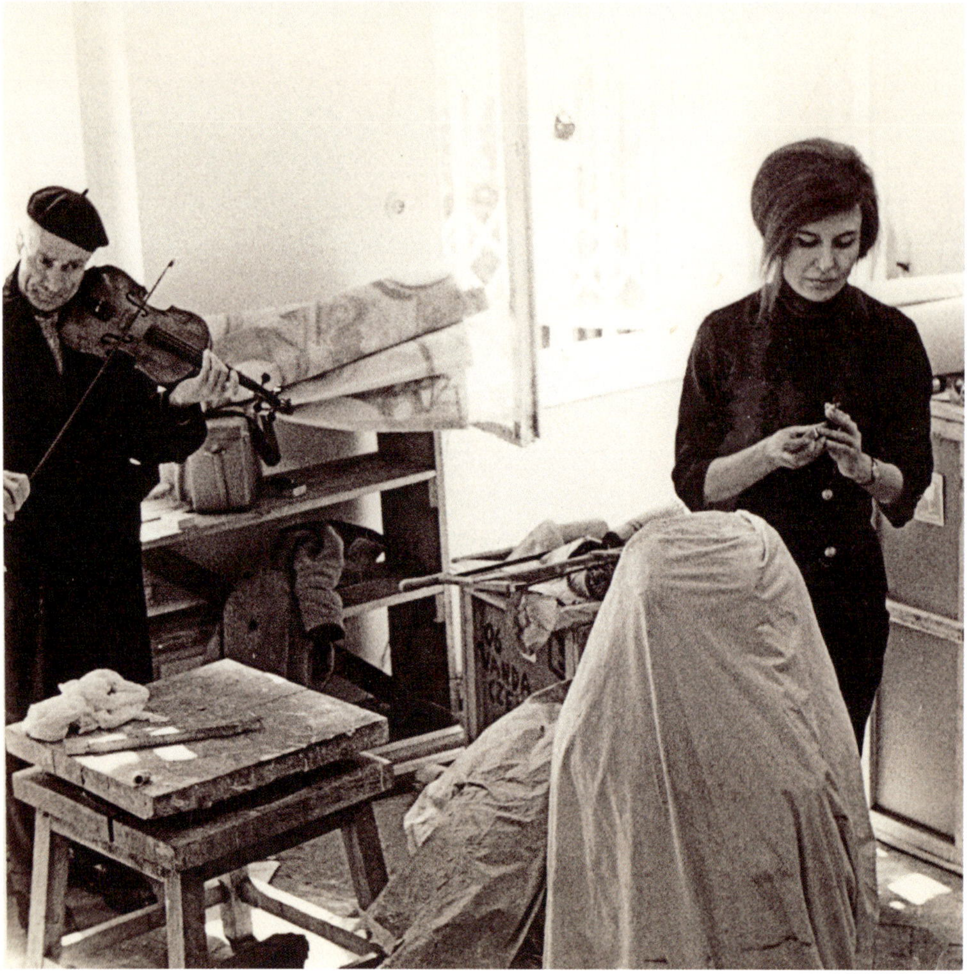

Wanda Czełkowska photographed in her studio at Wygoda Street in Kraków, 1968. Photo: Jacek Maria Stokłosa. The image was published in the catalogue of the 9th exhibition of the Second Kraków Group, 1968

Wanda Czełkowska, *Table* (*Stół*), 1968–1971, instruction manual

Czełkowska began to work on the concept for the monumental installation *Table* in 1968. She later presented the initial concept for the work during the 11th exhibition of the Kraków Group in 1971 in the form of a short instruction manual. It was enthusiastically received by Tadeusz Kantor and other Kraków Group members. A draft of the original leaflet remains in the artist's studio with the following instruction: "Table: dimensions 8 × 4 m, positioned at any one location, anywhere where it is possible to place a table. With sculptures of a head standing on top of the table. It is a sculpture of the head of a currently living man, encountered by chance [added in pen: it can be a direct cast]. It can be a head sculpted with the tools allowing for precise transfer of all reference points of the existing model as well as a sculpture made by me, entitled *Head*. The table is what's important, as an action of the divisions in which the multiplied head stands. Multiplied 18 times only, positioned at random, yet irreversibly. Placed on two fields, fully facing one another. 1968–71. W. Czełkowska".

▸

Stół - wymiary 8x4m, postawiony w dowolnym miejscu, wszędzie, gdzie można postawić stół. Na stole stoją rzeźby jednej głowy. Jest to rzeźba głowy współcześnie żyjącego, przypadkowo spotkanego człowieka. Może to być głowa wyrzeźbiona za pomocą przyrządów wiernie przenoszących wszystkie punkty istniejącego modela i może to być zrobiona przeze mnie rzeźba pt. głowa. Ważny jest stół, jego akcja podziałów w których stoi zwielokrotniona głowa. Zwielokrotniona tylko 18 razy, ustawiona przypadkowo lecz już nieodwracalnie, Ustawiona na dwóch polach, frontalnie zwrócona do siebie.
1968 - 71r.

W.Czełkowska

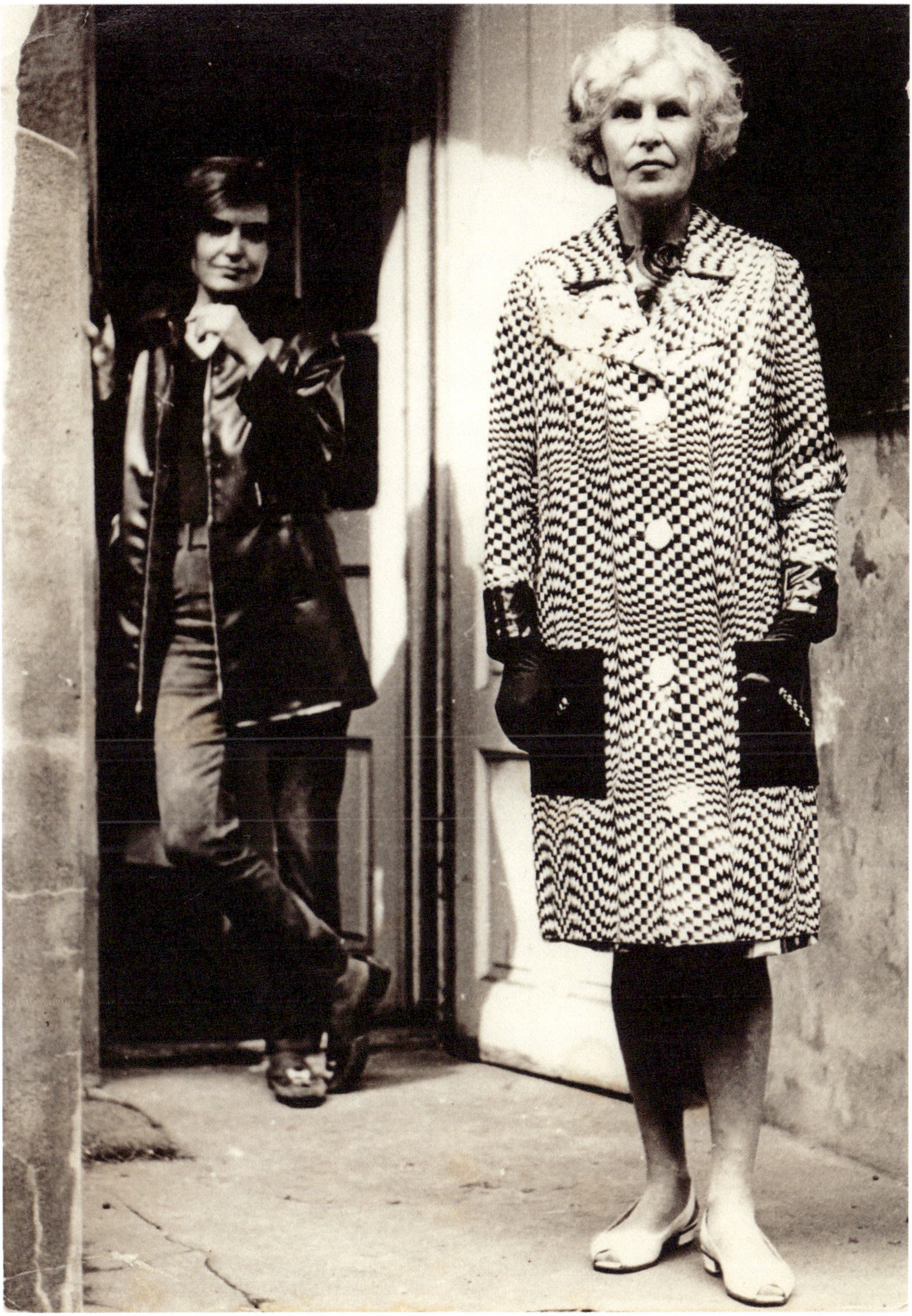

Czełkowska with her mother Franciszka (1911–2010) outside the artist's studio at Wygoda Street, Kraków, c. 1968

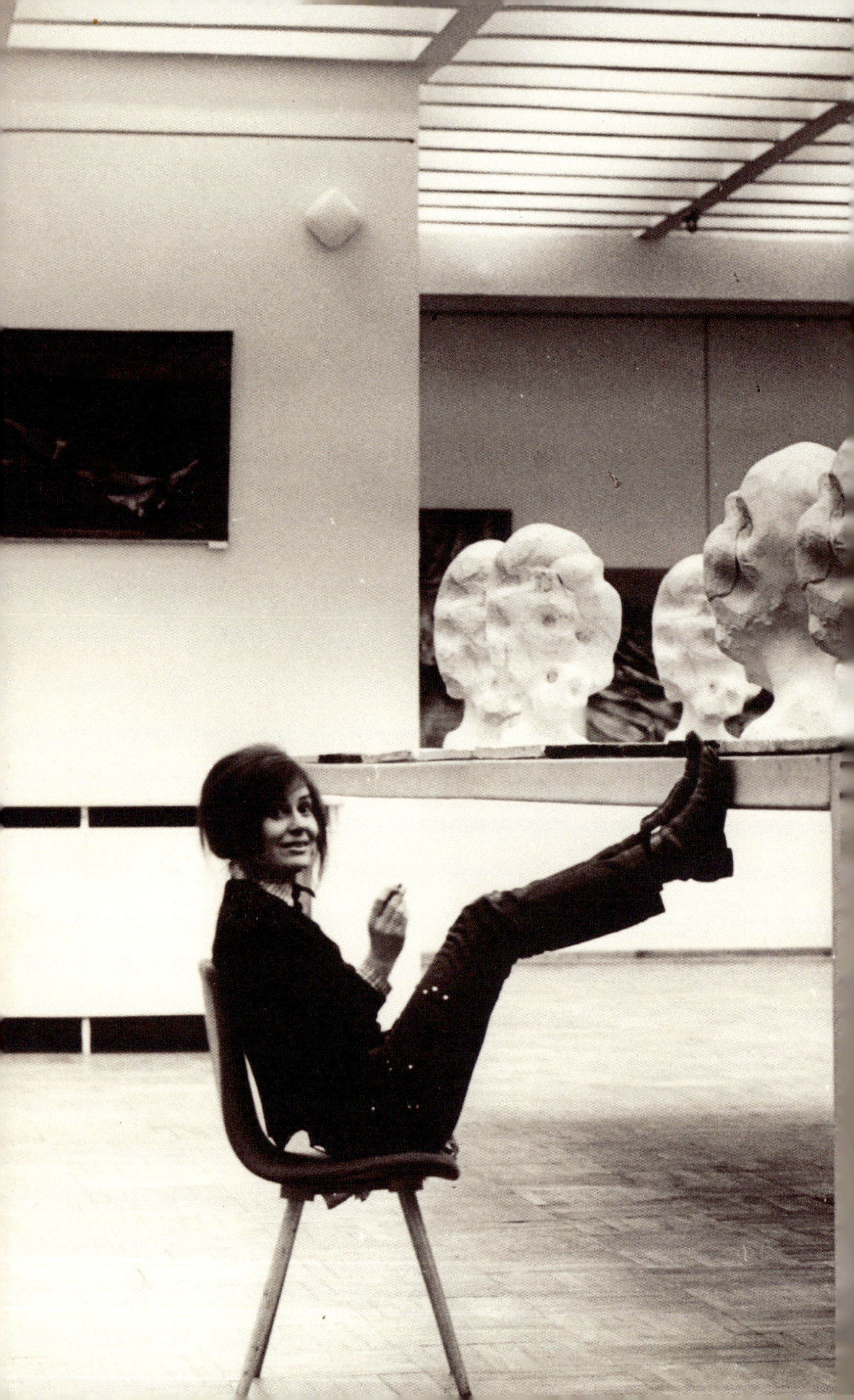

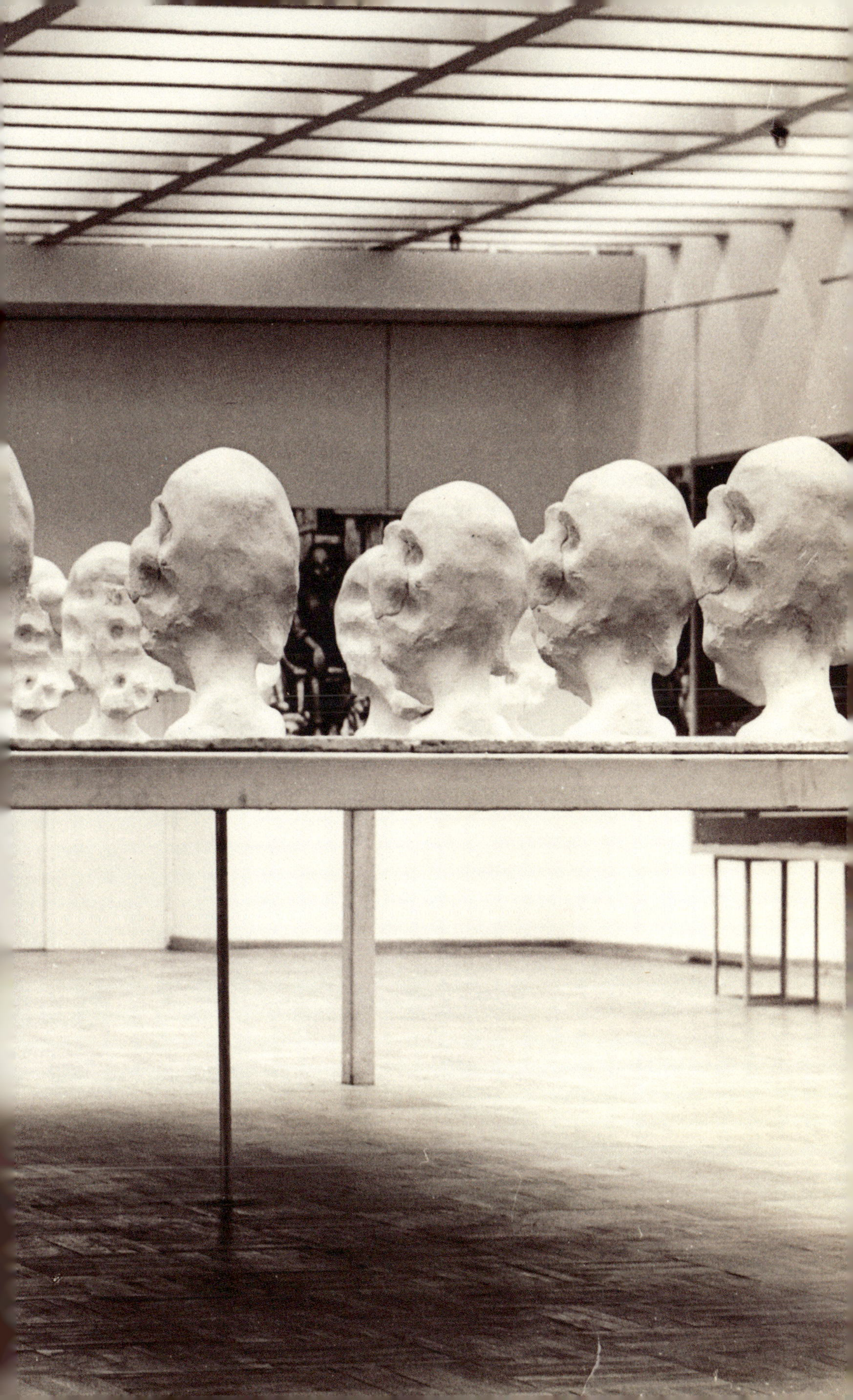

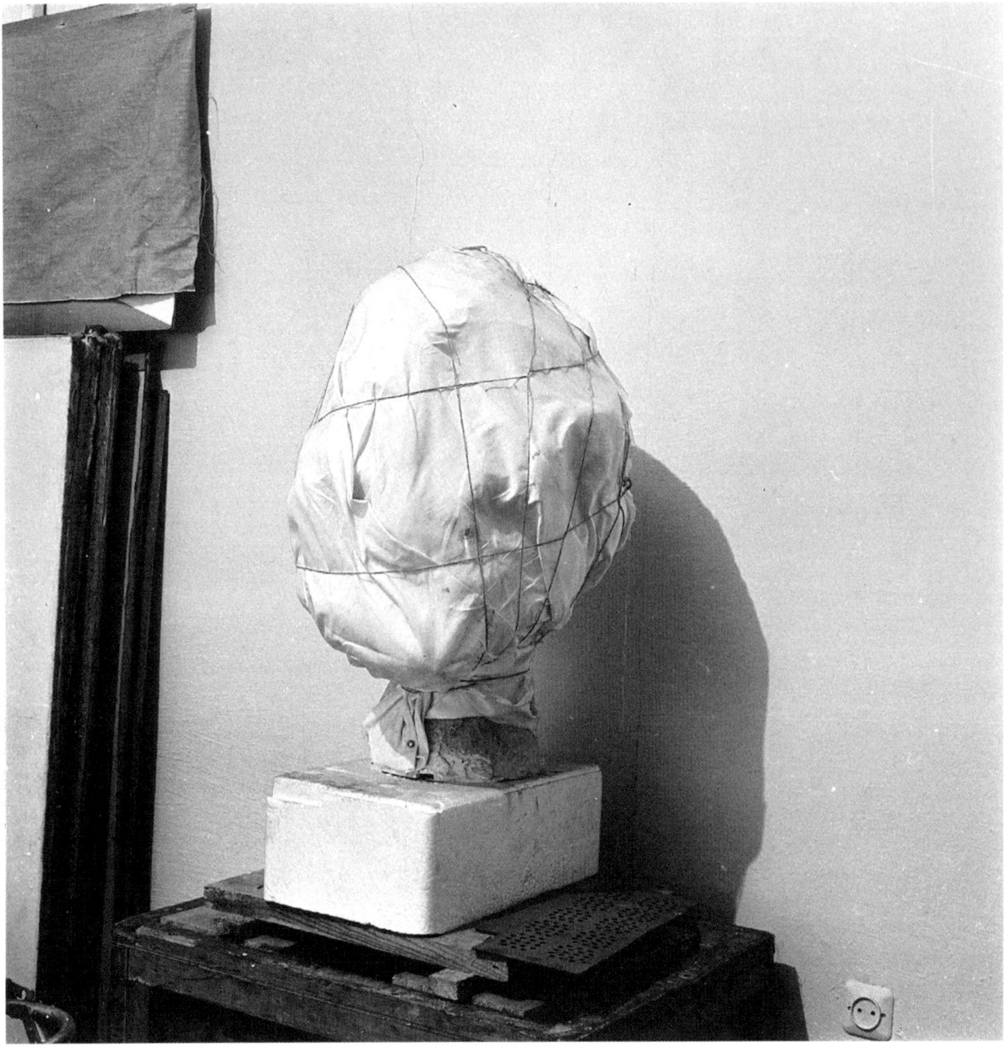

Previous pages:
Wanda Czełkowska next to the first public installation of *Table* (*Stół*), 1968–1971, during the 4th Kraków Encounters at the Art Exhibition Office in Kraków, 1971. Photo: Wacław Nowak, courtesy of Szarota Nowak

The work, which was considered bold and controversial at the time of its first presentation, met with general acclaim of the local artistic community. The following year Czełkowska was able to present her concept and photographic documentation of the installation to Richard Demarco during his studio visit in Kraków. This meeting resulted in Czełkowska being invited to participate in the *Atelier '72* exhibition at the International Edinburgh Arts Festival, marking yet another turning point in the artist's career.

Wanda Czełkowska, *Untitled* (*Wrapped Head* [*Zawinięta głowa*]), c. 1975, black-and-white photograph

In an unpublished conversation with Ewa Opałka from 2016,[7] the artist recalls flying to Scotland with the still damp *Edinburgh Head* (*Głowa edynburska*) in her hand luggage. The wrapped head is a recurring theme in the artist's oeuvre from the 1970s onwards.

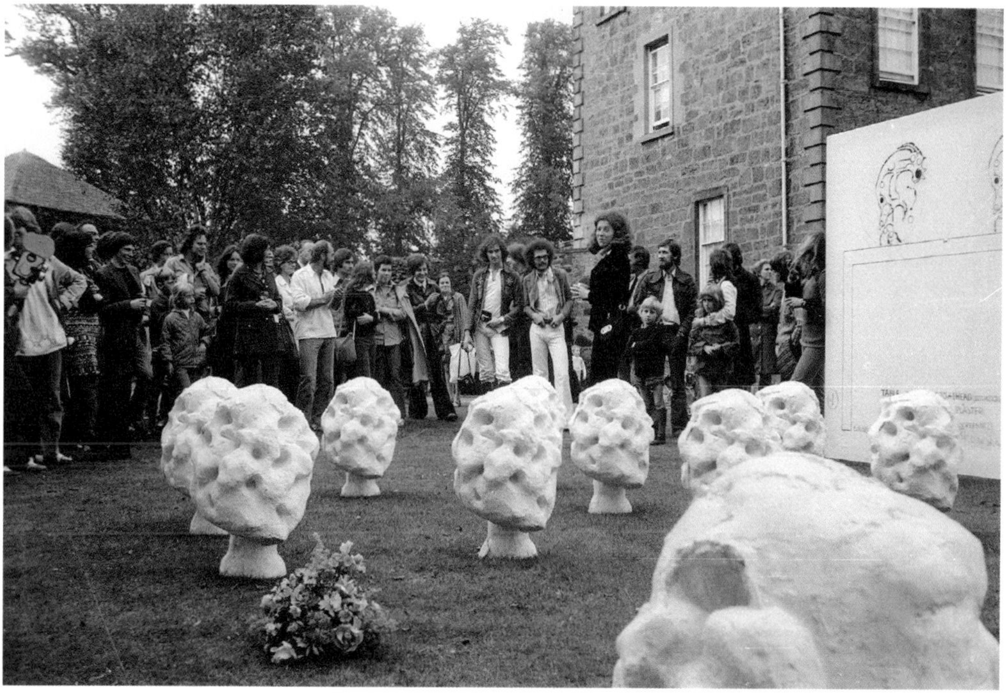

Wanda Czełkowska (eighth from the right) with her installation *Conceptual Information about "The Table"* (*Informacja pojęciowa o "Stole"*), 1972, at the Scottish National Gallery of Modern Art, Inverleith House, Edinburgh, exhibited in *Atelier '72* (dedicated to contemporary Polish art), presented by Richard Demarco Gallery in collaboration with Łódź Museum of Art for the Edinburgh Festival, 1972. Photo: George Oliver, courtesy of Demarco Digital Archive (University of Dundee) & Richard Demarco Archive

Czełkowska arrived in Scotland in the summer of 1972, ready to present the Edinburgh version of the installation *Table*. Due to a technical error made by the on-site production team, the artist had to make a last-minute change to her exhibition. Czełkowska decided not to show the incorrectly cast *Table* and instead present a new installation under the title *Conceptual Information about "The Table"*. The new work consisted of a group of eighteen casts of the *Edinburgh Head* sculpture placed directly on the ground, as well as panels with drawings discussing the idea behind the work, skewing the artist's practice even further in the direction of conceptual art.

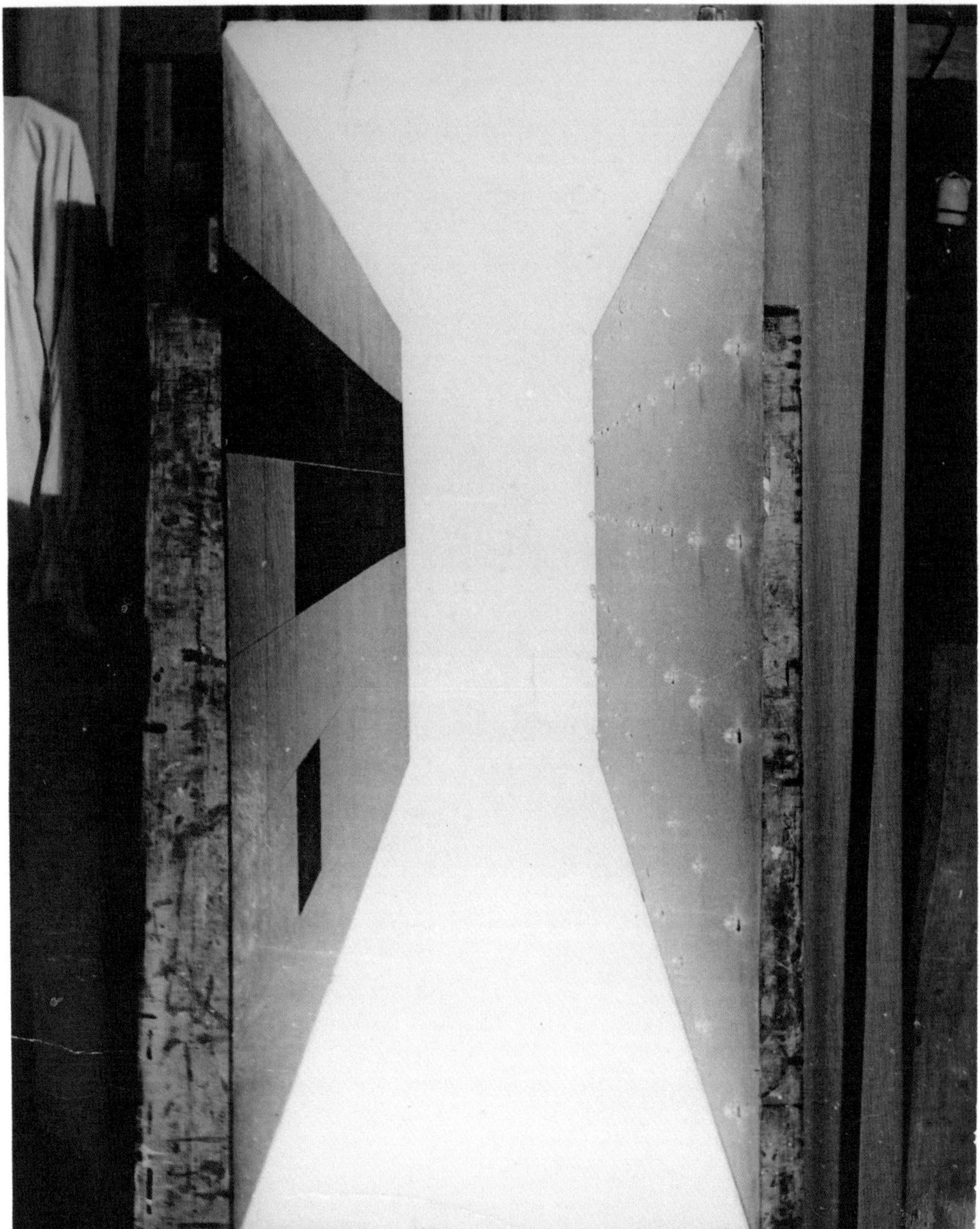

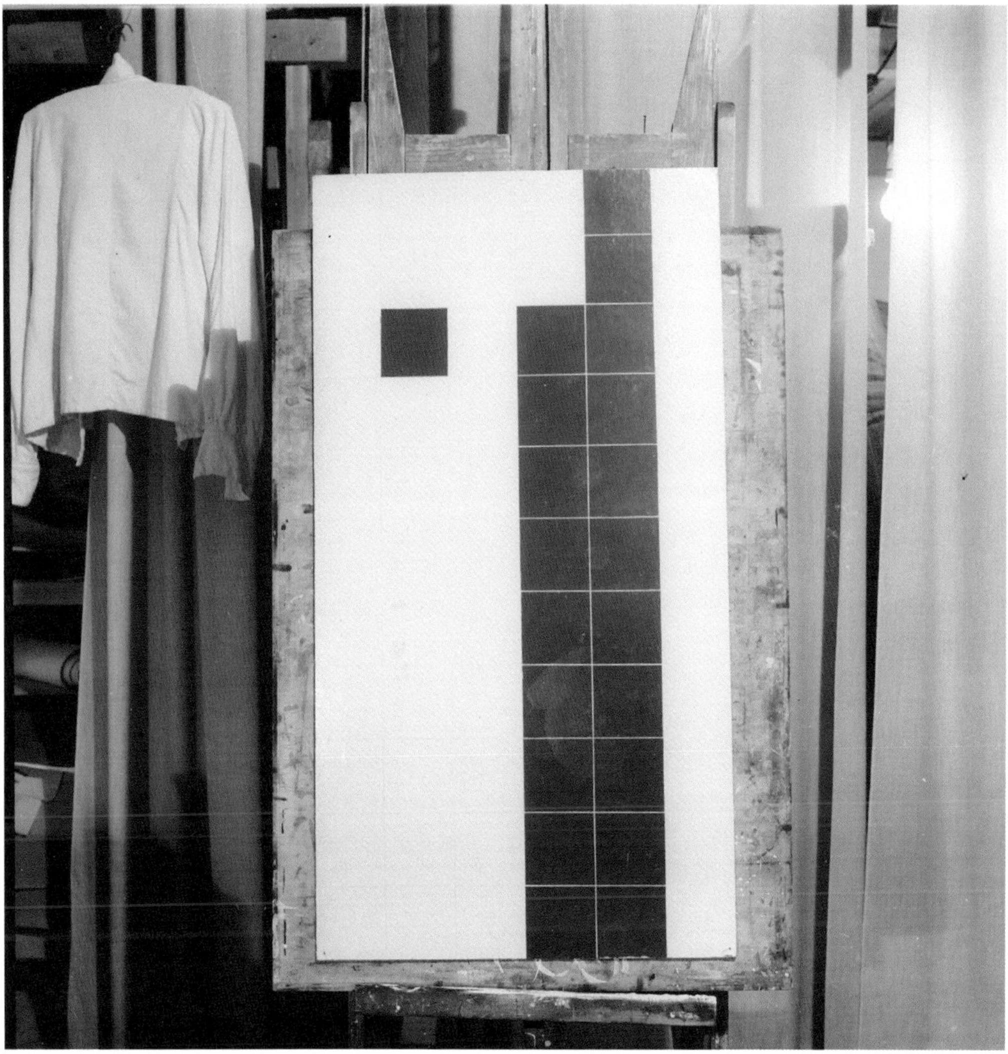

Wanda Czełkowska, 3D model of *Absolute Elimination of Sculpture as a Notion of Shape* (*Bezwzględne wyeliminowanie rzeźby jako pojęcia kształtu*), 1972. Photo: c. 1972

While still in Edinburgh, the idea for Czełkowska's next installation, entitled *Absolute Elimination of Sculpture as a Notion of Shape*, 1972, came to life. Despite an invitation to remain in Scotland for another exhibition, the artist was keen to return to Kraków to finalise her new project – an installation consisting of 66 same-size concrete plates in two different colours, space in between, 66 lightbulbs protruding linen coffers, distributed evenly, reproducing the geometrical pattern on the floor. The "empty" in-between space was at the centre of the artist's interest.

◄

Wanda Czełkowska, 3D model of *Absolute Elimination of Sculpture as a Notion of Shape* (*Bezwzględne wyeliminowanie rzeźby jako pojęcia kształtu*), 1972. Photo: c. 1972

Upon her return to Kraków, Czełkowska prepared technical drawings, 3D models and photographic renditions of the future installation. The artist first presented this concept in May 1973 during the exhibition of the laureates of the Art Criticism Awards at the Pryzmat Gallery in Kraków. On this occasion, Czełkowska was awarded the title of Sculptor of the Year 1972.

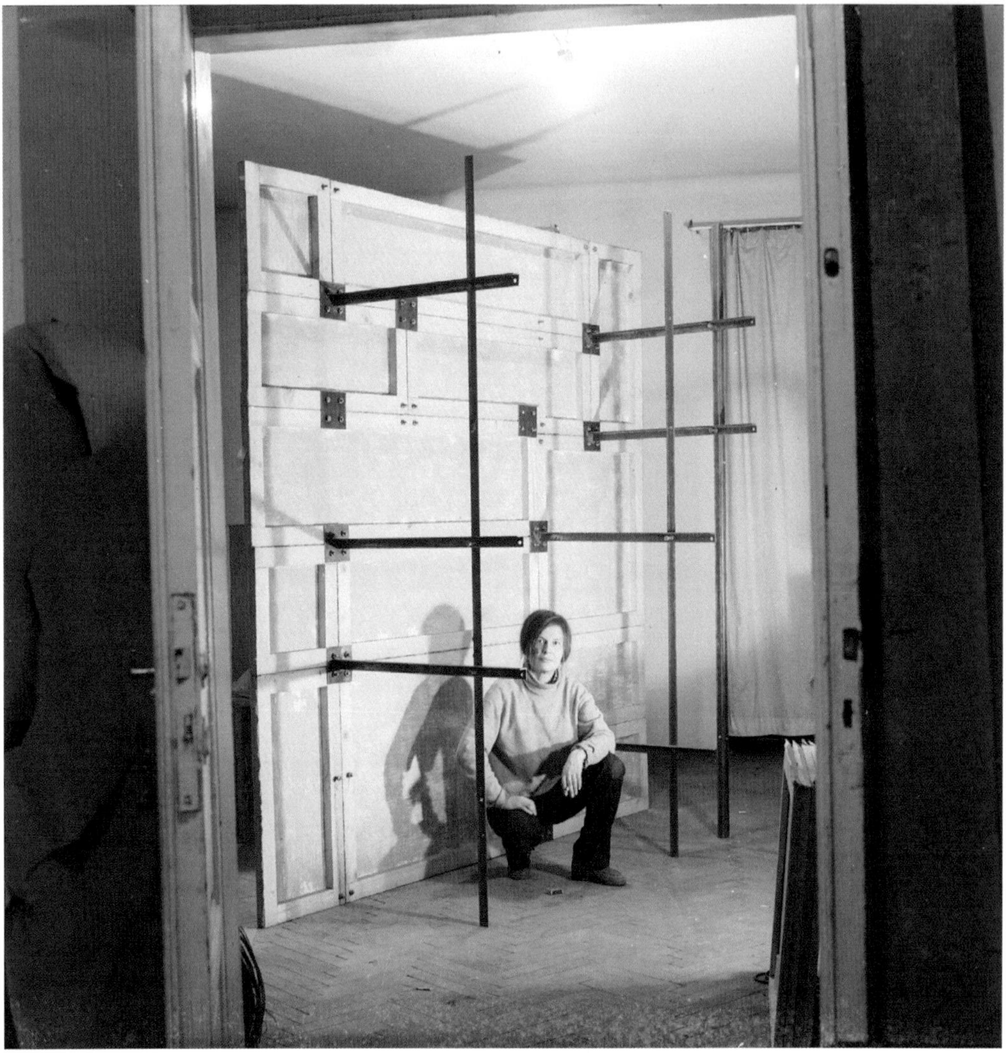

Wanda Czełkowska with *Wall* (*Ściana*), 1975

The work *Wall* was first exhibited in 1975 during a group exhibition at the CBWA Zachęta in Warsaw, as an homage to Xawery Dunikowski. The installation, which today belongs to the National Museum in Kraków, consists of a three-dimensional dark metal construction (the front of the piece) framing a puzzle-like composition of white canvas with drawings of the motif of a "wrapped head", bound together by shiny metal strips. A separate element of the installation is the *Edinburgh Head*, 1972, wrapped up in cloth and string, resting directly on the floor behind the wall.

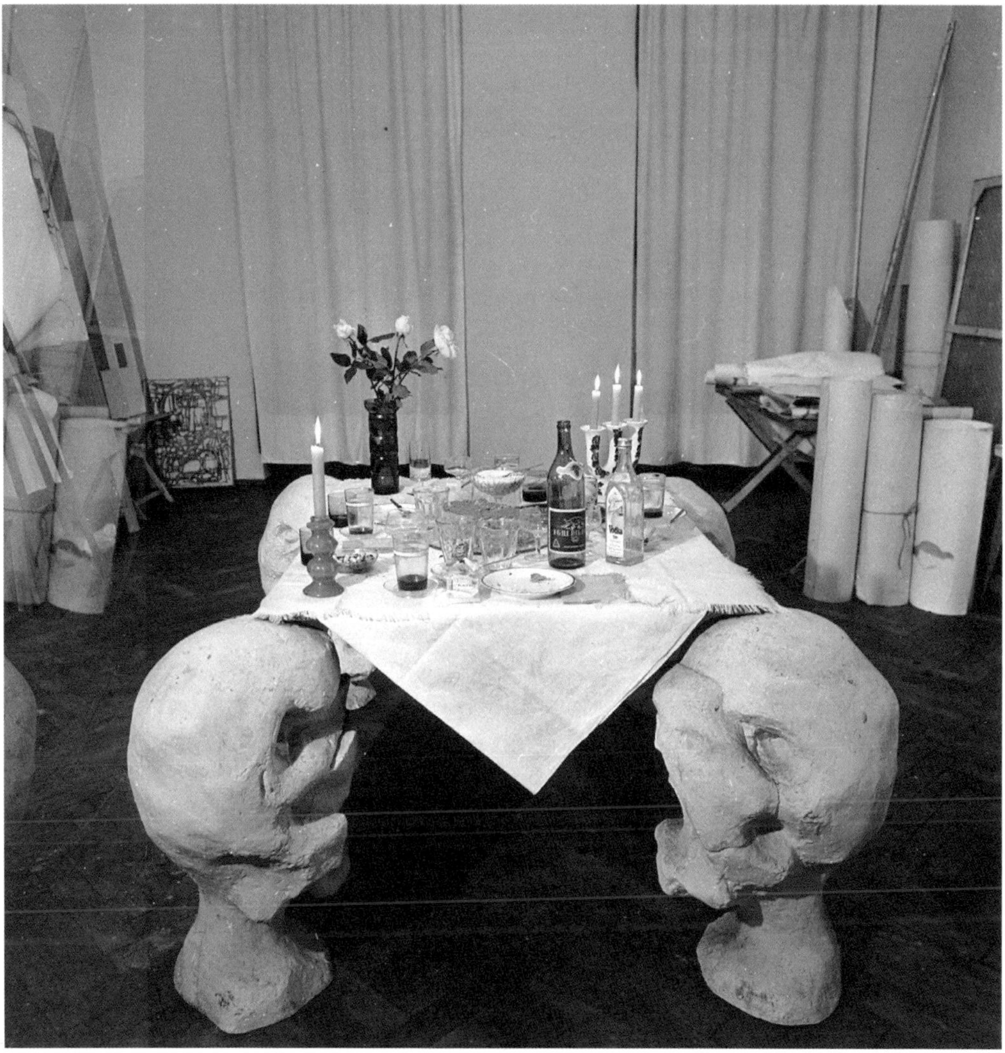

Private installation made with *Head* (*Głowa*) sculptures, 1970s to early 1980s. Photo: post-1971

During the international conference *Minimal, Conceptual and Material: The Phenomenon of Wanda Czełkowska's Sculptures* held in February 2017 at the National Museum in Warsaw, the contemporary art restorer Anna Kłosowska recalled that for many years Czełkowska had been unable to secure proper conditions to store her sculptures, and so she developed a utilitarian approach to her works, using them as table stands, whenever she threw a small dinner party.[8]

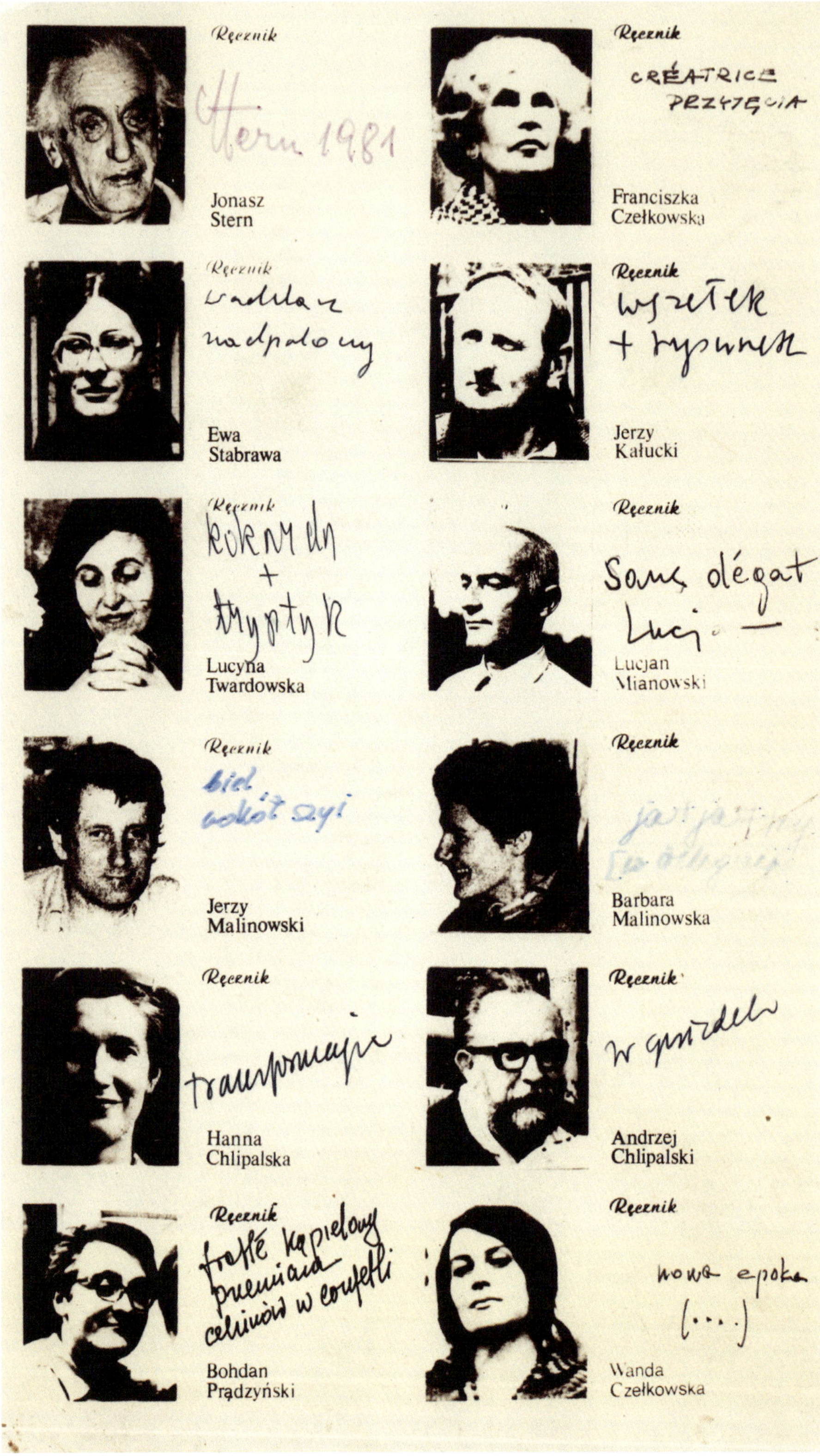
Ręcznik
Stern 1981
Jonasz Stern
Ręcznik
CRÉATRICE PRZYJĘCIA
Franciszka Czełkowska
Ręcznik
Ewa Stabrawa
Ręcznik
Jerzy Kałucki
Ręcznik
Lucyna Twardowska
Ręcznik
Lucjan Mianowski
Ręcznik
biel wokół szyi
Jerzy Malinowski
Ręcznik
Barbara Malinowska
Ręcznik
transformacje
Hanna Chlipalska
Ręcznik
Andrzej Chlipalski
Ręcznik
Bohdan Prądzyński
Ręcznik
nowa epoka
(...)
Wanda Czełkowska

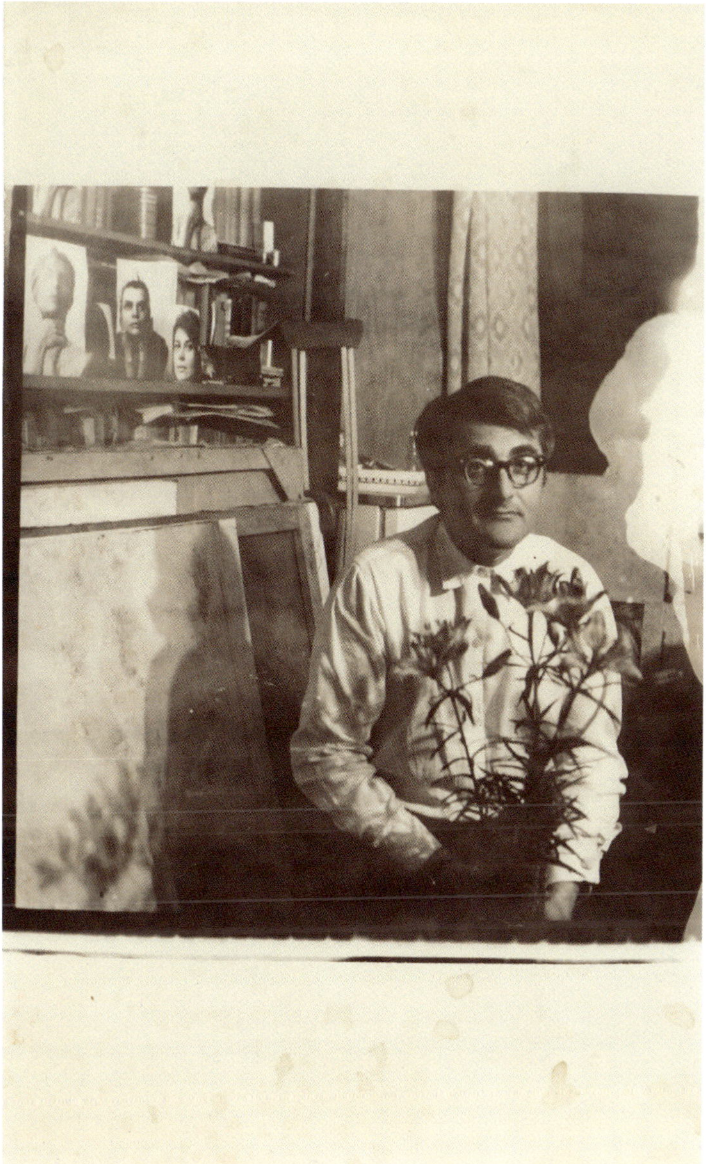

Bohdan Prądzyński (1930–2000), graphic designer and Czełkowska's long-time partner. Some photographic prints of the artist's self-portraits can be seen in the background, c. 1972

The reverse of the invitation card to the New Year's Eve party held on 31 December 1980 in her apartment at 27 Karmelicka Street. The guest list consisted of the artist's close family and friends
◂

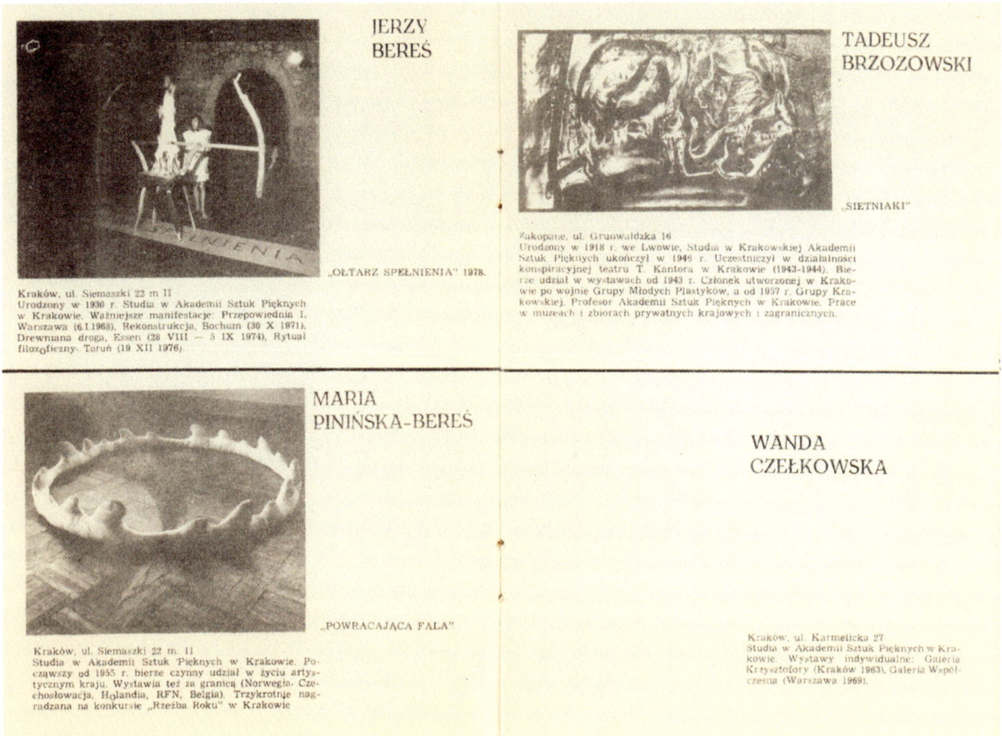

JERZY BEREŚ

„OŁTARZ SPEŁNIENIA" 1978.

Kraków, ul. Siemaszki 22 m II
Urodzony w 1930 r. Studia w Akademii Sztuk Pięknych w Krakowie. Ważniejsze manifestacje: Przepowiednia I, Warszawa (6.I.1968), Rekonstrukcja, Bochum (30 X 1971), Drewniana droga, Essen (28 VIII — 5 IX 1974), Rytuał filozoficzny. Toruń (19 XII 1976).

TADEUSZ BRZOZOWSKI

„SIETNIAKI"

Zakopane, ul. Grunwaldzka 16
Urodzony w 1918 r. we Lwowie. Studia w Krakowskiej Akademii Sztuk Pięknych ukończył w 1948 r. Uczestniczył w działalności konspiracyjnej teatru T. Kantora w Krakowie (1943-1944). Bierze udział w wystawach od 1943 r. Członek utworzonej w Krakowie po wojnie Grupy Młodych Plastyków, a od 1957 r. Grupy Krakowskiej. Profesor Akademii Sztuk Pięknych w Krakowie. Prace w muzeach i zbiorach prywatnych krajowych i zagranicznych.

MARIA PINIŃSKA-BEREŚ

„POWRACAJĄCA FALA"

Kraków, ul. Siemaszki 22 m. 11
Studia w Akademii Sztuk Pięknych w Krakowie. Począwszy od 1955 r. bierze czynny udział w życiu artystycznym kraju. Wystawia też za granicą (Norwegia, Czechosłowacja, Holandia, RFN, Belgia). Trzykrotnie nagradzana na konkursie „Rzeźba Roku" w Krakowie

WANDA CZEŁKOWSKA

Kraków, ul. Karmelicka 27
Studia w Akademii Sztuk Pięknych w Krakowie. Wystawy indywidualne: Galeria Krzysztofory (Kraków 1963), Galeria Współczesna (Warszawa 1969).

Spread from the 1981 Second Kraków Group exhibition catalogue (Lublin: BWA Gallery, 1981), 3–4

On 13 December 1981, in an attempt to defeat the Solidarity movement, which had arisen in political opposition to the communist government, a military junta headed by General Wojciech Jaruzelski, was formed and Martial Law was introduced in the Polish People's Republic. This was followed by a period of harsh restrictions and political invigilation in everyday life. Shortly afterwards, Czełkowska decided to leave the Kraków Group. In a letter to fellow artists in February 1982, she expressed her feelings about censorship and the group's lack of political engagement.[9] This marked the beginning of almost a decade of declining public activity on the part of the artist.

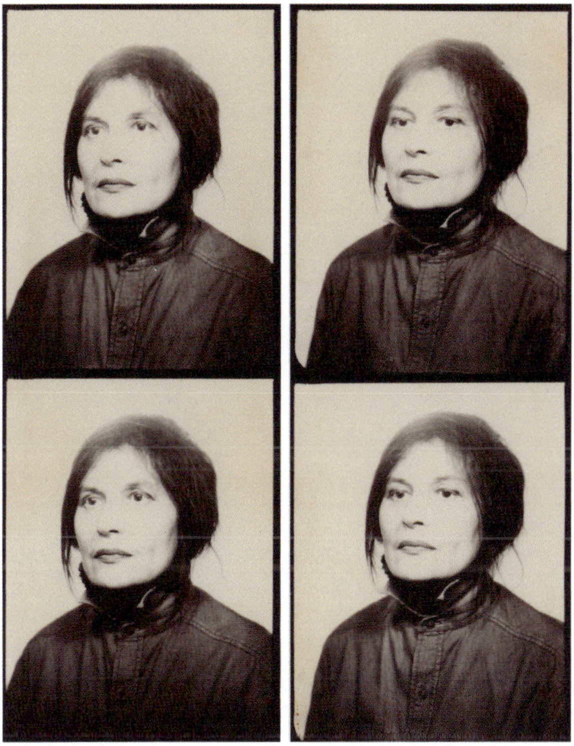

Wanda Czełkowska's ID photographs, 1980s to 1990s

Wanda Czełkowska, from the series *Tree – My Tree* (*Drzewo – Moje drzewo*), 1988, exhibition in the crypt of the Piarist Fathers in Kraków. Photo: 1988

As the artistic community began to boycott the state cultural institutions during the time of Martial Law, the Catholic Church became an unexpected ally for some artists. Churches throughout Poland, often in collaboration with independent curators, offered artists the opportunity to exhibit their work at this difficult time.[10] Having left the Second Kraków Group, Czełkowska turned to the church as a place that welcomed art which was in opposition to the official doctrine.

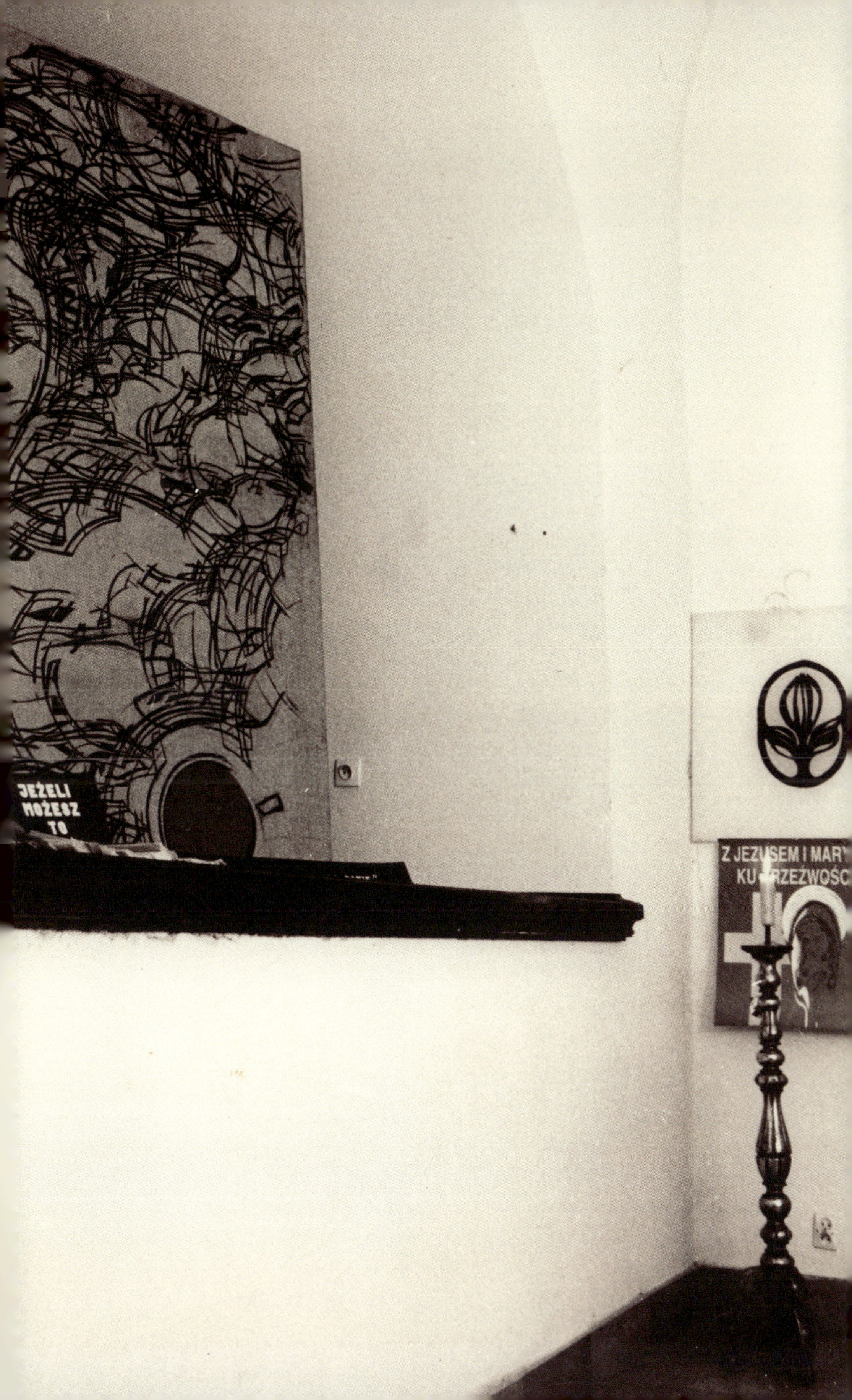
JEŻELI
MOŻESZ
TO
Z JEZUSEM I MARY

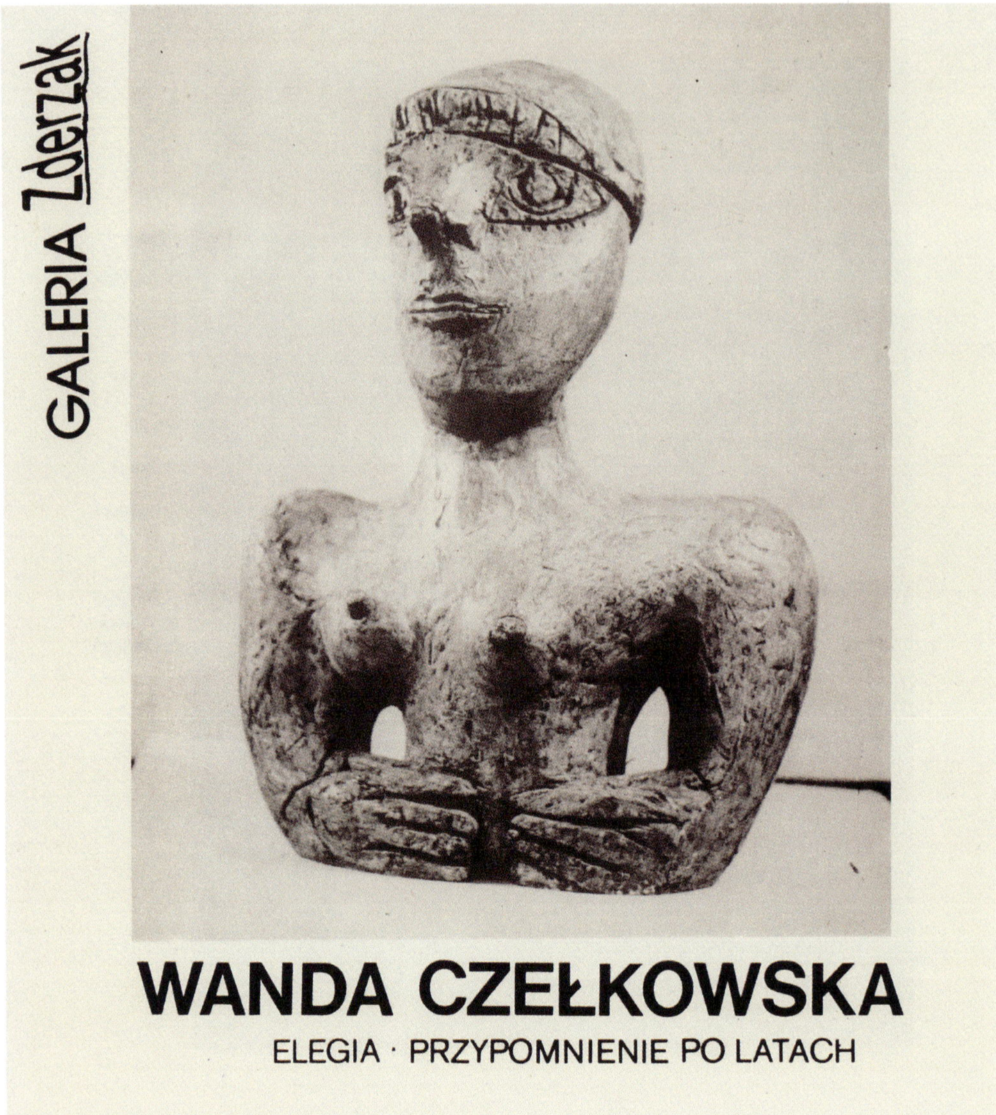

Cover of the catalogue published on the occasion of the artist's solo exhibition *Wanda Czełkowska. Elegia. Przypomnienie po latach* (Wanda Czełkowska. Elegy. A Recollection after Many Years) at the Zderzak Gallery in Kraków, 1990. Courtesy of Zderzak Gallery

In March 1990, two solo exhibitions of the artist were held at the Zderzak Gallery in Kraków run by Bettina Bereś (b. 1958) and Marta Tarabuła, bringing Czełkowska back into the limelight. The artist was finally able to show works that she had been developing in the 1980s, amongst them the monumental *Elegy* (*Elegia*), 1990 (4 × 4 metres).

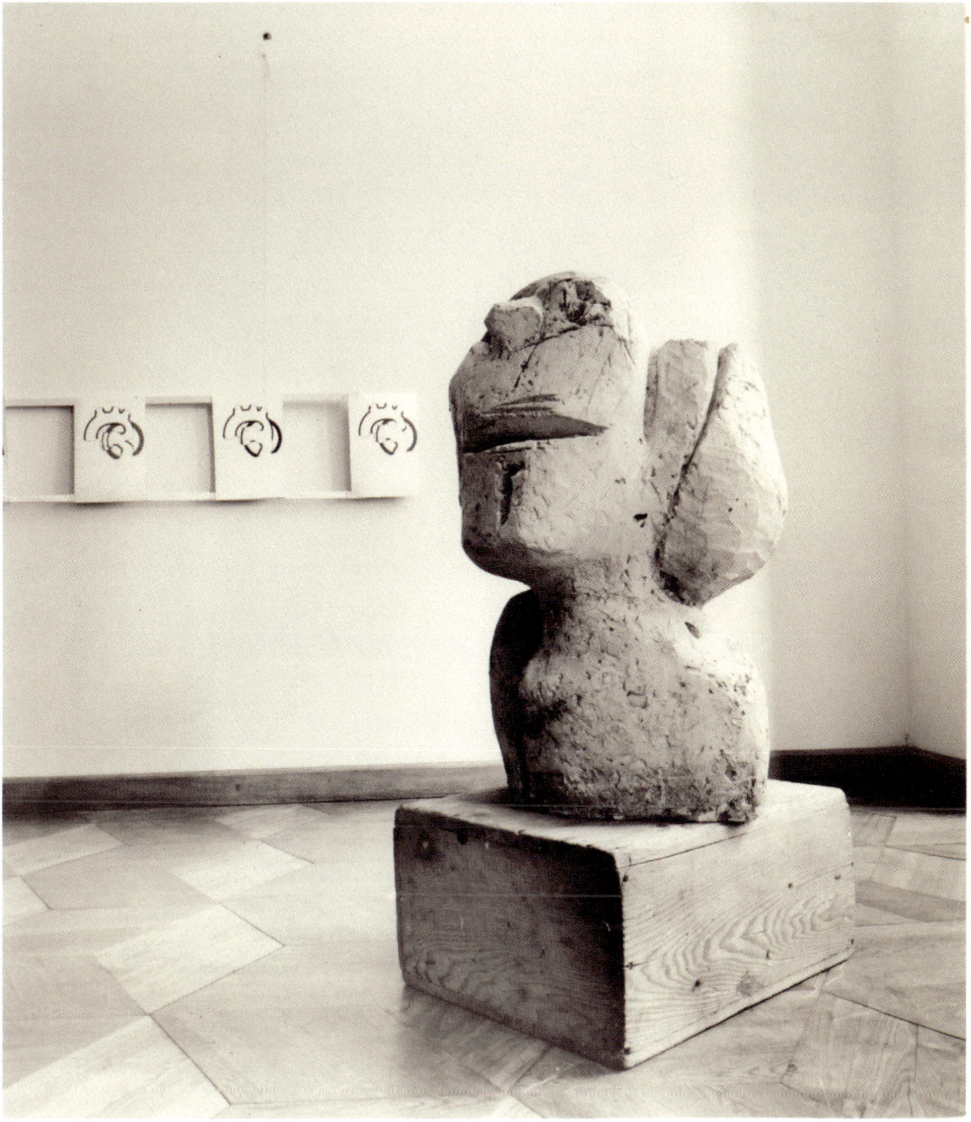

Wanda Czełkowska. Elegia. Przypomnienie po latach
(Wanda Czełkowska. Elegy. A Recollection after Many Years),
exhibition view, Zderzak Gallery, Kraków, 1990. Sculptures featured
include, from left to right: *Untitled*, 1976 or 1977, drawing on
paper, and *Head* (*Głowa*), 1964, sculpture, cast, painted plaster.
Photo: Paweł Zechenter, courtesy of Zderzak Gallery

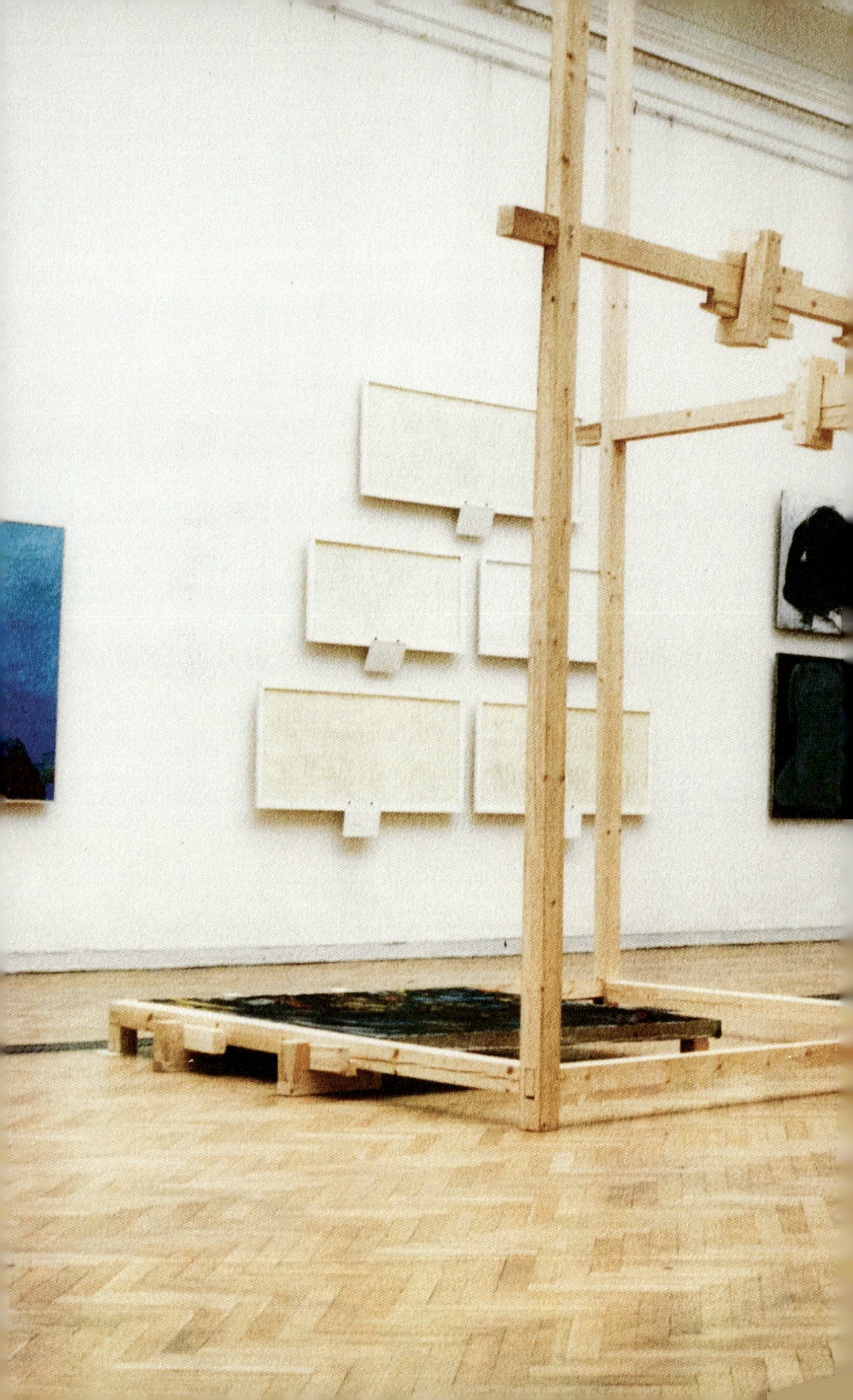

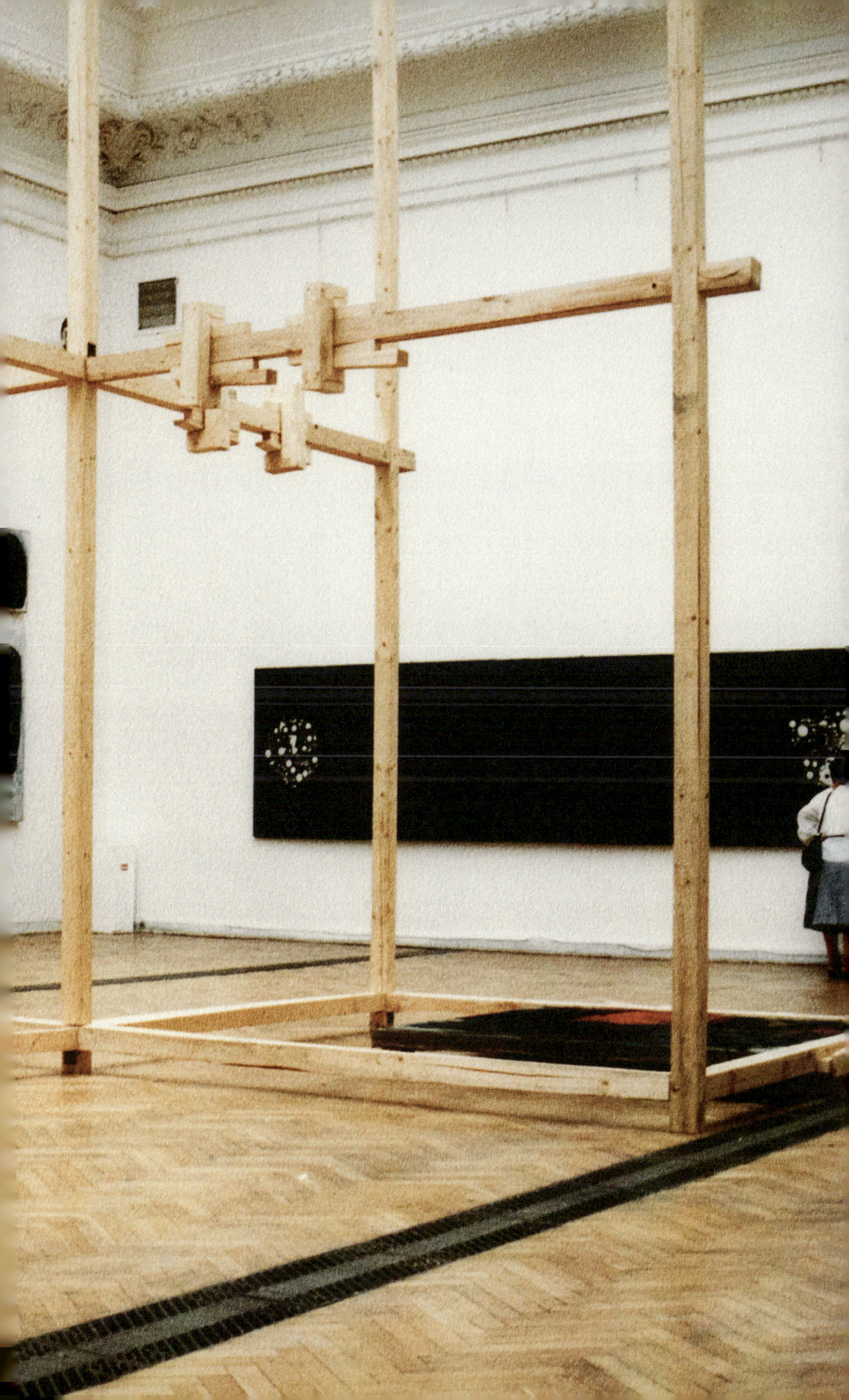

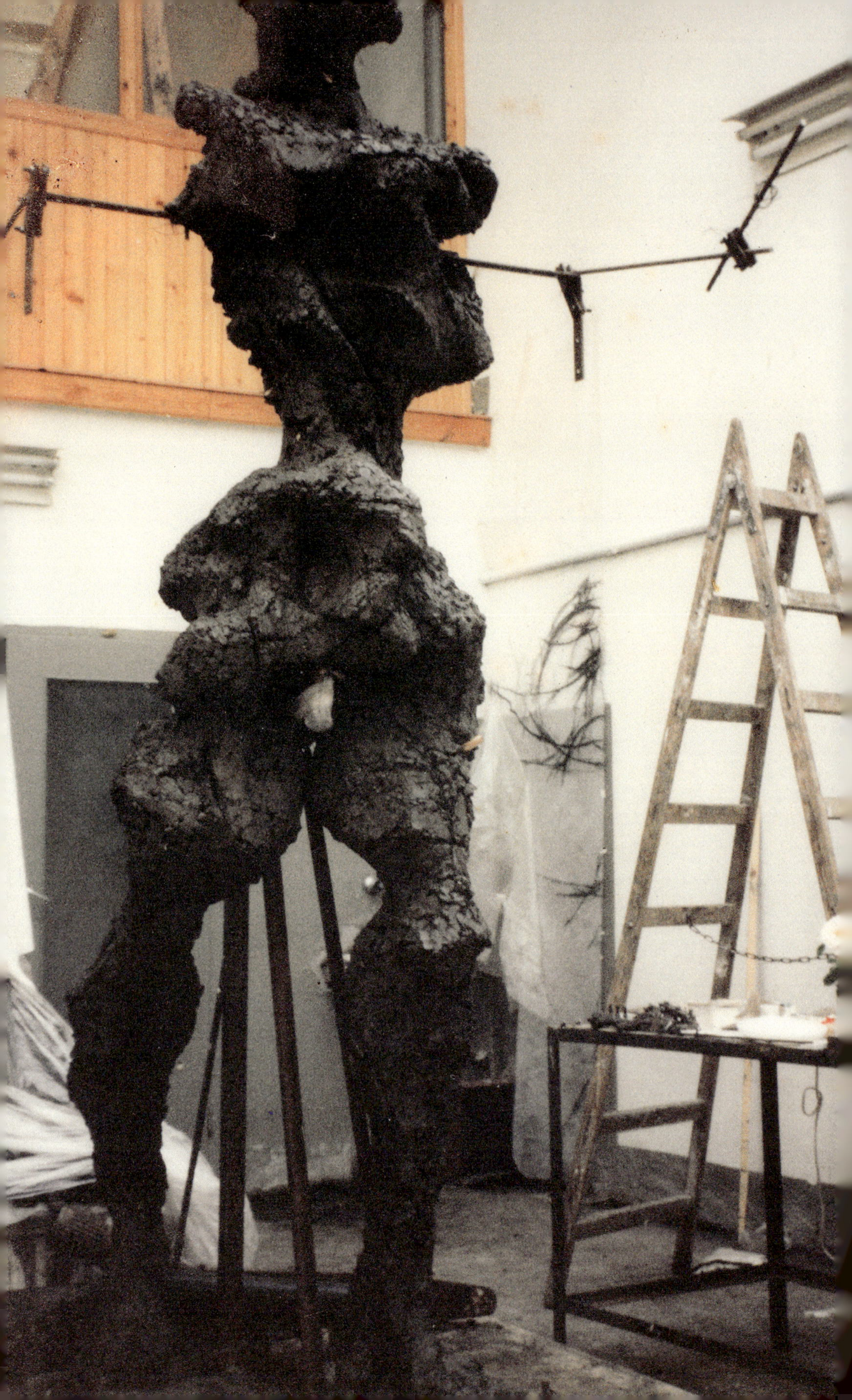

Previous pages:
Artyści z Krakowa (Artists from Kraków), exhibition view, Zachęta National Art Gallery in Warsaw, 1993. Featured artworks: *Black Frieze* (*Czarny fryz*), 1968–1969–1971–1973, acrylic, tempera, canvas [in the catalogue it appears with the title *Nostalgia*] and *Evening Full of Ears of Grain II* (*Wieczór pełen kłosów II*), 1992–1993, wood, charcoal, pastel, canvas

Wanda Czełkowska's rented studio at the Centre for Polish Sculpture in Orońsko, 1995

In 1995, Adolf Ryszka (1935–1995), Czełkowska's friend and fellow artist, invited her to rent a studio at the Centre for Polish Sculpture in Orońsko. The artist's residency lasted six months and resulted in a series of large-format drawings which she later dedicated to Ryszka. In the following years the Centre in Orońsko became an important ally for Czełkowska, inviting the artist to participate in a number of exhibitions and helping her with the cost of materials and technology to produce demanding installations.
◀

Following pages:
Wokół polskiej rzeźby lat 70-tych i lat 80-tych XX wieku (Polish Sculpture of the 1970s and 1980s), exhibition view, Centre for Polish Sculpture, Orońsko, 1995. Featuring Wanda Czełkowska, *Absolute Elimination of Sculpture as a Notion of Shape* (*Bezwzględne wyeliminowanie rzeźby jako pojęcia kształtu*), 1972 [1995]

In 1995, Czełkowska was finally able to execute the concept for *Absolute Elimination of Sculpture as a Notion of Shape*, 1972 [1995] in its full scale. The artist reproduced her original design to almost the exact shape as it was conceived back in 1972, introducing a few minor changes in order to adapt to the architectural layout of the gallery.

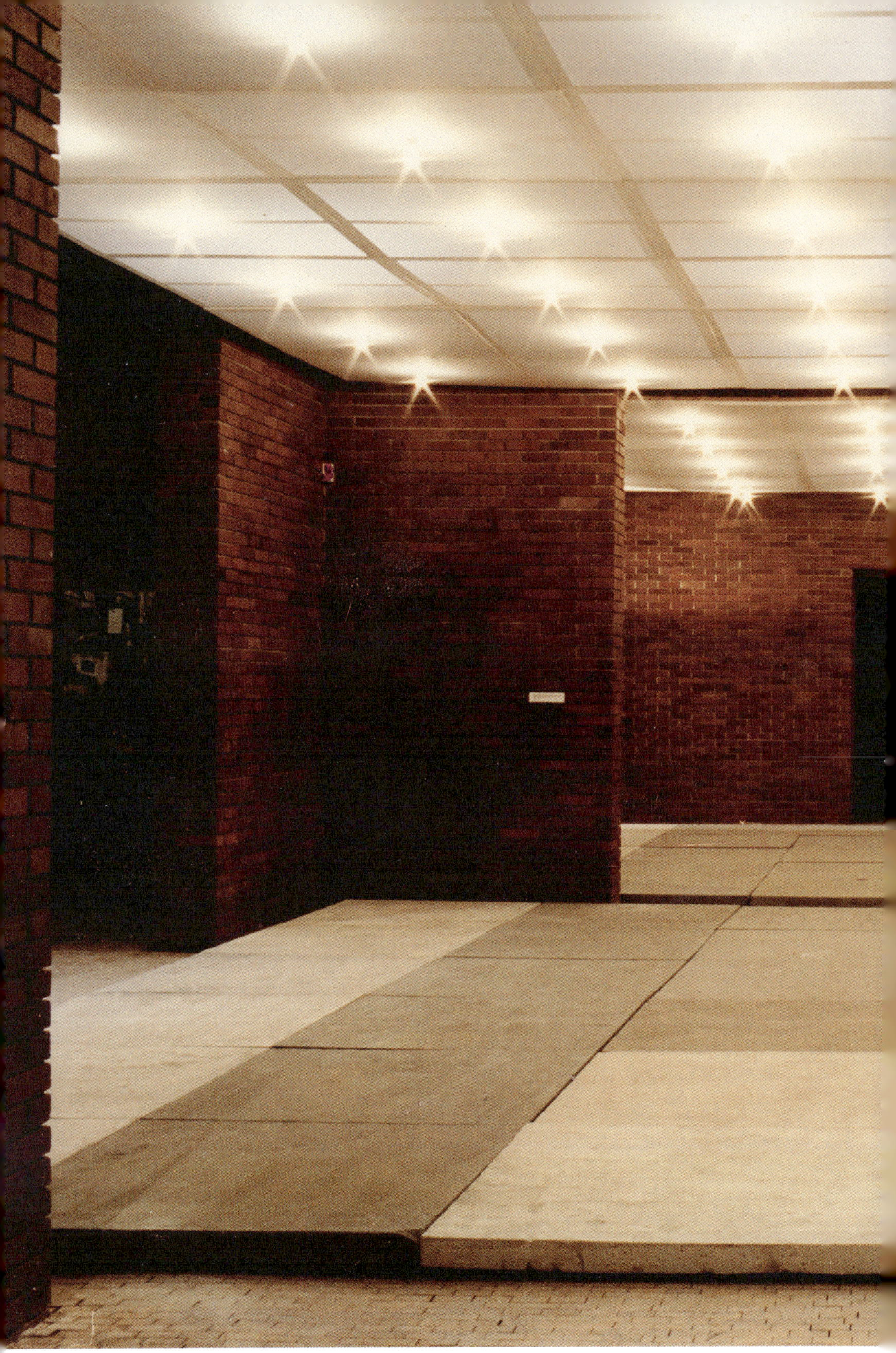

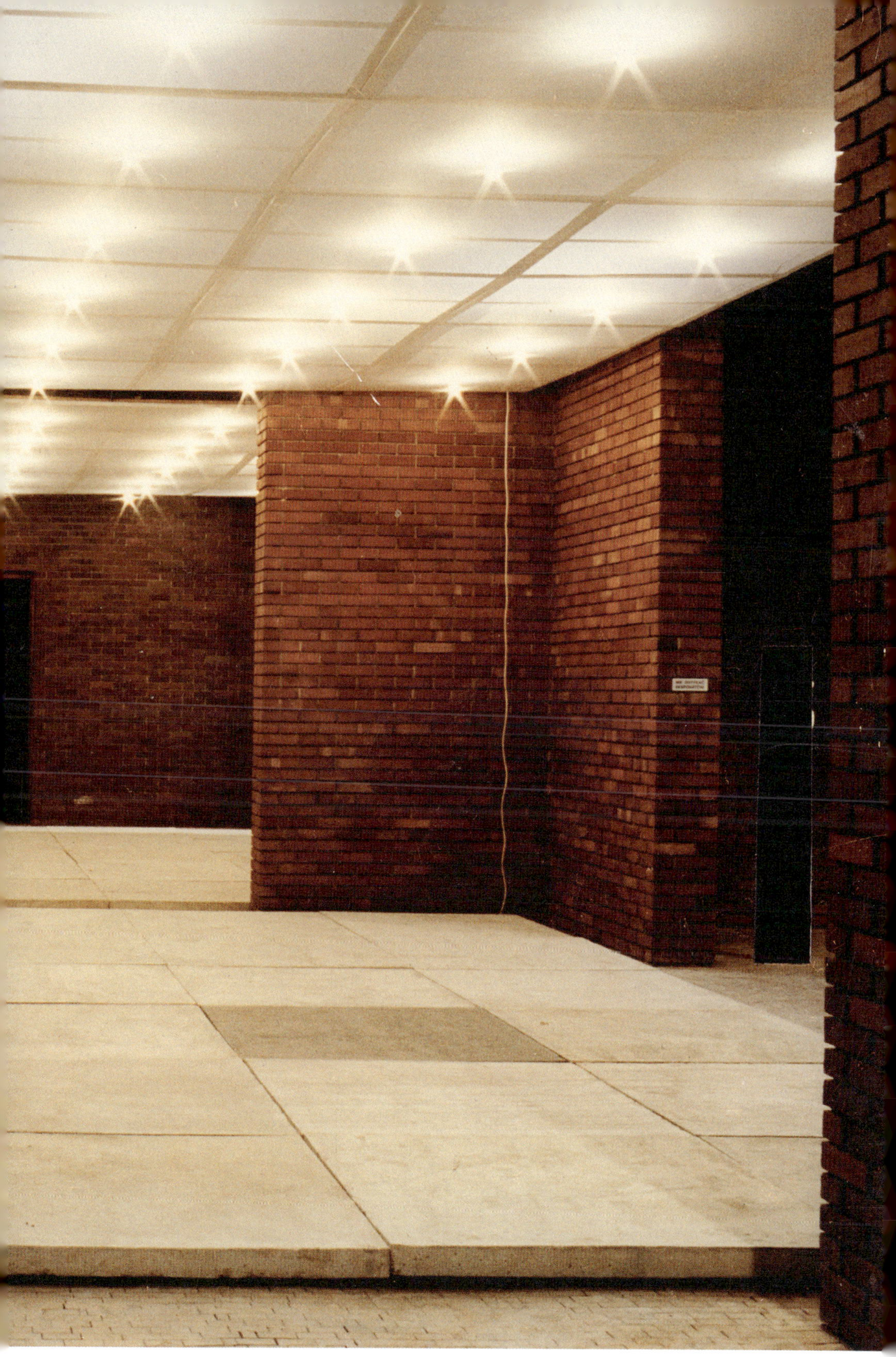

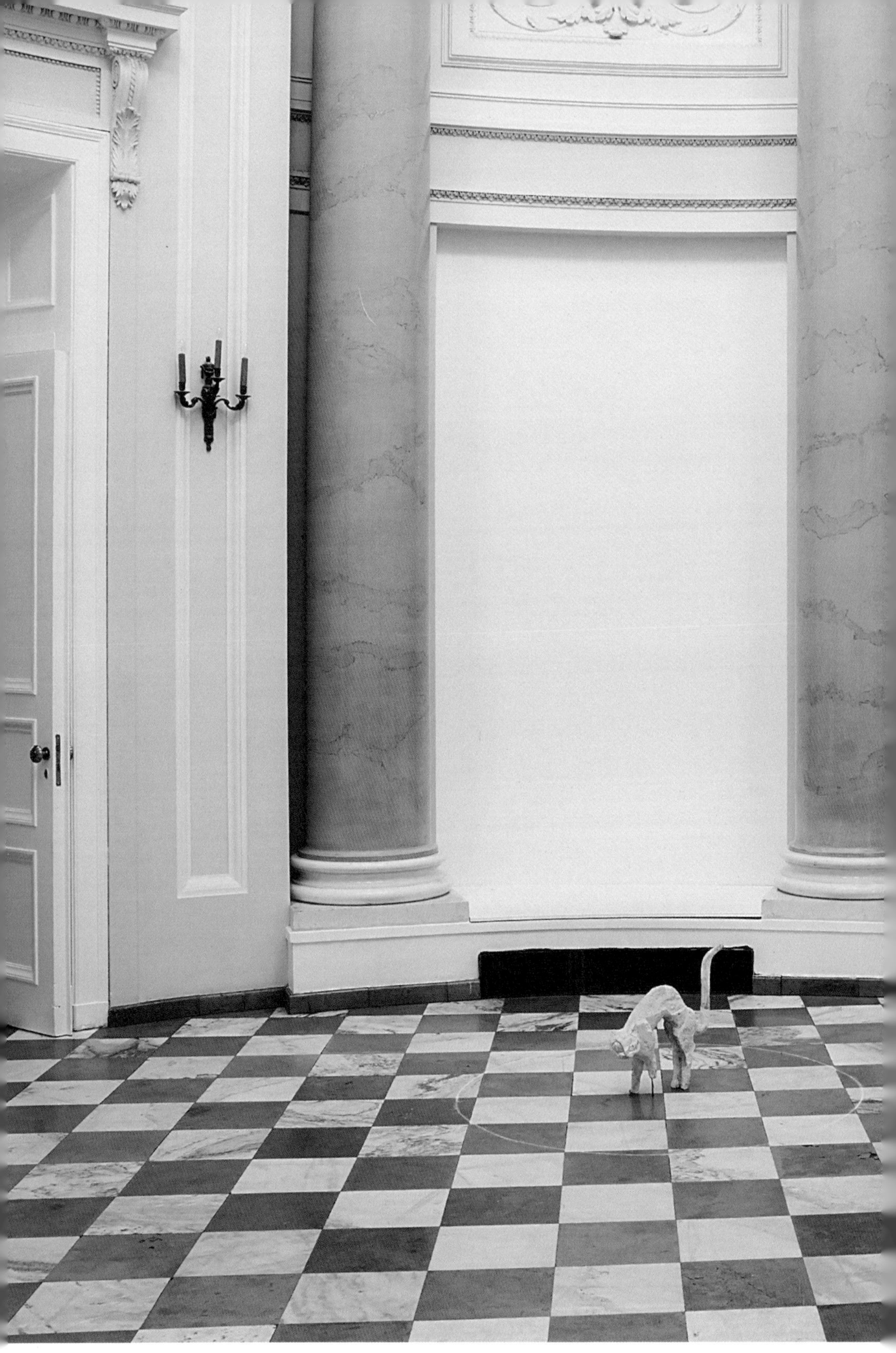

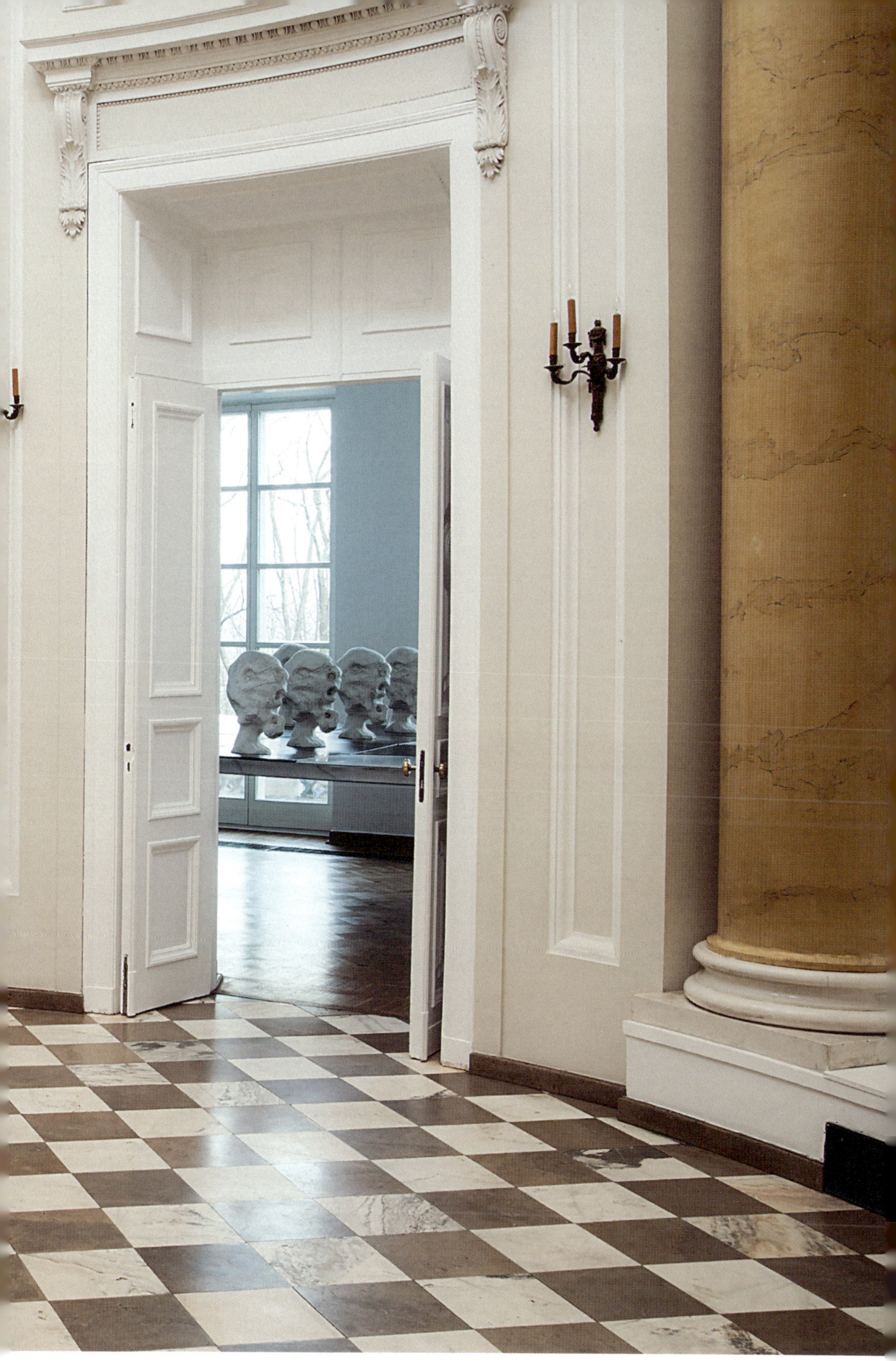

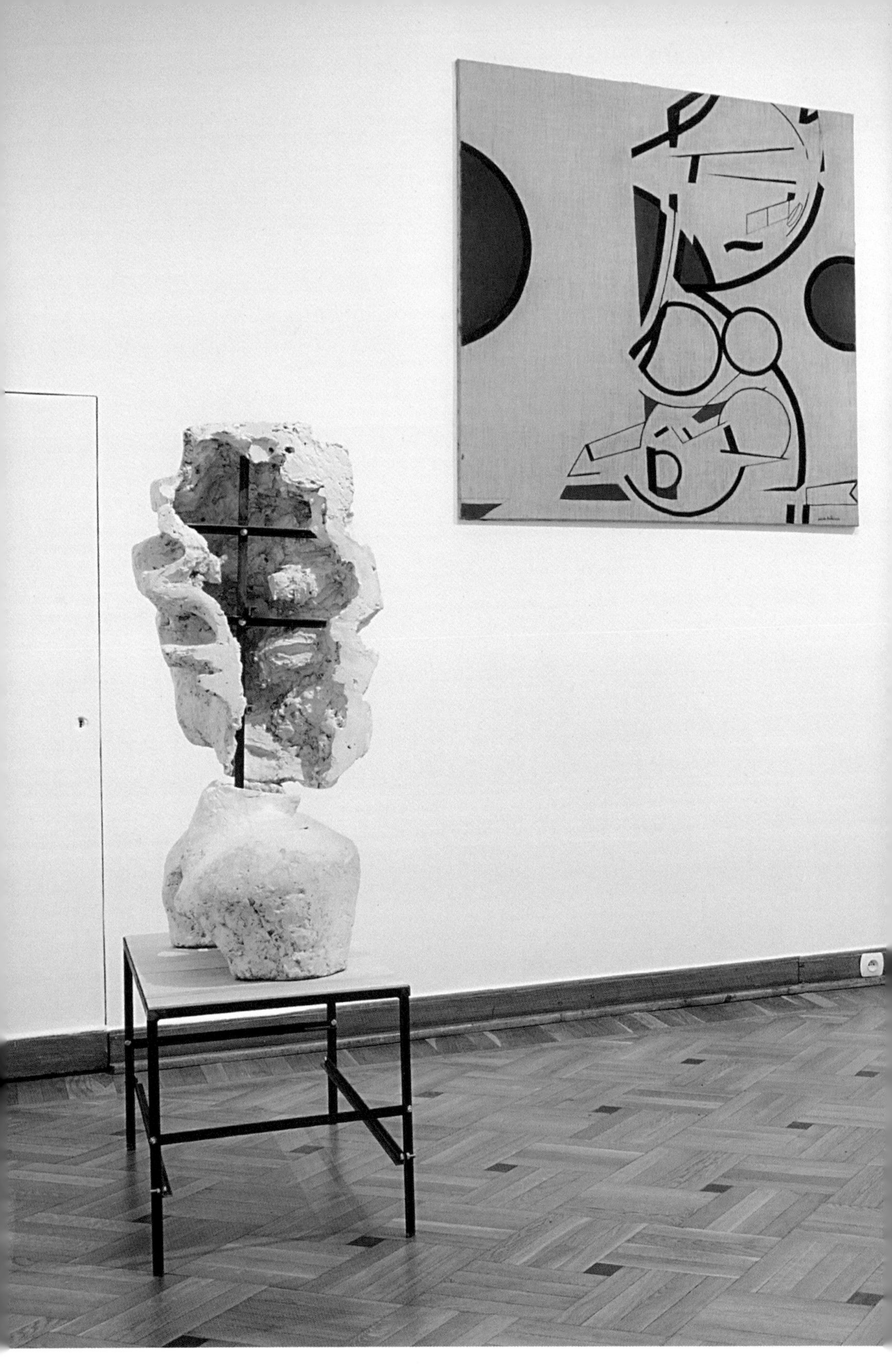

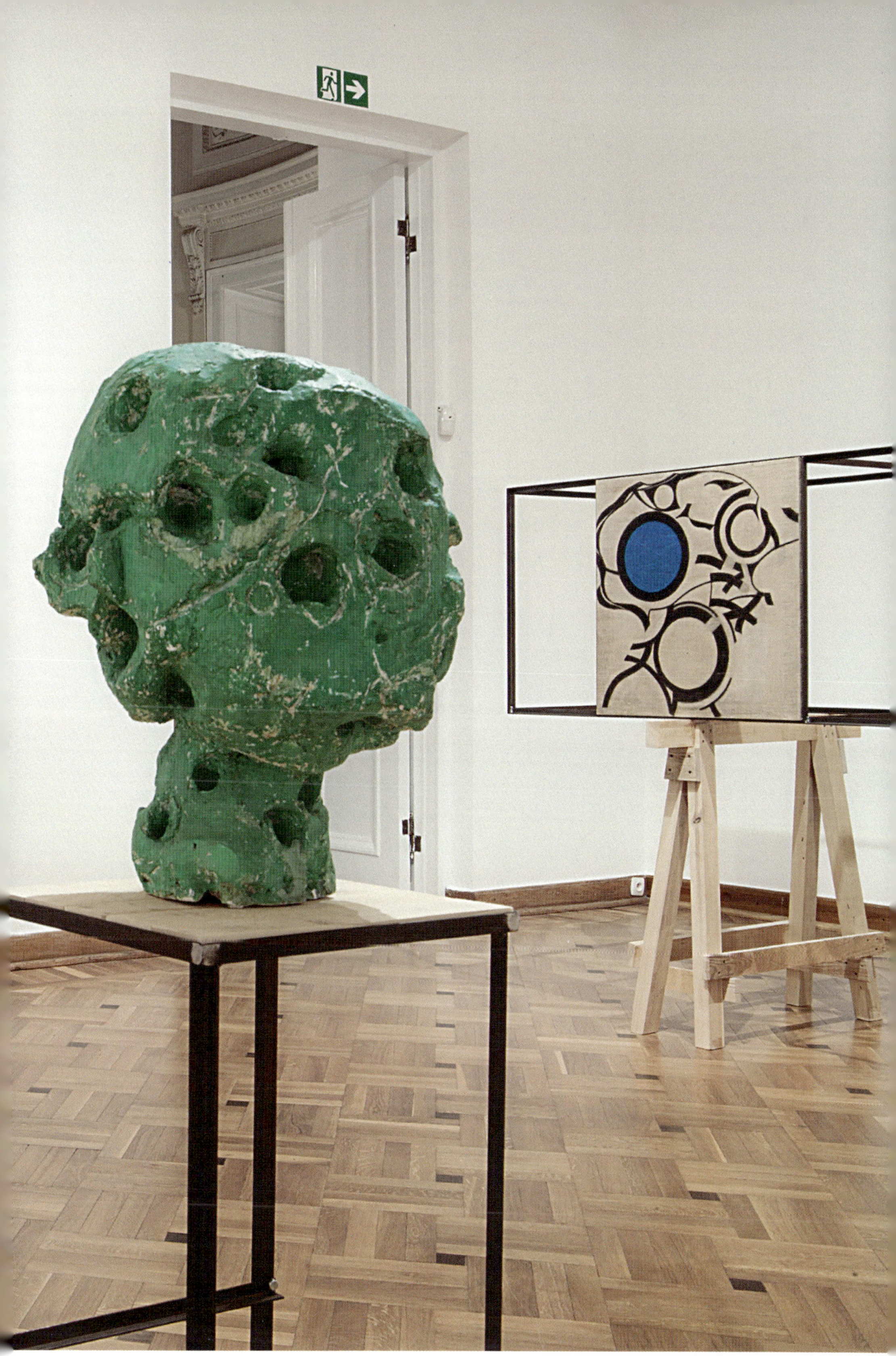

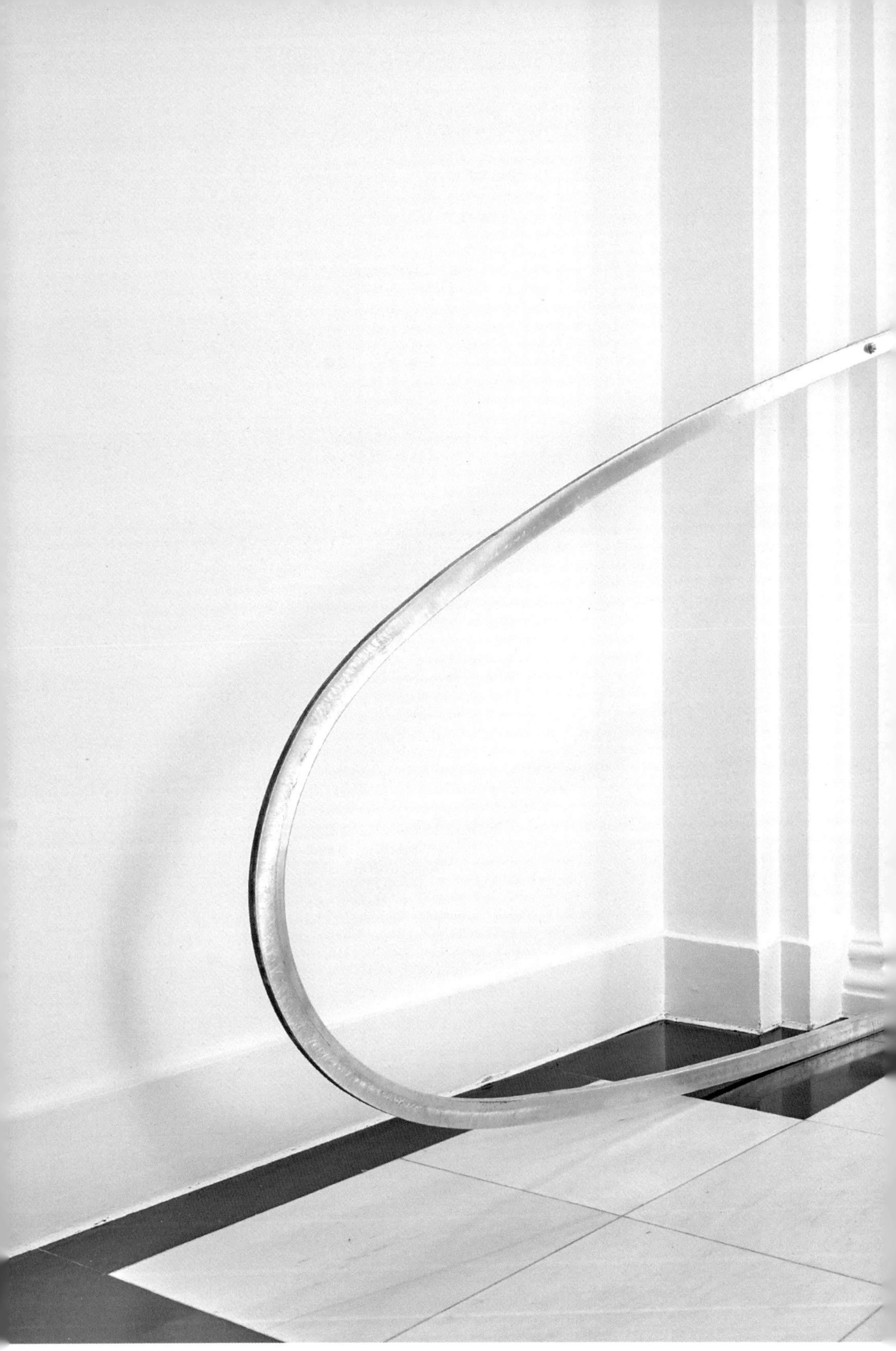

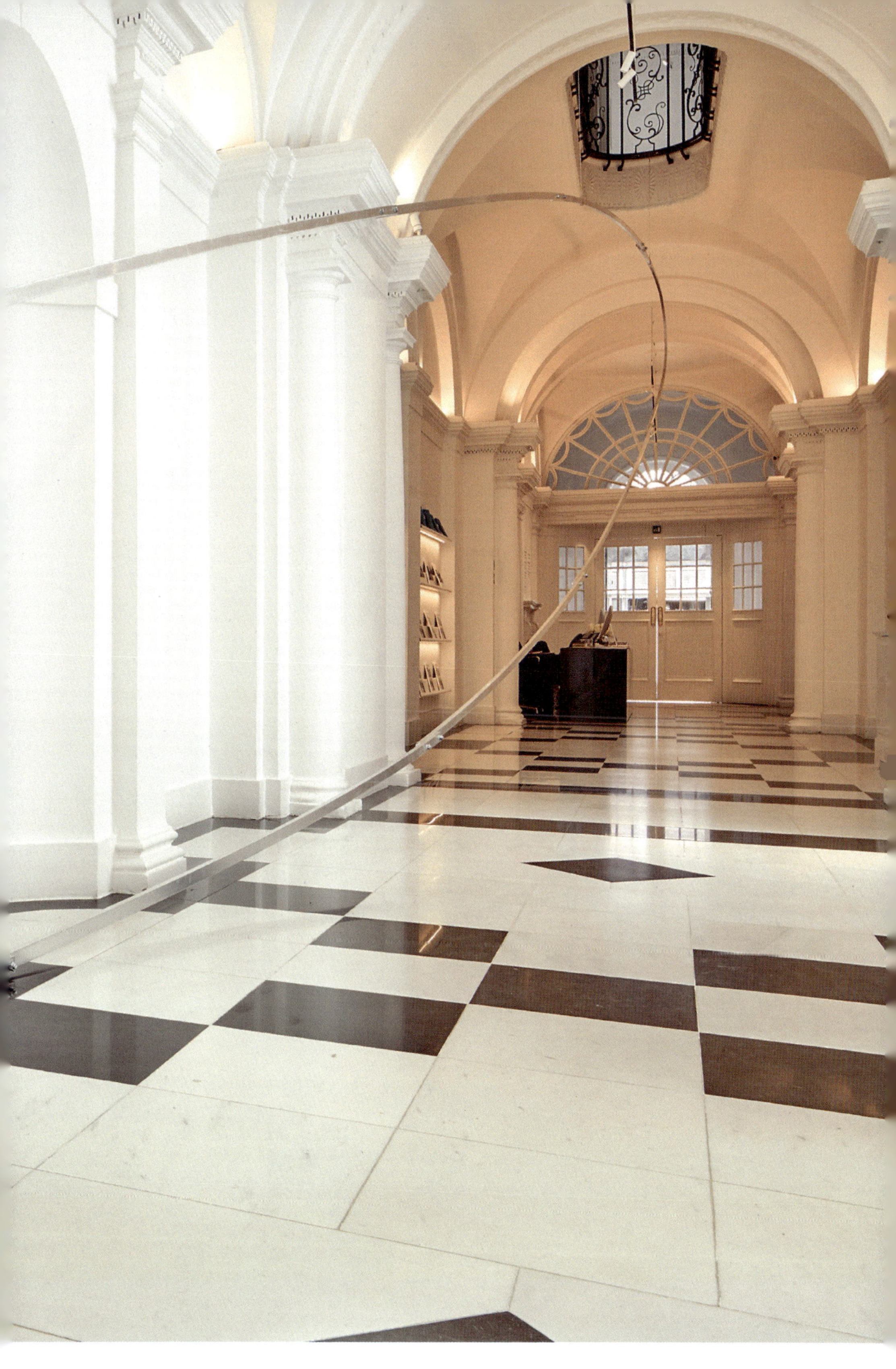

Pages 66–67:
Wanda Czełkowska. Retrospekcja (Wanda Czełkowska: Retrospection), exhibition view, Królikarnia – Xawery Dunikowski Museum of Sculpture (National Museum in Warsaw), 2017. Featured artworks (from the left): *Cat* (*Kot*), 1955, plaster; *Table* (*Stół*), 1968–1971, installation, mixed media. Photo: Szymon Rogiński

Pages 68–69:
Wanda Czełkowska. Retrospekcja (Wanda Czełkowska: Retrospection), exhibition view, Królikarnia – Xawery Dunikowski Museum of Sculpture (National Museum in Warsaw), 2017. Featured artworks (from the left): *Head* (*Głowa*), 1968, sculpture, plaster cast; *Sea Bird* (*Ptak morski*), 1977–1978, charcoal and tempera on canvas; *Green Head* (*Zielona głowa*), 1973, sculpture, cast and painted plaster; *Head – Kinetic Sequence* (*Głowa – Ciąg kinetyczny*), 1981, charcoal and tempera on canvas. Photo: Szymon Rogiński

In 2013, Wanda Czełkowska met Agnieszka Tarasiuk, chief curator at Królikarnia – Xawery Dunikowski Museum of Sculpture (National Museum in Warsaw). Shortly after, they embarked on the preparation of a retrospective exhibition of the artist, with Ewa Opałka appointed curator of the show.

Pages 70–71:
Land of Lads, Land of Lashes: Rosemarie Castoro, Wanda Czełkowska and Lydia Okumura, exhibition view, Thaddeus Ropac gallery, London, 2018. Featuring Wanda Czełkowska's *Ellipse* (*Elipsa*), 2016. Photo: Tom Carter, courtesy of Thaddeus Ropac gallery, London–Paris–Salzburg

In 2018, Czełkowska was invited to participate in the exhibition *Land of Lads, Land of Lashes: Rosemarie Castoro, Wanda Czełkowska and Lydia Okumura*, conceived by Anke Kempkes.

Wanda Czełkowska in her studio at 14 Magazynowa Street in Warsaw, 2016. Photo: Tadeusz Rolke, courtesy of Le Guern Gallery

In 2004, Wanda Czełkowska moved from Kraków to Warsaw, and a few years later was able to find a studio space large enough to accommodate her lifetime's body of work, located in a post-industrial area of the city, in a building which not long before served as a car service station. The artist spent the last decade of her life (2011–2021) working and living in her studio.
▶

[1] Marek Piasecki (1935–2011) was an artist who specialized in photography and assemblage. In 1958, he became a member of the Second Kraków Group.
[2] All translations from the original sources by Antonina Gugała.
[3] Unpublished letter to Juliusz Garztecki, editor-in-chief, *Ty i Ja* magazine, 1963.
[4] Piotr Krakowski, *Wanda Czełkowska*, Stowarzyszenie Artystyczne Grupa Krakowska, Kraków, 1963.
[5] Ewa Opałka, "Mam chyba skłonność do negacji", *La Vie Magazine* 4, 2015, 139–141.
[6] From the artist's unpublished notes, undated.
[7] Ewa Opałka, "Głowa w bagażu podręcznym", in *Eliminacje. Rozmowy z Wandą Czełkowską* (Eliminations. Conversations with Wanda Czełkowska), Warsaw, 2016, unpublished, 234.
[8] Anna Kłosowska, "The fifth leg of the table or the conservator's dilemmas: A few thoughts on Czełkowska's composition from the collection of the National Museum in Cracow", during the conference *Minimal, Conceptual and Material – the Phenomenon of Wanda Czełkowska's Sculptures*, 10–11 February 2017, National Museum in Warsaw.
[9] Unpublished draft of letter from 18 February 1982.
[10] Piotr Policht, *Nadeszła godzina ciężkiej próby. Sztuka w stanie wojennym*, culture.pl, https://culture.pl/pl/artykul/nadeszla-godzina-ciezkiej-proby-sztuka-w-stanie-wojennym

The first-ever "Wanda Czełkowska: Artistic Timeline" was published by Dorota Grubba-Thiede for the exhibition *Wanda Czełkowska. Retrospekcja* in 2017 (National Museum in Warsaw, pp. 92–135). It served as the starting point for my research, for which I am most grateful. I would also like to thank Dorota Grubba-Thiede and Maria Hussakowska for their help in identifying some of the artists in the archival photographs, as well as Ewa Opałka for sharing the unpublished version of her book manuscript. My thanks also go to Ona Winogrodzka, from the artist's estate, for her kindness in allowing me to spend endless hours combing through the artist's archive.

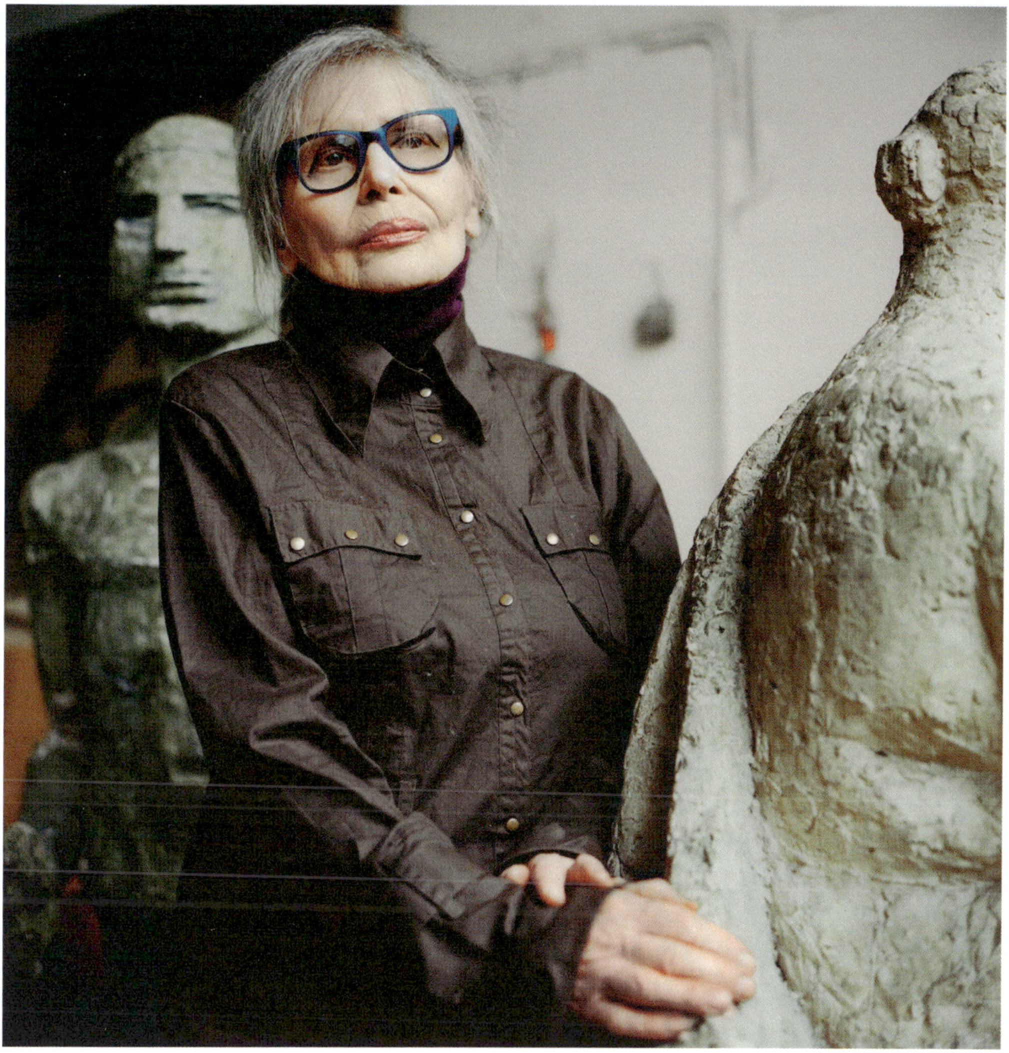

The Elliptical Trajectory of Wanda Czełkowska

Matylda Taszycka

"What I don't do now, I will never do … the presence of an artist in their studio at a given, unique moment cannot be questioned, postponed."[1] In Wanda Czełkowska's (1930–2021) former studio notes are piled up everywhere, in notebooks, on loose sheets of paper, sometimes illegible and more often than not without dates. Her hasty hand reflects the urgency of the thought, a faculty she assimilates with the creative act. I read this note several times. And I wonder about our meeting that never was. What is the position of the art historian and their inevitably deferred perspective? Examining an artist's work retrospectively is akin to turning up too late to an appointment.

The expectations, however, seem clear: to make a body of work and a career known and give it recognition, to form connections with better known artists, and propose avenues for interpretation. Behind this work lies the thorny question of its inscription *a posteriori* into the canon. Wanda Czełkowska is obviously not the only sculptor to have been neglected. "Social representations have long held that the qualities associated with the female condition and the virile imaginary world of the sculptor (physical strength, confrontation with the materials, the authority of the master over assistants and practitioners…) are incompatible. If one adds to this the economic constraints of traditional sculpture, such as the high cost of casting, we can gauge the multiple obstacles that face female sculptors."[2] In 1959, on the death of Germaine Richier, one of the rare female artists to have experienced international success in her lifetime, French weekly *L'Express* ran the headline: "Sculpture. So a woman can create". The paucity of consideration for women's work in this field may explain why Czełkowska always preferred the masculine noun "sculptor" to "sculptress".

To the observation of the derogation and marginalisation of women sculptors, another difficulty can be added. Wanda Czełkowska was an artist who spent most of her career in the Polish People's Republic. The geographical estrangement, the specific political and cultural context in which she worked, the absence of her work in the collections of international museums, the language barrier that makes access to the archives all the more laborious… these are just some of the reasons for her omission from reference works dedicated to sculpture.[3] However, one question has preoccupied me since embarking on this book. What is my role, as a Polish art historian, who has trained and always worked in France, in the journey of Czełkowska's art through consciousnesses, texts, and exhibition spaces? This text is naturally the expression of my situated gaze. Is Czełkowska's inclusion in the Western canon necessary to ensure her recognition? How can one avoid falling into the trap of the discourse of the "discovery" of a "forgotten" artist?[4] In the long term, only in-depth research is the most effective remedy against amnesia. As Anne Lafont has rightly commented: "[T]he goal is not so much neutrality as transparency in the production of knowledge".[5]

1. Wanda Czełkowska with *Self-Portrait* (*Autoportret*), 1959, sculpture, cast, painted plaster, 87 × 55 × 30 cm, National Museum in Kraków. Photo c. 1959. Courtesy of the artist's estate

Art historians and curators Dorota Grubba-Thiede, Maria Hussakowska, Anke Kempkes, Ewa Opałka, and Agnieszka Tarasiuk[6] have studied and sought to place the work of Wanda Czełkowska in a national and international context. Their work has been published in a catalogue accompanying the artists retrospective, *Wanda Czełkowska. Retrospekcja* (Wanda Czełkowska: Retrospection), which was held in 2016 at Królikarnia – Xawery Dunikowski Museum of Sculpture, a branch of the National Museum in Warsaw, and curated by Ewa Opałka. The ambition of this book is to contribute to their discussion.

Wanda Czełkowska is not an unknown on the Polish scene. Nor is she one of its celebrities. Born in 1930 in Brześć nad Bugiem (now Brest in Belarus), Czełkowska spent her early years in Vilnius (now in Lithuania). She was not yet nine years of age when the Second World War broke out. Several years later, as the conflict was coming to a close, she left the city of her childhood to escape the expanding Soviet Union. After meeting the sculptor Xawery Dunikowski,[7] she decided to enrol at the Academy of Fine Arts in Kraków, where she studied sculpture in Jerzy Bandura's studio from 1949 to 1954.[8] Her studying years corresponded with the height of Stalinism in Poland, which is mirrored in art with the imposition of the socialist-realist doctrine. The artist took refuge in

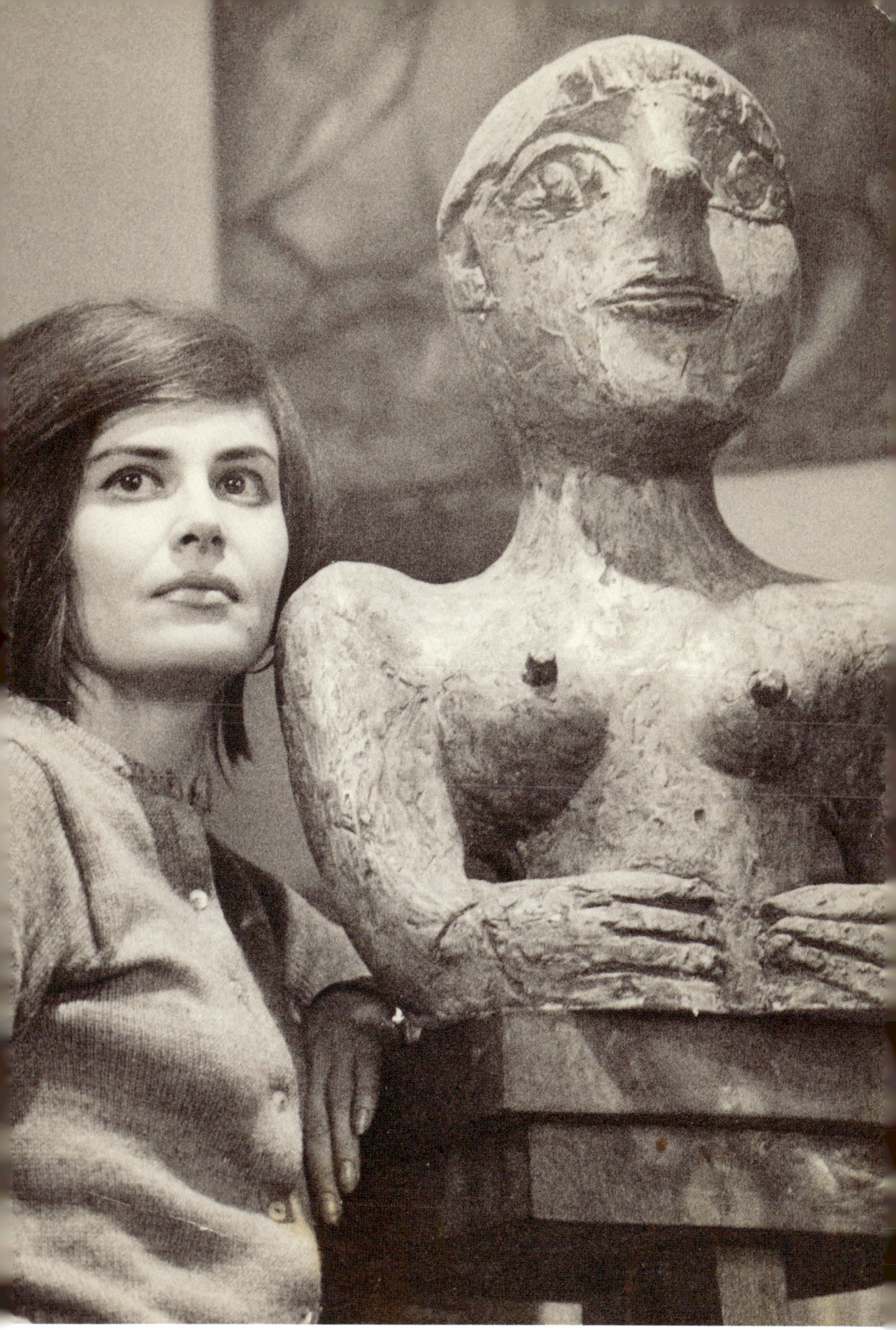

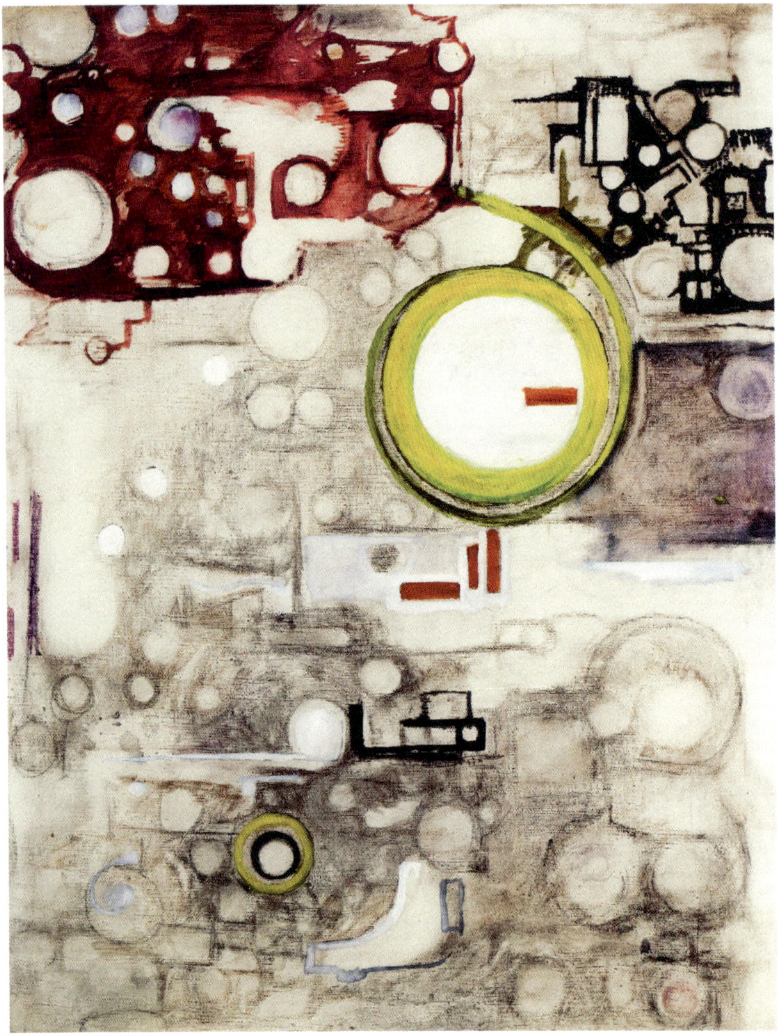

2. Wanda Czełkowska, *Untitled*, c. 1970, charcoal and tempera on canvas, 73 × 92 cm. Courtesy of the artist's estate Photo: Antonina Gugała

the libraries of Kraków to study works devoted to art, philosophy (French in particular) and contemporary music.

Between 1955 and 1959, a period that coincides with the start of her professional career and a time of relative political liberalisation in Poland, she created figurative sculptures that reflected her interest in classical sources (notably Greek and Etruscan sculptures), which is particularly evident in the full-length figure *Man* (*Mężczyzna*, 1956; fig. p. 17) and the bust *Self-Portrait* (*Autoportret*, 1959). This is also the first time that the artist explicitly identifies herself with one of her own works (fig. 1 and figs. pp. 20, 21). During the same period, she began designing an anti-gravity space composed of a sphere and a cube (1959–1969).[9]

3. Wanda Czełkowska, *Head* (*Głowa*), 1968–1970, oil, pencil and charcoal on canvas, 90 × 121 cm. Courtesy of the artist's estate
Photo: Paulina Staszkiewicz

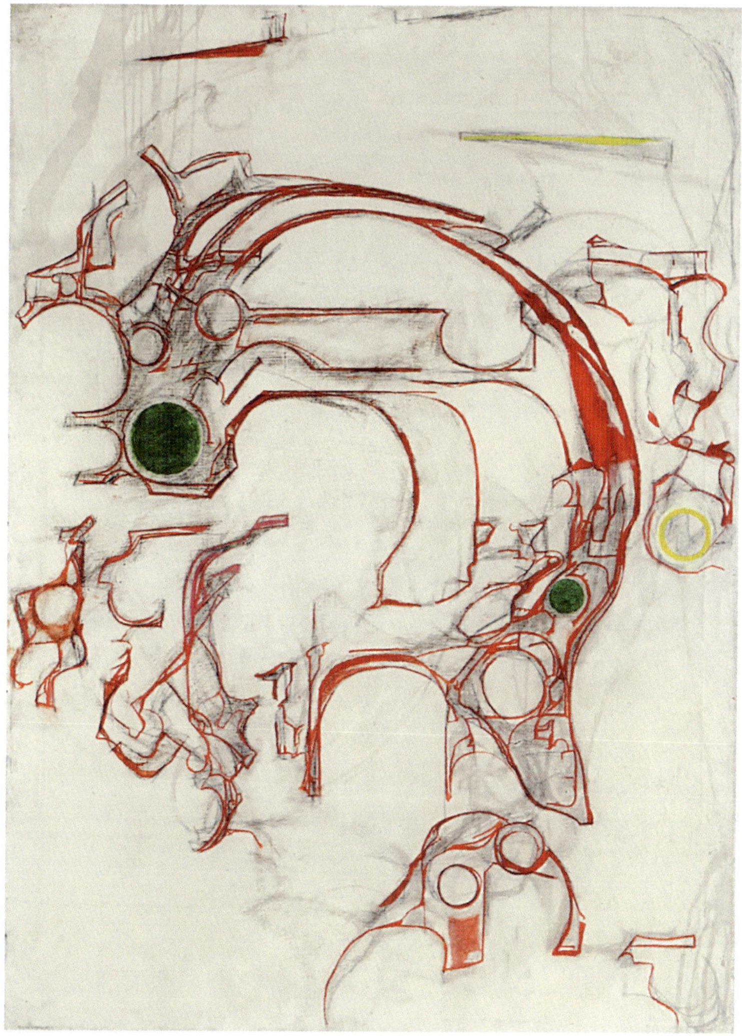

The piece, which remained in the draft phase, is a proto-environment and foreshadows her future preoccupations, particularly with space and geometry.

In 1961, Wanda Czełkowska was awarded first place in a competition for a medal to mark the 50th anniversary of the Związek Polskich Artystów Plastyków (Association of Polish Artists and Designers) for her representation of the myth of Pygmalion. The *Players* (*Gracze*) group (figs. pp. 22, 23) also won first prizes for a sculpture in a public space (never realized). This piece showed her nascent interest in the relationship her work has with its viewers by inviting them to take their place amongst figures gathered around a table. Formally, her sculptures, mostly busts, became more schematic. As Dorota

Grubba-Thiede demonstrates, from the 1960s onwards, one can observe the porosity between her drawing and sculpting practice (in particular, through her way of working the plaster with a chisel).[10] The figures became simpler, facial features more geometric, but also more expressive. Occasionally, it is possible to recognise individuals from the artist's entourage, even if the sculptor herself refuted any comparison with a real-life portrait.

From 1963 onwards, her engagement in the artistic scene intensified. She opened her first solo exhibition in Galeria Krzysztofory.[11] In a passage published in the small accompanying catalogue, the critic Piotr Krakowski described her work as "neo-expressionist".[12] In the same year, her sculpture *Self-Portrait* was exhibited at the Third Paris Biennale. Czełkowska was awarded a grant that allowed her to travel to France and Italy. In Paris, she visited the graphic artist Roman Cieślewicz, her friend, and the sculptor Alina Szapocznikow. Back in Kraków, she worked intensively on new sculptures, including *Head* (*Głowa*, 1964), an imposing plaster head with the appearance of a stone[13] and deeply hollowed features (fig. p. 59).

The following ten years were extremely rich for Czełkowska on an artistic level. From the mid-1960s onwards, the artist produced a series of drawings and paintings on canvas that pre-empted the development of her sculptural work (fig. 2). In these abstract compositions, which can bring to mind organic and urban fabrics, Czełkowska experiments with the form thanks to the interplay of solids and voids. The circular motif also made its appearance in her work (fig. 3), heralding the *Heads* series, created from 1968 onwards (including the literally "exploded" head displaying its metal structure; fig. pp. 68–69). That same year, the artist was also invited by Tadeusz Kantor to join the Second Kraków Group.[14]

1969 marks a break. Invited to present her work in a solo exhibition at Galeria Współczesna in Warsaw,[15] she preferred to show recent drawings rather than her older sculptures. Shortly after, she unveiled the object of her research. On the occasion of the 11th exhibition of the Second Kraków Group (1970–1971), she published the instructions for the installation *Table* (*Stół*;

4. *Wanda Czełkowska. Retrospekcja* (Wanda Czełkowska: Retrospection), exhibition view, Królikarnia – Xawery Dunikowski Museum of Sculpture (National Museum in Warsaw), 2017. Featured artworks (from the left): *Green Head* (*Zielona głowa*), 1973 (from the collection of National Museum in Kraków); *Head – the Kinetic Sequence* (*Głowa – Ciąg kinetyczny*), 1981. Courtesy of National Museum in Warsaw Photo: Szymon Rogiński

figs. pp. 44–45 and 116). The work was presented in December 1971 as part of the *Spotkania krakowskie* (Kraków Encounters) exhibition and impressed with its monumentality. In parallel with this, Czełkowska produced a series of photographs *Theme* (*Temat*, 1970–1971; fig. p. 37). in which she depicts herself veiled, transforming her own head into an ephemeral sculpture. She immediately received an invitation from Richard Demarco to reproduce *Table* as part of the *Atelier '72* event in Edinburgh. In 1972, she travelled to Scotland with other Polish artists, but due to technical difficulties, she finally presented *Conceptual Information about "The Table"* (*Informacja pojęciowa o "Stole"*) in which she gave up the three-dimensional structure, replacing it with informative panels (figs. pp. 110 and 126).

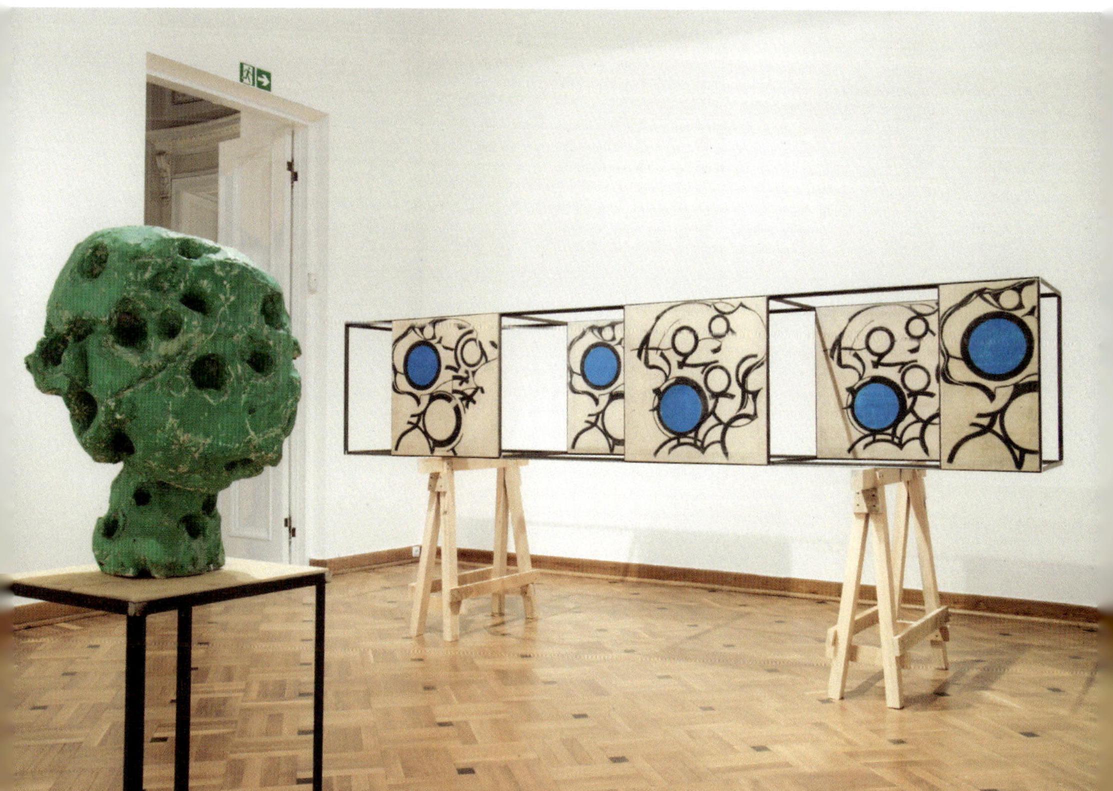

Czełkowska then returned to Kraków to work on the concept for *Absolute Elimination of Sculpture as a Notion of Shape* (*Bezwzględne wyeliminowanie rzeźby jako pojęcia kształtu*), the model and photographic documentation of which she presented in 1973 at the Pryzmat Gallery in Kraków (fig. p. 122), then in Sopot as part of the *Porównania* (Comparisons) exhibition. This installation constitutes her most radical achievement, thanks in particular to its perfectly assumed modular character (already present in the *Table*). She conceived the sculpture as a negative space, 'framed' by the floor, which is made up of 66 white and black concrete slabs, and the ceiling with 66 points of light. Through this work, the artist crystallised her research on the notions of structure and space. This also corroborated her interest in the viewer's perspective. In 1975, at an exhibition in Warsaw dedicated to Dunikowski, she exhibited *Wall* (*Ściana*) for the first time. Although at first glance this work seems to break with the conceptual installation produced a few years earlier, the artist is in fact pursuing the same subjects while continuing her formal experiments (figs. pp. 150 and 152).

As for many other Polish artists, the 1980s was a time of protest and refusal to exhibit at official events. In February 1982, Czełkowska officially left the Second Kraków Group.[16] In 1981, the sculptor produced *Head – the Kinetic Sequence* (*Głowa – Ciąg kinetyczny*), a cycle of paintings on canvas presented initially in the form of a frieze (fig. 4).[17] The organic character present in her works of the 1970s disappears in favour of geometric features. The circles are reminiscent of cogs, as if to express the idea of the intellectual process of creation. The head now resembles a machine in motion, presaging the debate around the relationship between man and technology.

In March 1990, in the midst of political and economic transformation, Czełkowska was given two solo exhibitions at Galeria Zderzak in Kraków. Presented as a comeback after years in obscurity, it was a genuine artistic event reported in one of the first issues of the Polish daily *Gazeta Wyborcza*.[18] The artist notably exhibited *Elegy* (*Elegia*, 1990; fig. p. 136), in which she explores the principle of a physical and visual barrier already present in *Wall* (*Ściana*). The work is composed of 9 frames that rest on a monumental wooden structure. Czełkowska made a return to abstract language, but her geometric design softened and became more gestural.

During the 1990s, she took part in numerous group exhibitions, including *Artyści z Krakowa* (Artists from Kraków) at Zachęta National Art Gallery in 1993, where she presented the polyptych *Black Frieze* (*Czarny fryz*, 1968–1969–1971–1973), then titled *Nostalgia* (*Nostalgy*). In the same year, her work was shown in the *Nowoczesna rzeźba polska 1955-1992* (Modern Polish Sculpture 1955–1992) exhibition at the Centre of Polish Sculpture in Orońsko. It was also in Orońsko that she created *Absolute Elimination of Sculpture as a Notion of Shape* on a 1:1 scale (figs. pp. 64–65 and 142). Although the 1970s instructions do not mention the role of the spectator, he or she can move freely on the gridded floor of the installation created in 1995. In 1996, she presented *The Closed Park Sculpture, i.e. the Infinite Right* (*Rzeźba parkowa zamknięta, czyli prosta nieskończona*) there, an installation of spruce beams that crisscross the Orangery building.

In the 2000s, a new generation of researchers and curators became interested in her work, notably Dorota Grubba-Thiede, who analysed her work in the context of post-war developments in Polish sculpture, and Ewa Opałka, who proposed a feminist reinterpretation of it.

In the closing years of her life, she continued to receive artists, art historians and art critics in her studio. Her works can be found in Polish museum collections, including the National Museum in Kraków, which owns her monumental works such as *Table* and *Wall*.[19]

Wanda Czełkowska's invitation to join the Second Kraków Group, "an exclusive club and an informal academy of modern art",[20] is an undeniable sign of recognition. The exhibition at Galeria Współczesna and her collaborations with Richard Demarco and Ryszard Stanisławski, director of Muzeum Sztuki in Łódź, in the 1970s, show that she was well integrated into various avant-garde circles. Her participation in retrospective exhibitions of Polish sculpture and the renewed support from the Centre for Polish Sculpture in Orońsko are also

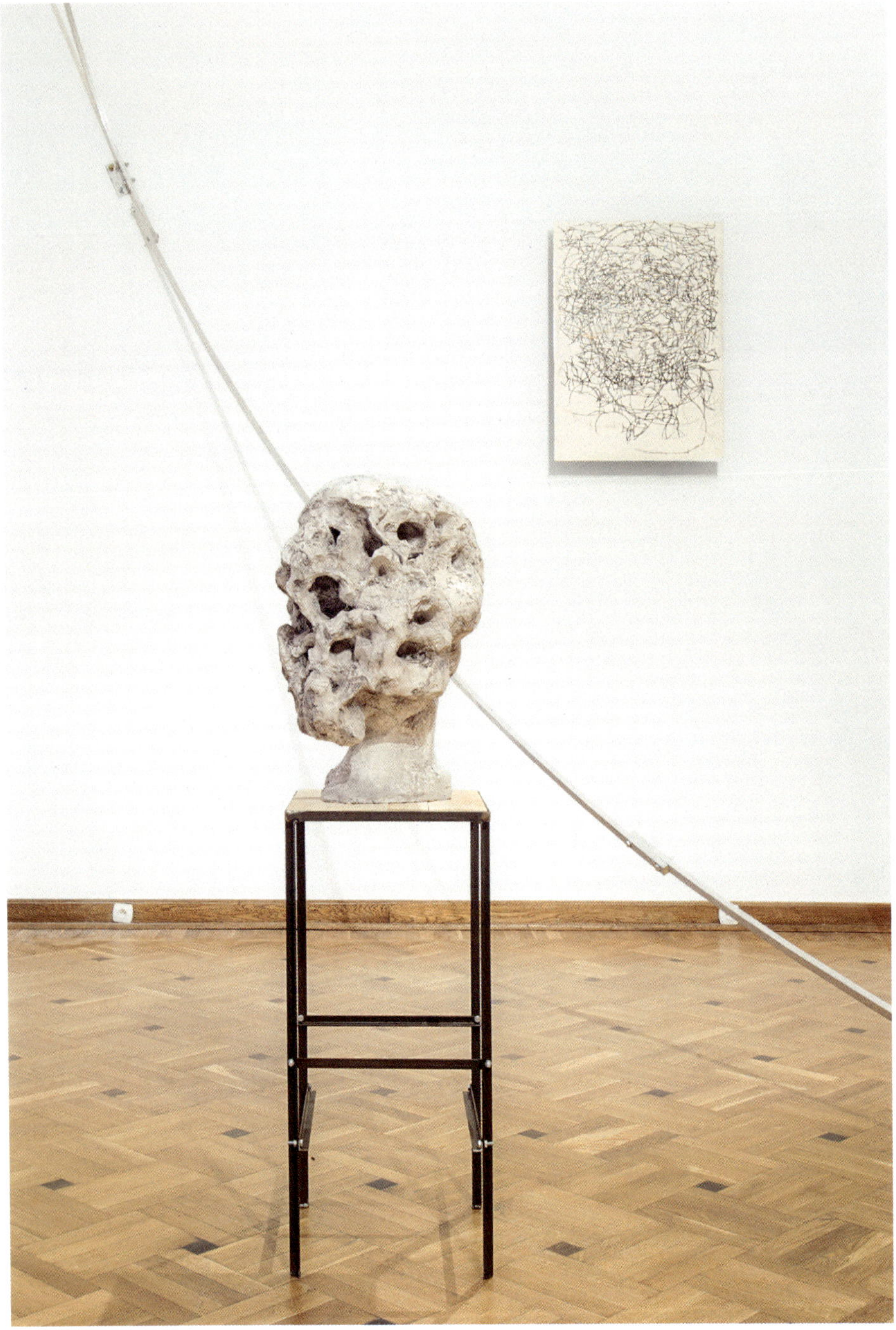

5. *Wanda Czełkowska. Retrospekcja* (Wanda Czełkowska: Retrospection), exhibition view, Królikarnia – Xawery Dunikowski Museum of Sculpture (National Museum in Warsaw), 2017. Featured artworks (from the left): *Head* (*Głowa*), 1972/2016; *Ellipse* (*Elipsa*), 2016; *Analysis* (*Analiza*), 1986. Courtesy of National Museum in Warsaw Photo: Szymon Rogiński

testimony to the acknowledgment she received within her profession. And lastly, the artist seized those rare opportunities to exhibit her work abroad.[21]

The specific context in which Czełkowska lived can at least partially shed light on her career choices, her way of working and the conditions in which her works have been handed down to us today. The end of socialist realism (the dominant doctrine at the time Czełkowska was studying), the 1956 'thaw' that accompanied the advent of a modernist counter-doctrine (the period when the sculptor began to work professionally), the liberalisation of cultural policy in the 1970s and, conversely, the repression following the proclamation of martial law in December 1981, as well as the political and economic transformation of the 1990s, are generational experiences that link her to other Polish artists of her time. The return of private property in the 1990s, for example, confronted cultural circles with the brutal realities of the property market. Based in Kraków after completing her studies, Czełkowska also had to contend with evictions. Some of her sculptures and canvases were badly damaged after the cellar in which she kept her works was flooded. After the loss of her last apartment in Kraków, she moved to Warsaw at the age of 74. Between 2010 and 2018, she moved into a disused truck repair garage in the Mokotów district, which she transformed into a studio and rather precarious living quarters. It was only towards the end of her life that the artist benefited from an apartment that allowed her to separate her living space from her working space.

Following pages:
6. *Wanda Czełkowska. Retrospekcja* (Wanda Czełkowska: Retrospection), exhibition view, Królikarnia – Xawery Dunikowski Museum of Sculpture (National Museum in Warsaw), 2017. Featured artworks (from the left): *Ellipse* (*Elipsa*), 2016; *Blue Head* (*Niebieska głowa*), 1967; *Pink Head* (*Różowa głowa*), 1962; *Head* (*Głowa*), 1962 (from the collection of National Museum in Kraków); *The 10th Study* (*Studium X-te*), 1957; *Head* (*Głowa*), 1972/2016. Courtesy of National Museum in Warsaw Photo: Szymon Rogiński

Her career was composed of moments of acceleration and pause, which it would be difficult to interpret unequivocally. The artist claimed that she was able to interrupt her work when the material conditions were not met. Numerous accounts refer to her strong character, difficult collaborations and an unwillingness to compromise.[22] It is also interesting to note that for years the artist 'slipped through the cracks' of the feminist art history and criticism that had developed in Poland from the 1990s onwards. Czełkowska, for her part, was wary of the gendered reinterpretation of her work.[23]

Finally, one aspect brings the phenomenon of Wanda Czełkowska closer to the paths of many female artists, in Poland and elsewhere: the late institutional

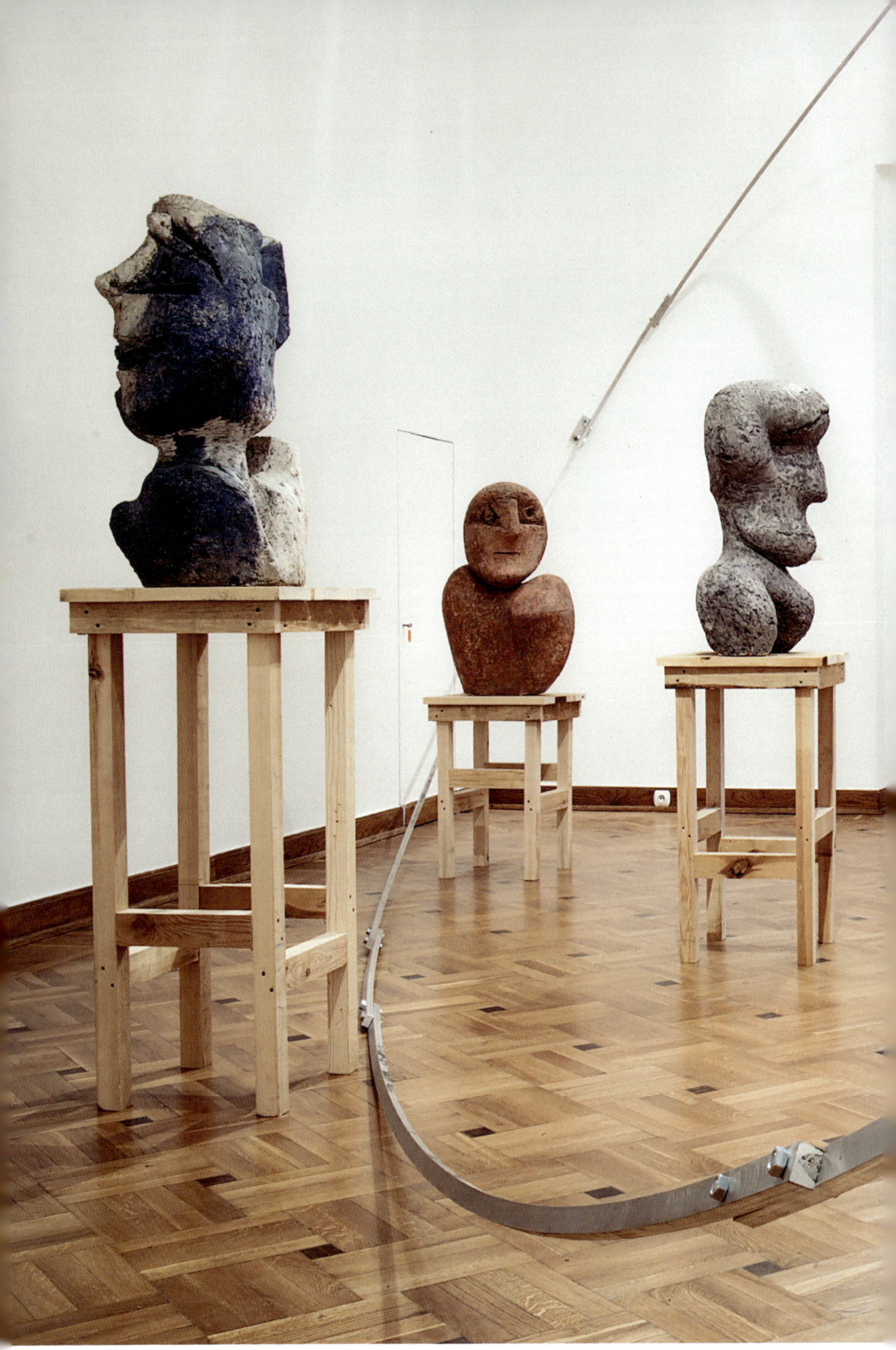

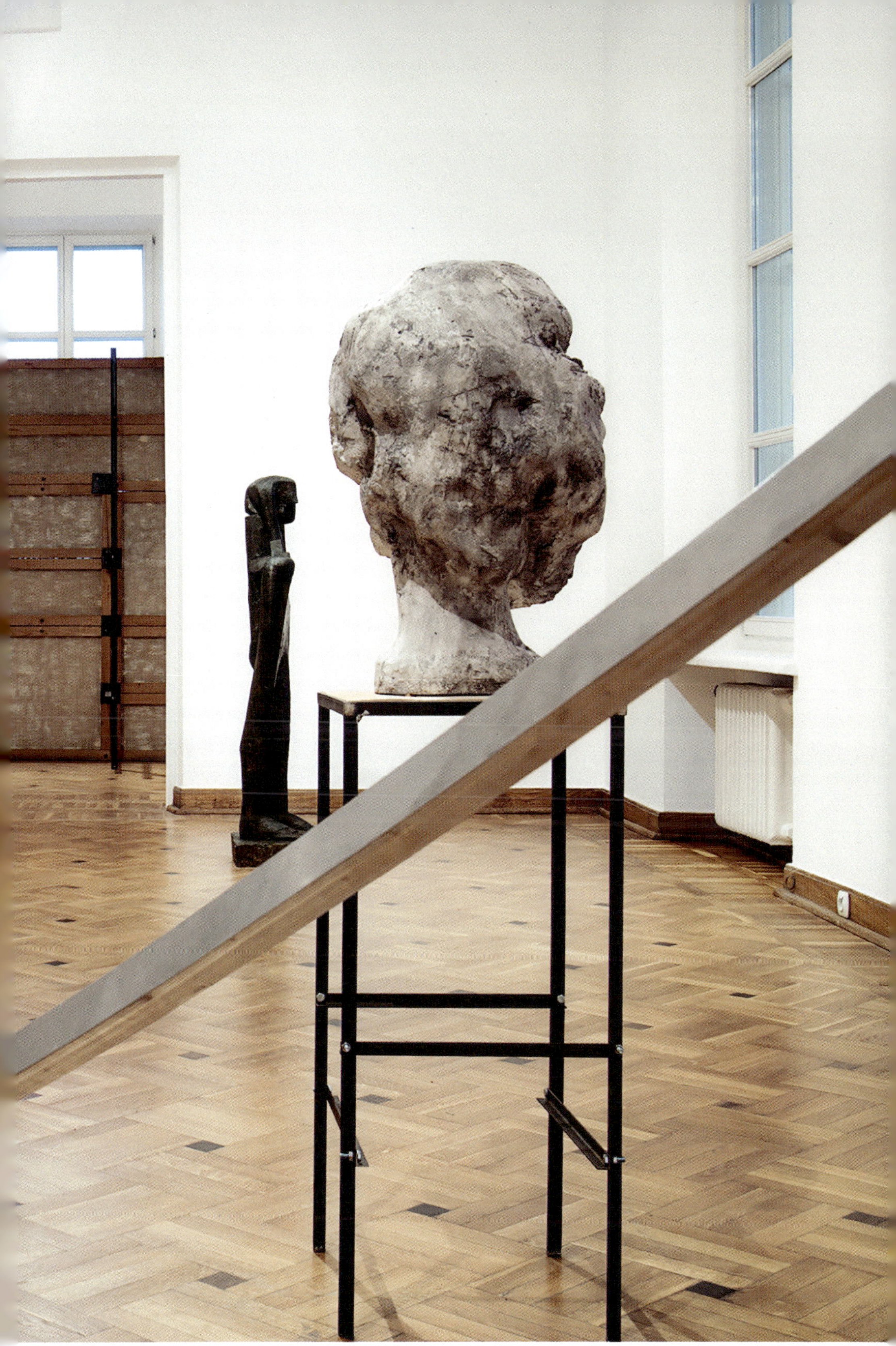

consecration of her work. At the time of the opening of her retrospective in Królikarnia in Warsaw, the artist was already 86 years old. To this day, no modern art museum in Poland or abroad has dedicated a solo exhibition to her.

This phenomenon is well known to feminist art historians. While the most famous example is that of Louise Bourgeois, by far the best known of the artists who gained recognition late in life, it illustrates a pattern that could be applied to dozens of women artists who achieved late renown. We have learned to value the continuous and progressive careers of male artists, without taking into account the pause often represented by maternity or other responsibilities borne by women in our societies. We rarely consider the difficulties involved in 'restarting' a career after a break.[24]

Like time machines, retrospective exhibitions and publications seek to situate forgotten or neglected artists in the artistic trends of their time. The objective is laudable: to place a practice in its time and space, to act as a marker for future studies. More often than not, these initiatives also aspire to demonstrate retroactively the "compatibility" of these artists with the canon by highlighting the existence of their personal and professional relationships with more established artists (to prove their legitimacy) or by proposing formal connections (to prove their contemporaneity). Consequently, any compensatory effect can only be partial. In the catalogue for the Królikarnia exhibition, Maria Hussakowska also returns to this question: "*every* comeback assumes the distortion of the original signal, a deformation",[25] she writes. As Griselda Pollock remarks about Louise Bourgeois, "[t]he absence of a critical acknowledgement at the right moment means that there is no recovery of that lost chance to be seen in one's own history, as the absence in the historical record or archive can never be retrospectively filled by what was never said."[26]

For a career spanning almost 60 years, the critical literature on Wanda Czełkowska is comparatively modest. The book published in 2017 for her exhibition at Królikarnia remains the most comprehensive to date. Her archive contains very few traces of the artist's social or worldly life. In the testimonies of her acquaintances and relatives, the expression *artystka osobna*[27] (individual artist, apart, separate from the others) is often used, as if this insistence on her individualism made it possible to avoid the question of her absence from the canon of Polish and Western sculpture.

"For posterity, we build houses, not art",[28] Czełkowska writes in her notes. She offered very few keys to understanding her work. She did not write manifestos or theoretical papers. She rarely granted interviews and could be uncompromising in her refusal to have some of them published. On the rare occasions she did talk about her work, she blurred the lines and definitions (sculpture as movement? as space? as thought?).

The art historian that I am can only assume our dialogue, which is carried out in an offbeat way. This is not an attempt to compensate but a new narrative in the making. To this end, I would like to reflect on one of Wanda Czełkowska's final creations, *Ellipse* (*Elipsa*), presented at Królikarnia in 2016 (fig. 5). Her oval aluminium sculpture, of which there are two versions of different sizes (fig. pp. 70–71), is presented as a monumental design, perfectly geometric, diagonally crossing the space of the museum. The installation serves as a framework for showing a group of sculptures captured within it: *Blue Head* (*Niebieska głowa*), 1967; *Pink Head* (*Różowa głowa*), 1962; *Head* (*Głowa*), 1962; *The 10th Study* (*Studium X-te*), 1957; and *Head* (*Głowa*), 1972/2016 (fig. 6). I would like to argue that the way *Ellipse* puts these works into perspective makes it an expression of Czełkowska's late style, as defined by Edward W. Said. "We meet the accepted notion of age and wisdom in some last works that reflect a special maturity, a new spirit of reconciliation and serenity … But what of artistic lateness not as harmony and resolution but as intransigence, difficulty, and unresolved contradiction?" asks Said.[29]

In the context of Czełkowska's museum exhibition, as the organisers state, *Ellipse* becomes a tool for thinking about the relationships between the works, the materialisation of the idea of "retrospection", namely the subjective view of the artist herself on her own journey.[30] As the polar opposite of the exhaustiveness of the classic museum retrospective, the artist executes an activation of her past which she selectively captures and which, through her gesture, becomes current. "[I] perceive what I do", she says, "as an ever-present presence within me."[31] More than 40 years after *Absolute Elimination of Sculpture as a Notion of Shape* and a few years before her death, the artist continued the work of redefining her favourite medium. Czełkowska designed a radical, hollowed-out form, a simple outline in the space, which she filled with her past achievements.

At first glance, the work seems to be a metaphor for the time loop and the return of the sculptor to prominence. In reality, it is a more equivocal staging that sometimes reveals and sometimes puts in parenthesis a part of her past production. The all-encompassing, unifying, triumphantly retrospective character of the ellipse is only a delusion when we return to the etymology of the word, which in ancient Greek means lack, and applies to both grammatical ellipsis (something is removed) and geometrical ellipsis (something is missing from it for it to be a perfect circle). In music, the term means the removal of a chord required for regular harmony.[32]

The artist's practice is built around oppositions and paradoxes. First of all, Czełkowska calls herself a "sculptor" but her work encompasses many media such as painting (often with sculptural characteristics), drawing (on canvas, paper and tracing paper) and photography. Throughout her life, she skilfully juggled figurative art, which she practised while refusing to attribute a representative function to it, and abstraction, which bears the traces of the presence of bodies (hers first and foremost, but also that of the viewer). The engineer who designs an anti-gravity space or the scientist who represents the human brain in action in the form of an abstract drawing, in a vision that seems to anticipate post-humanist projections, Czełkowska is also preoccupied by a form of mysticism that it would be reductive to attribute to religiosity. Finally, her work is formed in a tension between the materiality of her creations and their conceptual dimension. On the one hand, we have formal research, an attachment to the tools and the traditional materials of sculpture (wood, plaster, metal), on the other, there is the affirmation of her work's intellectuality. "Art is born of thought", said the artist, but she immediately added "you have to think and do."[33] The relationship between these two actions lies at the heart of her approach. For Czełkowska, art is "grey matter" in both the literal and figurative sense.

The question of her inclusion in the *bigger picture*, which is the subject of the present book, is an issue that needs to be addressed. Firstly, at the heart of this work is the voice of Czełkowska herself. In this book, we reproduce an interview published by Richard Demarco in 1972, but never reissued. A visual essay by Antonina Gugała completes the process of making the artist's character more present. Then, the voices of those who knew the artist are represented through the pen of Agnieszka Tarasiuk, a Polish curator and sculpture specialist, who took the initiative of giving the artist the opportunity to hold her first museum retrospective. Finally, in an inversion of the standard centre-periphery relationship, we look to the voices of Western art historians, whom I have invited to reflect on specific works by the artist with reference to the subjects of their own research. Amelia Jones, June Geddes and Sarah Wilson, Mathieu Copeland, Émilie Bouvard, Abigail Solomon-Godeau, Charlotte Matter and David Crowley accepted my invitation to explore Czełkowska's trajectory in relation to the canon represented by artistic currents such as the post-war revival of figurative art, informal art, minimalism, conceptual art and feminism. By introducing ideas and movements sometimes outside of her work, we hope to shed a different light on it.

"I have never identified myself with any of these trends", she said.[34] Indeed, there is no orthodoxy in Czełkowska's work. Between the neoclassical sculptures of her youth, the expressionist heads, the conceptual installations, the back-and-forth between figurative art and abstraction, a path composed of innumerable beginnings takes shape.[35] Throughout her career, the artist produces works to which we could attribute a programmatic value. This is the case with her bust *Self-Portrait* and her installations *Table, Absolute Elimination of Sculpture as a Notion of Shape, Wall,* but also *Ellipse,* each of which opens up a new reflection on sculpture. When she wrote "art is created in a state of constant mortality",[36] it is not her own destiny she is thinking of but her work that never ceases to start afresh.

Compared with the sculptures of the past, *Ellipse* surprises us with its difference which presents itself as a final break. The artist does not surrender to the reality of the passing of time and continues to renew herself. The late style characterizes the works that bear the contradictions, absences and silences. It is a testimony to the artist's uncompromising relationship with the world and the aesthetic canons of her time. *Ellipse* is a late work which outlines the contours of a unique artistic path. Wanda Czełkowska's work evades categorisation by tracing its own elliptical trajectory.

[1] Wanda Czełkowska, notes kept in the artist's studio, undated. I would like to convey my thanks to Ona Winogrodzka for giving me access to Wanda Czełkowska's complete archive and for facilitating my research.

[2] Collective, "Sculpture. So a woman can create. Careers, practices, visibility and the reception of women sculptors from the 19th to the 21st century", symposium, https://awarewomenartists.com/en/nos_evenements/sculpture-une-femme-peut-donc-creer-parcours-pratiques-visibilite-et-reception-des-sculptrices-xixe-xxie-siecle/

[3] Czełkowska's name does not appear, for example, in the *Dictionnaire des sculptrices* by Anne Rivière (Mare et Martin, 2017).

[4] The dialectic between recognition and oblivion can go on indefinitely. On this subject, read for example the article by Katie da Cunha Lewin https://lareviewofbooks.org/article/the-politics-of-rediscovery/

[5] Magali Lesauvage, Marine Vazzoler, "Société : l'histoire de l'art change la donne", *L'Hebdo du Quotidien de l'art* 2320, 4 February 2022, 11.

[6] I also wish to thank them for accompanying and helping me in my research by making their texts available to me, patiently responding to my questions, and sharing their thoughts. To these names, I feel it's important to add those critics and art historians who supported the artist at different times in her career: Piotr Krakowski and other critics close to the artists of the Second Kraków Group, Jerzy Malinowski, art historian; Marta Tarabuła and Jan Michalski from Galeria Zderzak; as well as several generations of curators at the National Museum in Kraków.

[7] Xavery Dunikowski (1875–1964), Polish sculptor and painter. Dunikowski taught sculpture at the Academy of Fine Arts in Kraków. Although encouraged by him to become an artist (she said she was persuaded by his intelligence and erudition), Wanda Czełkowska did not choose his studio to train in (she preferred Jerzy Bandura's). She did, however, maintain more personal links with Dunikowski (she lived in the sculptor's former flat in Kraków) and had great admiration for his work.

[8] Jerzy Bandura (1915–1987), Polish sculptor.

[9] Dorota Grubba-Thiede, "Rzeźby koniecznością życiową, jak powietrze, woda i ogień… Wanda Czełkowska, Ludmila Stehnova, Maria Pinińska-Bereś circa 1960", in Ewa Toniak (ed.), ***Jestem artystką, we wszystkim, co niepotrzebne. Kobiety i sztuka około 1960*** (Warsaw: Neriton, 2010), 75–92; Dorota Grubba-Thiede, *Nurt figuracji w powojennej rzeźbie polskiej* (Warsaw–Toruń: Tako, 2016), 216–222.

[10] Ibid.

[11] Galeria Krzysztofory was created in 1958 in the basement of a house in Szczepańska Street in Kraków. In the 1960s, Galeria Krzysztofory was the main exhibition site for artists associated with the Second Kraków Group as well as for productions by the Cricot 2 theatre and the Jerzy Grotowski troupe.

[12] Piotr Krakowski, *Wanda Czełkowska* (Kraków: Stowarzyszenie Artystyczne Grupa Krakowska, 1963), n.p.

[13] Dorota Grubba-Thiede, *Nurt figuracji w powojennej rzeźbie polskiej*, 216.

[14] The Second Kraków Group, an association of artists created 1957 along the lines of the group with the same name that was founded in the inter-war period. Amongst the best known members of the group are Tadeusz Kantor, Tadeusz Brzozowski, Jonasz Stern and Maria Jarema. As Anna Markowska writes, the group consisted mainly of male artists. The place of women was secondary and their work was rarely taken seriously. They usually adopted the role of 'mediators' with the past (Maria Jarema, Jadwiga Maziarska, Erna Rosenstein) or of wives (Teresa Rudowicz, Danuta Urbanowicz). From this perspective, Wanda Czełkowska was a special

case. See Anna Markowska, "Artystki Grupy Krakowskiej", in Ewa Toniak, ***Jestem artystką, we wszystkim, co niepotrzebne***, 105–122.

[15] Founded in 1965 by Janusz and Maria Bogucki, Galeria Współczesna was an important exhibition site for the Polish avant-garde in the 1960s and 1970s.

[16] On 13 December 1981, martial law was declared in Poland and remained in place until 22 July 1983. Against this backdrop, a section of the Polish art community renounced any official activity and retreated to private flats and apartments as well as other confidential places (including churches).

[17] When it was exhibited at Królikarnia in 2016, the work was mounted on a metal structure and installed on two trestle tables.

[18] Dorota Jarecka, "Przeciw pomnikom", ***Gazeta Wyborcza***, Warsaw, no. 68, 21 March 1990. See also Tomasz Fijałkowski, "Wydarzenie w 'Zderzaku'", ***Tygodnik Powszechny***, Kraków, 8 April 1990. I would like to thank Jan Michalski for sharing the Galeria Zderzak archives with me.

[19] This biography is a subjective selection of the artist's exhibitions. For a more complete biography, take a look at the timeline written by Dorota Grubba in collaboration with Ewa Opałka. Wanda Czełkowska, "Kalendarium artystyczne", in Ewa Opałka, Jennifer Moore-Tymowska (eds.), ***Wanda Czełkowska. Retrospection***, exhibition catalogue (Warsaw: National Museum, 2017), 92–132.

[20] Anna Markowska, "Artystki Grupy Krakowskiej", 105.

[21] At the end of Czełkowska's life, the international art market was no longer indifferent to her work either. In 2016, her work was exhibited twice at the Broadway 1602 Harlem gallery in New York. In 2018, the artist also participated in a group exhibition at the Thaddaeus Ropac gallery in London, alongside Rosemarie Castoro and Lydia Okamura (Anke Kempkes curated all three exhibitions).

[22] These same personality traits are considered to be qualities in male artists (who are more often described as "exacting" rather than "difficult").

[23] In the 1990s and 2000s, the development of feminist methodology in Poland enabled some artists to benefit from the renewed interest of emerging female art historians and critics. Czełkowska, however, was not part of this corpus. This can be explained by the fact that she does not use "feminist phraseology" in her work, as Anna Markowska writes, but also by the fact that she distances herself from certain claims. See Anna Markowska, "Artystki Grupy Krakowskiej".

[24] The reasons are mostly structural: women cannot devote themselves fully to their work as artists. However, Czełkowska did not have children and was not in a relationship with a more famous male artist.

[25] Maria Hussakowska, "Wanda Czełkowska. The mechanism of the disappearance of the artist and the disappearance of the sculpture", in ***Wanda Czełkowska. Retrospection***, 71.

[26] Griselda Pollock, "Old Bones and Cocktail Dresses: Louise Bourgeois and the Question of Age", ***Oxford Art Journal*** 22, no. 2, Louise Bourgeois (1999), 87. The same excerpt from Pollock's essay is repeated by Paul B. Preciado, "Le membre fantôme : Carol Rama et l'histoire de l'art", in ***La passion selon Carol Rama*** (Paris: Paris Musées, 2015), 23.

[27] Hussakowska, "Wanda Czełkowska. The mechanism of the disappearance", 76.

[28] Wanda Czełkowska, notes kept in the artist's studio, undated.

[29] Edward W. Said, ***On Late Style. Music and Literature Against the Grain*** (New York: Pantheon Books, 2006), 6–7. An idea I first encountered in Linda Nochlin's text "Le style « tardif » de Louise Bourgeois", in exh. cat. ***Louise Bourgeois*** (Paris: Centre Pompidou, 2008), 158–167.

[30] Agnieszka Tarasiuk, "Introduction", in ***Wanda Czełkowska. Retrospection***, 92–132.

[31] Ewa Opałka, ***Eliminacje. Rozmowy z Wandą Czełkowską*** (Eliminations. Conversations with Wanda Czełkowska), Warsaw, 2016, unpublished. Opałka conducted this very extended interview between 2014 and 2019. I am grateful to her for sharing it with me and the co-authors of this book.

[32] Wanda Czełkowska was close to the North American composer of instrumental, vocal and electronic music, Daria Semegen.

[33] Wanda Czełkowska in conversation with Ewa Opałka and Agnieszka Tarasiuk as part of the conference dedicated to the artist in 2017 in conjunction with her exhibition ***Wanda Czełkowska. Retrospekcja*** (Wanda Czełkowska, Retrospection) at Królikarnia, https://www.youtube.com/watch?v=oJtTZ8Iba7s

[34] Ewa Opałka, ***Eliminacje.***

[35] In her introduction to ***Inside the Visible,*** Catherine de Zegher recalls the notion of the beginning analysed by Edward Said in his work ***Beginnings: Intention and Method*** (New York: Columbia University Press, 1985): "Beginning is making or producing difference … Beginning is basically an activity which ultimately implies return and repetition rather than simple linear accomplishment; beginning and beginning-again are historical whereas origins are divine". Catherine de Zegher, "Introduction", in ***Inside the Visible: An Elliptical Traverse of 20th Century Art, in, of, and from the Feminine*** (Cambridge, Mass.: MIT Press 1996), 19–41.

[36] Wanda Czełkowska, notes kept in the artist's studio, undated.

Sculpture Is an Intellectual Event[1]

Agnieszka Tarasiuk

I well remember my first visit to the studio of Wanda Czełkowska. I had to get to a not too distant but forgotten part of town. Between abandoned factories, find the building where a lorry garage used to be and knock on a small door next to a steel gate that had not been opened for ages. A prolonged grinding of keys in several locks. The hostess, wearing sports slacks and work boots, the signature red lipstick on her lips and eyelids heavily outlined in black, cordially invites me in. To enter this space is, however, far from easy; you have to navigate a labyrinth – bending down, bending over and avoiding obstacles, the visitor's body is drawn into a spatial game. The space is cramped, even though the room is the size of an industrial hall. The smell of dust and grease comes from the inspection pits set into the floor that were once used to repair cars. The setting sun streams in through dozens of small cracked panes of glass, accentuating the surplus of accumulated objects. Heavy tools seem to be most at home here: a car jack, ladders, industrial beamlights, piles of metal angle and panes of glass. The paraphernalia of the car workshop, however, are mixed with the telling props of the sculptor's studio: a sculptor's stand, chisels, rams, bags of plaster and piles of dry clay. Right next to it there is an easel, rolls of cardboard, a photographic tripod and an enlarger (figs. 1–2).

Hidden between the tools and boxes filled with who-knows-what are some pieces of ornate nineteenth-century furniture. They are not in mint condition; the missing leg of an armchair has been propped up with a baking tray. A makeshift bookcase made of unhewn boards contains an impressive library: classic novels, philosophy, journalism, exhibition catalogues, albums. Side by side with items the worse for wear and the passage of time there are the latest publishing bestsellers. As befits a car repair shop, a small, grease-stained radio is on, only here it is tuned to a station broadcasting experimental contemporary music. Despite the overabundance of objects, arranged in a way that defies the usual rules, there is a mysterious order to the workshop, seductive from the moment one steps over the obstacle-race threshold. This order is based on the premeditated arrangement of the artist's works throughout the space. Amidst all this swirling matter, the paintings and sculptures create dominant tensions and counterpoints.

Czełkowska's installations seem to combine all the paradigms of order present: classical sculpture, mechanics, structural engineering and theatre. The silent presence of hieratic figures (*Man* [*Mężczyzna*], 1956; *The 10th Study* [*Studium X-te*], 1957) and mangled sculpted heads (*Pink Head* [*Różowa głowa*], 1962; *Blue Head* [*Niebieska głowa*], 1967) commands seriousness, but an expressive plaster animal (*Cat* [*Kot*], 1955), whose broken paw has been replaced by a steel screw, winks. The paintings, heedless of the damage

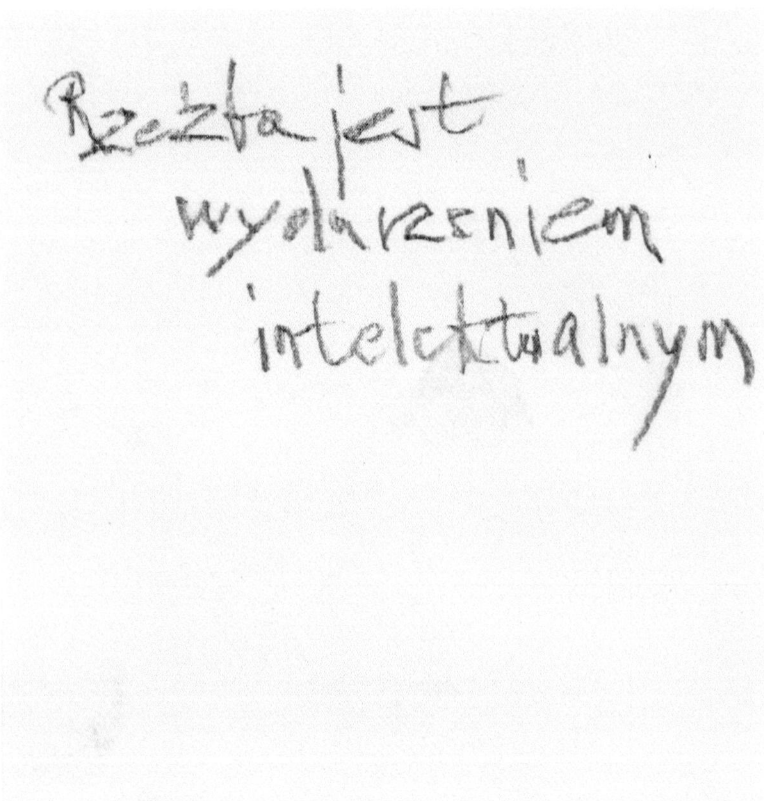

1. *Sculpture Is an Intellectual Event* (*Rzeźba jest wydarzeniem intelektualnym*), undated from Wanda Czełkowska's notes. Courtesy of Wanda Czełkowska Studio

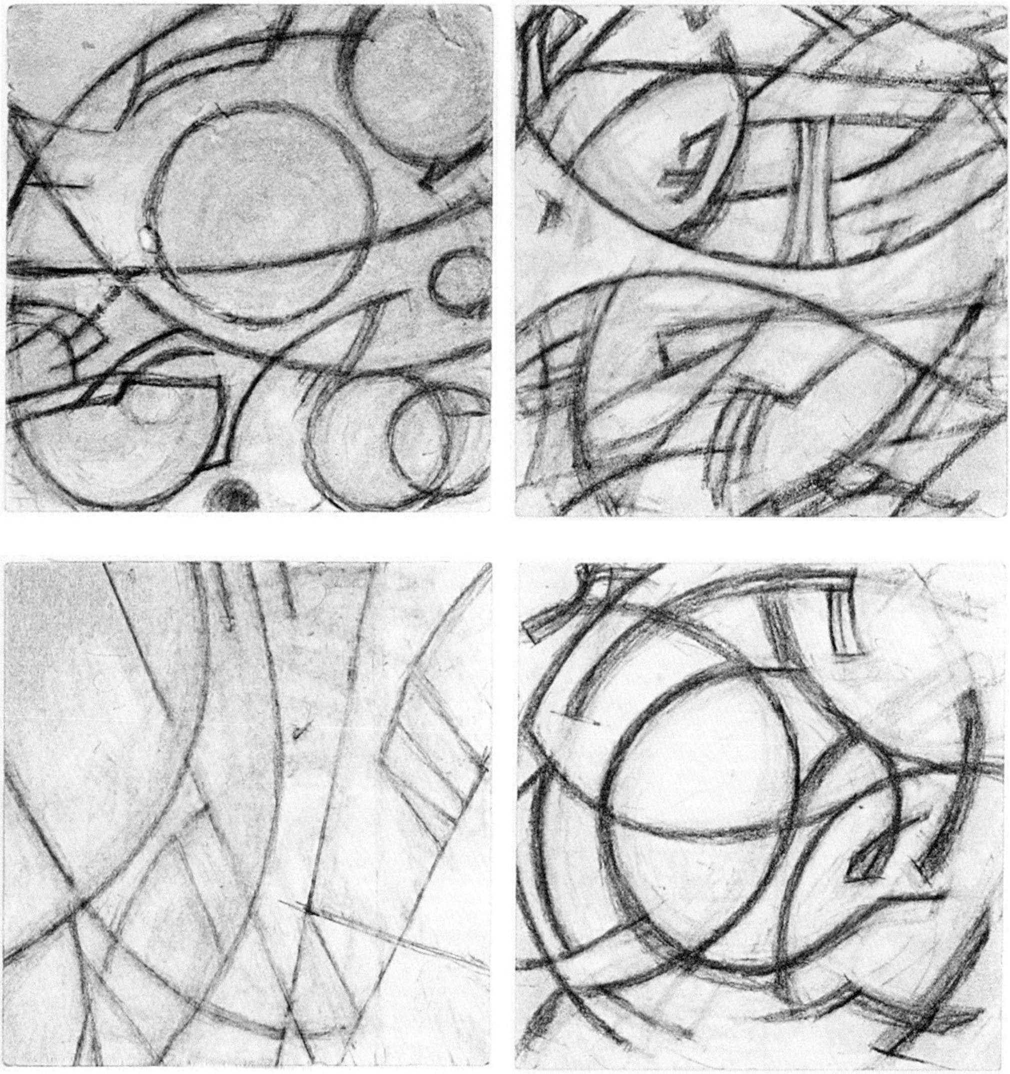

2. Wanda Czełkowska, pencil on post-its, 2021, 10 × 10 cm each. Courtesy of the artist's estate

done to them by the sunlight, function as shutters. The large-scale drawings divide the space and are executed in charcoal on raw linen canvas stretched on painterly looms (*Elegy* [*Elegia*], 1990). I do not know if the geometric construction of pine beams joined together by steel bolts is a sculpture or an infinite building structure (*Closed Park Sculpture* or *Infinite Line* [*Rzeźba parkowa zamknięta* lub *Prosta nieskończona*], 1996). The steel skeleton of the would-be sculpture, standing on a three-legged stool, has been given a head made from a tin bowl. The heavy screen of an archaic computer and a slide projector have also been elevated to the dignity of sculpture by the solemnity of the pedestal on which they are set. The unfinished drawing is mysteriously

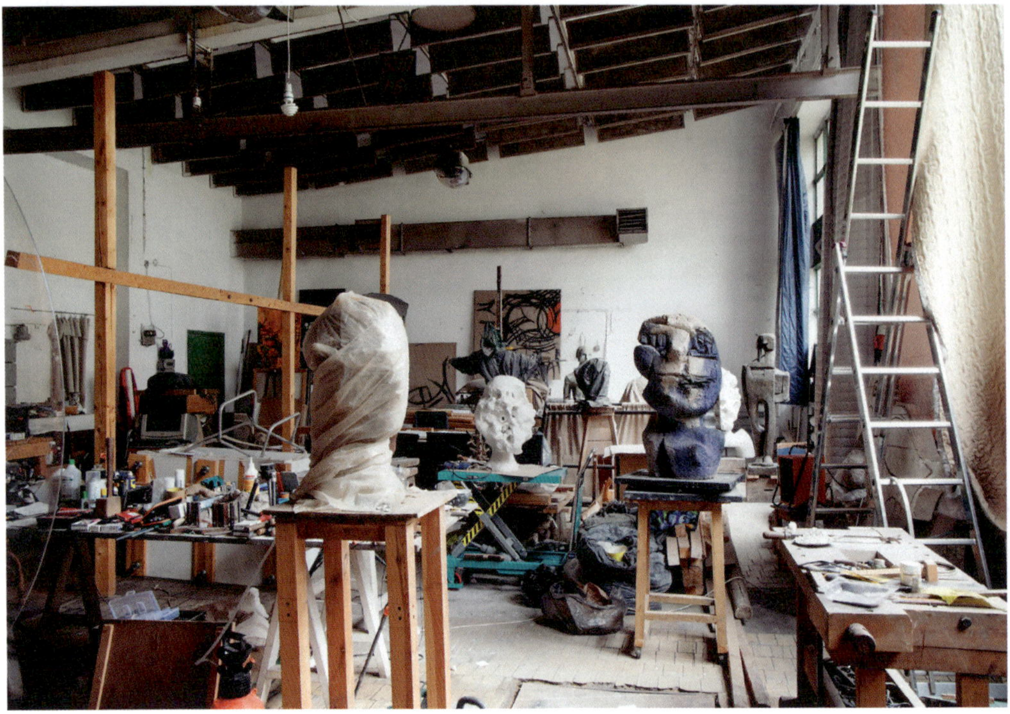

hidden behind a makeshift curtain; the fragment protruding from beneath brings to mind Leonardo da Vinci's *Vitruvian Man*. The tools stacked next to it suggest a drawing process that has only just been interrupted (although the layer of dust on the erasers and pencils makes one wonder). This studio is a kind of long-term performance, a theatre of one performer and hundreds of things, gestures and thoughts. It is an active space, energetically charged; it is also a story about art and the ethos of artistic engagement (figs. 3–4).

3–4. Wanda Czełkowska's studio, Warsaw, 2016. Courtesy of National Museum in Warsaw Photo: Szymon Rogiński

On the table, Czełkowska places a chocolate bar, faience saucers, cups. Miraculously – since there is no kitchen cupboard – the artist manages to locate everything needed to make tea. We talk about her work, very specifically: about materials, tools, technical solutions and the eternal difficulties of finding and maintaining a suitable studio. And about the fact that in this space the sculptures "are content". Saying this, the artist tenderly strokes the large *Blue Head* standing nearby. The sculpture, however, does not look patted smooth – made up as it is of thick knots, as of carbuncles, the matter repeatedly dissected with a sharp tool. In many places, the blue skin is painfully abrased to a white plaster. On closer inspection, I recognize that *Blue Head* is in fact a self-portrait (fig. 5).

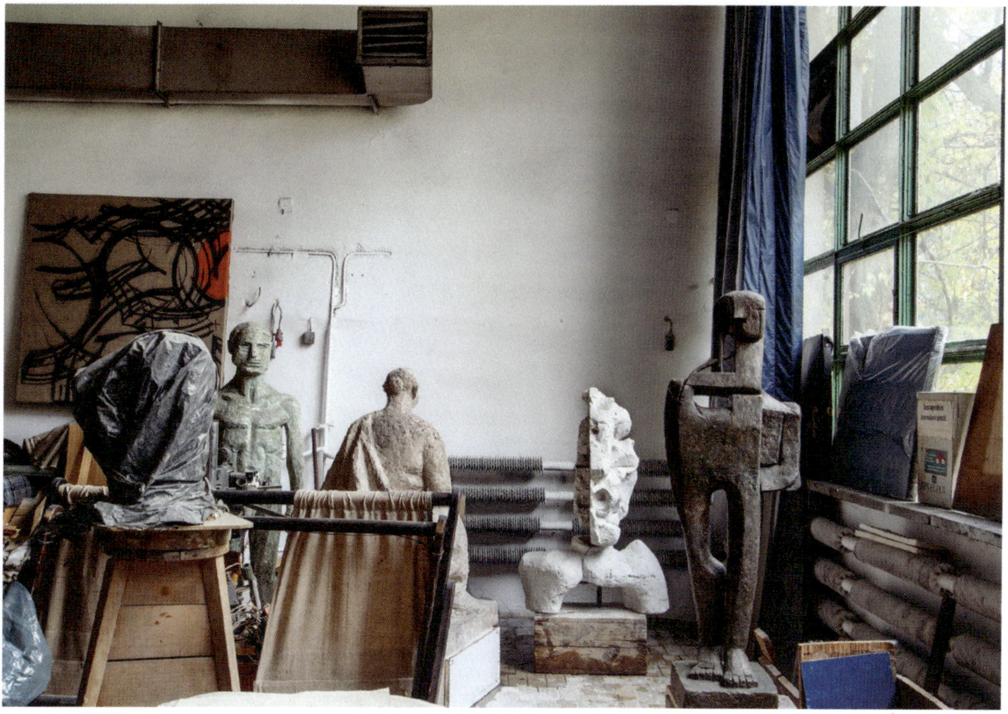

When the sun goes down, we turn on the studio lights, which further emphasizes the theatricality of the space. "Oh, she will probably come in soon and pretend she is not listening to us at all", says Czełkowska. And indeed, after a while, the creature in question, which the artist holds in high respect and is friends with, does turn up: a little grey mouse. She comes, looks on and goes about her own business under the table.

Only just before saying goodbye do I realize that there is another order of objects in the studio, the least important and least visible – the order of everyday life. A shower and a dish cupboard encased in a sculptural installation of beams and flat bars, boxes of clothes next to plaster moulds, and a small bed, tucked into the corner of the atrium. In her eccentric, poorly heated studio, Wanda Czełkowska not only made sculptures and received visitors and students, but simply lived. It was 2012. The artist was eighty-two years old. She was the epitome of the mythical avantgarde artist. Her dedication to art was complete and unconditional. We artists, intellectuals and art lovers weary of the shallowness of the art world in the time of Poland's little capitalist stabilization, were drawn to Wanda Czełkowska like moths to a candle. Although sometimes one could get burned.

Czełkowska was a believer in the unconditional autonomy of art; she wanted to see it "untainted even by the noblest commercialism or journalism".[2] She dismissed the demand for social involvement of artists, on this occasion raised by the grass-roots – representatives of the critical art generation of the 1990s – saying that "the attempt to exploit art as a tool for social change offends both art and society".[3] Perhaps at the root of this stance was a rebellion against any imposed convention or artistic idiom that she had developed while she was still a student at the Kraków Academy of Fine Arts. The time of her studies (1949–1954) coincided with the years of forcible implementation of the doctrine of socialist realism in art by the communist authorities. "Such a thing as socialist realism simply does not exist", Wanda would say, using her time at the academy to learn in depth the sculptural craft that would later prove to be the axis of her mature artistic language.

For Czełkowska, as a young student, it was a formative experience to be immersed in the intellectual atmosphere of post-war Kraków, which, unlike the destroyed Warsaw, was the undisputed artistic capital of Poland. In 1958, Tadeusz Kantor's experimental theatre company Cricot II had set up on the premises of Kraków's Krzysztofory Palace, and the palace cellars housed a gallery presenting modern artists associated as the Second Kraków Group. The figure "two" in the names of both these groups hark back to the first-generation avantgarde formations that had operated under similar names in Kraków before World War II and indicate the deliberate desire to continue the autonomous ideas of that first avantgarde. In the brick interiors of the Krzysztofory Gallery, Czełkowska encountered expressionism, matter painting, surrealism, informel art and abstraction. The key personalities of the Second Kraków Group were the sophisticated abstractionist Maria Jarema, whose oeuvre is still waiting to be fully recognized worldwide, and the theatre demiurge Tadeusz Kantor, who needs no introduction. It was these artists, along with Xawery Dunikowski, that Czełkowska named as important to her own path, and she occasionally became involved artistically with their work. She assisted Dunikowski, who practised traditional sculpture, in the realisation of monumental classicist architectural and sculptural projects, but it was only avantgarde art that she only took seriously and engaged with personally. In 1963, she had her first solo exhibition at the Krzysztofory Gallery, and four years later she was formally accepted into the Second Kraków Group. Years later, she would recall these events as "beautiful crystalline episodes".[4] In 1975, she co-created the mannequins of the pupils for Kantor's production of *The Dead Class*, hailed a year later by *Newsweek* as the best theatrical performance in the world.

For half a century, Czełkowska was associated with Kraków's bohemia. Despite repeated invitations to emigrate, she kept returning from her travels to Kraków. It was not until 2004 that she moved to Warsaw, in search of a mental and physical space to work in. In 2008, Czełkowska contributed to the erection of an abstract monument in Kraków – a fountain dedicated to Frédéric Chopin, and designed almost five decades earlier by the first lady of the Kraków avantgarde, Maria Jarema. Above the table in her Warsaw studio, for many years to come, there would be pinned the old invitation to the opening at the Krzysztofory Gallery, with a handwritten note "Ms Wanda, please come! Tadeusz Kantor".

Try not to enter – It will cause infinite upset

We do not know whether Czełkowska did go to the Krzysztofory opening. She was an individualist; in both her artistic and personal life she valued freedom above all and consistently defended her boundaries. She could befriend a mouse or a cherry tree, but sentimental she was not. Full of interest and respect for others, including non-human beings, she valued quiet intellectual friendship but avoided emotional entanglements. Her extraordinary beauty, energy and authenticity attracted many, but relationships based on romantic feelings did not last long. In 1959, she wrote in a letter to her mother:

"So, yes – we did part … I left so as not to have to explain myself. So that my life and my actions would be mine alone … So that I would be responsible only to myself. It was really worth it. Now I am a free person and happy. Very rarely can one use this word to fully describe a phenomenon; in fact, I have used it for the first time, and I used it with full, absolute awareness. It happened only now, when I took freedom for myself … But freedom

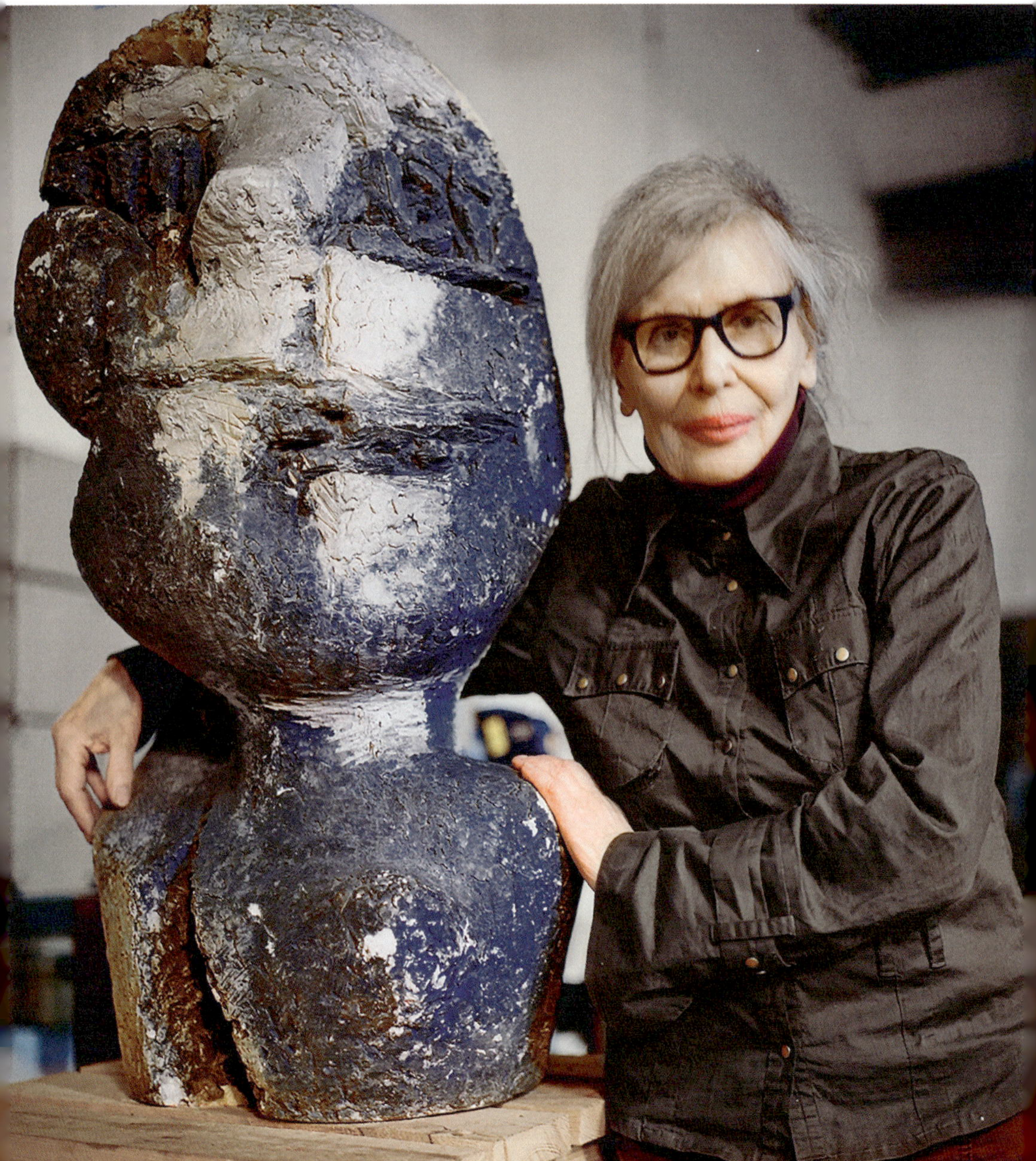

5. Wanda Czełkowska next to *Blue Head* (*Niebieska głowa*), 1967, in her studio at 14 Magazynowa Street in Warsaw, 2017
Photo: Tadeusz Rolke

cannot be taken. Freedom is arrived at. You have to have a huge life behind you. Many people only come to it when they are old, when they have a life behind them, when they are already tired, when they are already physically weak. I am happy precisely because I have reached freedom now, when I am young. When I am fully mature and strong. I am happy that my life has been strongly condensed, an essence."[5]

What was the "condensed essence" of Wanda Czełkowska's life and art? What was her "own path" and in which direction did it lead? The simplest answer to this question would be to say that Czełkowska's artistic path consisted of conceptualising the form of the sculptural portrait and led from classicist figuration, through expressive, archaic, drastic deformation and mechanical multiplication, all the way up to – as the title of her iconic work put it – *ruthless elimination*. It is worth noting that the process of arriving at abstraction and the abandonment of the idiom of shape in favour of an active field was the result of the artist's consistent work in the studio; all decisions had been worked out empirically, and working with matter had always preceded verbalized thought.

She referred to herself as a "professional" and had a great appreciation for the honest simplicity of her craft. The techniques and materials she employed are part of the stock in trade of the classical sculptural craft: the wooden rotating modelling stand, the precedence of the steel skeleton over the application of the clay body, and the system of wires ending in the wooden crosses necessary to hold the heavy clay mass. And finally, the wet rag in which the sculpture has to be wrapped during a break in the work to prevent the clay from cracking. She used scaffolding of wooden beams, traditional with larger sculptures, and heavy, rusty steel bolts to connect the structural elements, as well as a variety of moulds and casting. And then there were the forms taken from painting: wooden looms, linen canvas, initially primed as for a painting, but later just raw. Paper, tracing paper, pencil, paint, charcoal and glass are practically all the materials and techniques present in Czełkowska's art. The artist looks at them closely, discovering meanings previously unseen: the drastic nature of the rag wrapping a clay head or the steel screw piercing wood, canvas or glass. The artist transforms technical procedures into conscious gestures, making their hidden meaning more explicit: she wraps not only the sculptures but also her own head in fabric, cuts the plaster cast to reveal the inner emptiness and the steel skeleton supporting the form, and exposes the places where the rusting screw painfully pierces the canvas.

Abstraction – Yearning for the freedom of existence

Why use such drastic forms and gestures? Why did the artist deform, perforate and geometrize the shape of the human head, which she had so masterfully possessed? Why did she turn it into quasi-cybernetic shapes, only to finally completely reject it – along with the idea of representation as such? If one attempts to place this gesture in the world of art described by theoreticians, one can point to an anachronistic fidelity to the modernist paradigm or, alternatively, a surprisingly progressive parallel with minimalism and conceptualism which had been developing on the other side of the Iron Curtain or even the other side of the ocean.[6] Czełkowska was not familiar with the writings of Rosalind Krauss or Robert Morris, yet their theoretical texts describing the aesthetic and symbolic value of the "expanded field", simple materials or the use of the geometric grid pattern apply perfectly to her own work. Like Sol LeWitt or Carl Andre, the artist makes the viewer physically step on the installation lying on the floor. The artist herself dismisses such comparisons by calmly commenting that she was simply "present in her era". "I do not disavow conceptualism. But I have been going down such a very separate path since the beginning… I am constantly introducing new solutions … How is it possible for something similar to happen in two different places, on two continents, under different conditions? … It is natural; it is the realm of intellect, of intuition, because intellect is essentially intuition."[7]

At the same time, Czełkowska's oft-declared belief in "pure" art and her professed aversion to psychoanalytical or identity-based interpretations points to her very strong attachment to the modernist idiom. Ewa Opałka, a researcher, curator and for a while a close colleague of Wanda Czełkowska, saw a tragic undertone in this attachment.[8] Following the path of feminist corporate phenomenology and referencing such philosophers as Donna Haraway or Rosi Braidotti, Opałka problematizes the embodied female creative subject.

The elitist patriarchal idiom, which is at the root of modernism, identifies everything subjective, creative, intellectual and spiritual with the masculine, although it wants to see this as objective. Femininity remains the domain of absolute otherness – the emotional drives, the body and the lability. The female artist, wishing to tap into the "objective" intellectual heritage of the West, must ruthlessly eliminate negatively valorized corporeality and emotionality, and thus commit an act of symbolic violence against her own female identity.

The validity of this investigation seems to be confirmed by the resistance with which the artist herself received it. In Opałka's and Czełkowska's joint notes, which I have been reviewing, every sentence locating Czełkowska's work among other women artists, or even the mere mention of gender studies, has been crossed out by Czełkowska and marked repeatedly with "No! No!"

"I always had a pure mind, untainted by gender. And yes, this was evident in my work … For me, the problem is that women at some point, probably in ancient times, gave up the use of the head for life, the right to use this pure intellect. Because this intellect does exist, and this is my hobby horse: a third kind of human being. Because when there is a man and a woman, we have a constant conflict. It does not matter whether it is flowers or animals, there is still this conflict, because there has to be, because there is no way out."[9]

I want to believe that for Czełkowska, her refusal to participate in the social construct that Simone de Beauvoir termed "the second sex" – both radical and costly – was not a tragic choice but an emancipatory one. Like her refusal to produce commercial or propaganda art, or to live within the traditional, status framework of family, marriage and possessions. I want to believe that the painful blows that she inflicted on the blue self-portrait served to bring out its still-alive interior from under the polychrome of social clichés. When asked by Anke Kempkes about the gender of her sculptures, the artist would once again reply: "My heads are of the Third Gender".[10] I wish I could talk to Czełkowska today about the queer deconstruction of binarity. I am sure she would have loved to have put Paul

B. Preciado's *An Apartment on Uranus* on her rough wooden shelf: "… the violence generated by the dualist epistemology of the West. The entire universe cut in half and solely in half. Everything is heads or tails in this system of knowledge. We are human or animal. Man or woman. Living or dead. We are the colonizer or the colonized. Living organism or machine. We have been divided by the norm. Cut in half and forced to remain on one side or the other of the rift. What we call 'subjectivity' is only the scar that, over the multiplicity of all that we could have been, covers the wound of this fracture. It is over this scar that property, family and inheritance were founded. Over this scar, names are written and sexual identities asserted".[11]

Czełkowska always stood on the side of freedom, but refused to take on the role of the oppressed and participate in the emancipatory revolution. She acted as if the battle had already been won. "Indeed, reason is serene, it is pure, it is noble, it is independent."[12] Once we disentangle ourselves from the violent binary epistemology of the West, the interpretative possibilities of Wanda Czełkowska's art become limitless. The embodied causal subject can be a woman or a plant; it can be an integral part of the universe. Commenting on the creation of her monumental work *Elegy*, Czełkowska recalled: "It turns out that the tree spoke to me. The tree just absorbed me with its leaves… I… It was unheard of… I had been embraced and absorbed. It was a real feeling. It was a transmission of something unbelievable. The trees have it and the flowers have it … I experienced it, without knowing it, when I climbed into that tree on the ladder – because it was a big cherry tree and it probably never had much fruit. But up the ladder I climbed and all of a sudden… I was sucked in… I wanted to stay there, I had no need to detach myself from it".[13]

What if we completely change the scale? What if from the scale of the human body, which weighs each of us down from time to time, we move to the picoscale of elementary particles or to the 92 million light-years of the observable cosmos? When Wanda Czełkowska was working on *Elegy*, the space probe Voyager 1, leaving the Solar System, took a photograph of the Earth from a distance of 6.4 billion kilometres, named by the astronomer Carl Sagan, who had suggested taking the image, *Pale Blue Dot*. Four years later, Sagan wrote a book with the same title, and the phrase became an iconic text for the awakening planetary consciousness. Wanda had been incorporating the blue dot into her compositions since the 1970s (*Sea Bird* [*Ptak morski*], 1978; *Head – Kinetic Sequence* [*Głowa – Ciąg kinetyczny*], 1981). In space, spheres, luminous dots and ellipsoidal orbits are not theoretical geometries.[14] Let us take another look at Czełkowska's late heads. They look as if they have been clumped together from rocky material by the force of gravity, and the perfectly round holes resemble craters from meteorite impacts. Perhaps they are not heads but small planets? Or is the artist saying that they are one and the same?

The change of scale evens out the tension between the body and pure form. The relationship between the organic world and geometry has been explored by the mystical traditions of many cultures, and it is probably there that the roots of abstract art must be sought. Today, mathematics, astrophysics and quantum theories answer questions hitherto reserved for philosophy, religion and esotericism. How did the universe come into being? What do we exist for? And what are the fundamental building blocks of reality? We used to be taught that they were atoms, their 120 varieties filling up Mendeleev's periodic table; this is where geometry comes in again – with circular orbits, the mathematical principles of electric charge and atomic bonds. When quantum physics reached schools, we delved even deeper and found out that the whole world was made up of twelve types of particles: electrons, several varieties of quarks and the Higgs Boson, which initially only existed theoretically until it could be observed at CERN. Today we know that, in fact, the world is made up of fields stretching across the entire universe and that particles are only temporary perturbations of the field density. Physicists have begun to use the old Buddhist metaphor about the unity of all the waves in the ocean.[15]

Viewed from this perspective, by eliminating particularistic shapes in favour of an active field marked by a grid of geometric divisions, Czełkowska simply sculpted what is.

—

A decade has passed since that first visit I made to Czełkowska's studio. Those wild, post-industrial sites have been built up and covered with the new fabric of the city (Czełkowska loved to watch the work of large excavators and cranes). Shops and cafes have sprouted in the neighbourhood. The artist's professional career once again accelerated somewhat. One sculpture and two drawings by Czełkowska were presented at the 2016 Frieze New York art fair by New York's 1602 Broadway Gallery, run by Anke Kempkes. The same year saw the opening of a major exhibition curated by Ewa Opałka entitled *Wanda Czełkowska. Retrospekcja* (Wanda Czełkowska: Retrospection) at the Museum of Sculpture in the Królikarnia section of the National Museum in Warsaw, culminating in an international session devoted to the sculptor's work. In 2018, Czełkowska took part in the group exhibition *Shapeshifting: Eisenstein as Method* at the Museum of Art in Łódź, and in the summer of the same year, in the Kempkes-curated exhibition *Land of Lads, Land of Lashes: Rosemarie Castoro, Wanda Czełkowska and Lydia Okumura*. The following year, Czełkowska's work was present at Frieze London.[16]

This allowed the artist to rent a small flat in a newly built block of flats opposite her studio. It was there that she died on 17 June 2021, surrounded by her immediate family. A few weeks before her passing, she drew a series of drawings on sticky notes. Czełkowska's handwriting is immediately recognisable, produced with utmost concentration and clarity, curved lines and circles, drops of colour. Planets? Atoms? Or perhaps mitochondria – the energy centres of all living cells that, by producing energy from oxygen and food, temporarily reduce local entropy levels.

One of the fundamental laws of nature – the second law of thermodynamics – states that over time all isolated systems disintegrate. As long as we breathe, we can maintain our complex bodies at the expense of emitting large amounts of heat. Ultimately, entropy in the universe can only increase, and life seen from a cosmic perspective only accelerates this process.

After Wanda Czełkowska's death, the local entropy level rose dramatically. On the first day after her death, the long-term performance of the studio was still taking place, but very soon, despite the lack of anything having changed in physical terms, the mysterious harmony between objects began to vanish. The seductive labyrinth of active space was slowly turning into a mere mess. Heir to the artist's legacy and executor of her last will, architect Ona Winogrodzka has made an extraordinary effort: in just a few months, she has turned the studio building into a private museum dedicated to Wanda Czełkowska's work, where research and conservation work is constantly ongoing. The paintings, which have been carefully restored, no longer function as shutters, but – just as they did in the artist's lifetime – friends meet at the wooden table, above them on the wall the card with the inscription "Ms Wanda, please come!"

[1] Wanda Czełkowska would write down random thoughts or aphorisms on small pieces of paper. The title of this text and the section headings are quotations from these notes, left by the artist in her studio.
[2] The quotation is taken from Wanda Czełkowska in conversation with Agnieszka Tarasiuk and British artist Matthew Darbyshire, during the opening of the exhibition *Rhetorical Figures: Warsaw Architectural Sculpture* at Królikarnia – Xawery Dunikowski Museum of Sculpture, a section of the National Museum in Warsaw, 14 June 2015.
[3] Ibid.
[4] Wanda Czełkowska, in an as yet unpublished interview conducted by Ewa Opałka in 2018, courtesy of Ewa Opałka.
[5] Manuscript dated 9 November 1959. Wanda Czełkowska archive, courtesy of the artist's estate.
[6] See Ewa Opałka, Jennifer Moore-Tymowska (eds.), *Wanda Czełkowska. Retrospection*, exhibition catalogue (Warsaw: National Museum, 2017). Texts by Agnieszka Tarasiuk, Maria Hussakowska, Ewa Opałka, Anke Kemkes, Dorota Grubba; see also texts by Amelia Jones and Mathieu Copland in the present publication.
[7] Wanda Czełkowska, in an as yet unpublished interview conducted by Ewa Opałka between 2014 and 2019. Courtesy of Ewa Opałka.
[8] See Ewa Opałka's talk given on 11 February 2017 at the conference entitled *Minimal, Conceptual, Material: The Phenomenon of Wanda Czełkowska's Sculpture* at Królikarnia – Xawery Dunikowski Museum of Sculpture, a section of the National Museum in Warsaw, https://www.youtube.com/watch?v=89GZmIIkITY
[9] Wanda Czełkowska, in an as yet unpublished interview conducted by Ewa Opałka between 2014 and 2019. Courtesy of Ewa Opałka.
[10] Anke Kempkes, "The Third Gender: Wanda Czełkowska and Rosemarie Castoro – Life in the Studio", in *Wanda Czełkowska. Retrospection*, 63.
[11] Paul B. Preciado, *An Apartment on Uranus: Chronicles of the Crossing*, trans. Charlotte Mandell (South Pasadena: semiotext(e), 2020), 27; https://library.stationofcommons.org/Paul%20B.%20Preciado/An%20Apartment%20on%20Uranus_%20Chronicles%20of%20the%20Crossing%20(11)/An%20Apartment%20on%20Uranus_%20Chronicles%20of%20the%20-%20Paul%20B.%20Preciado.pdf
[12] Wanda Czełkowska, in an as yet unpublished interview conducted by Ewa Opałka between 2014 and 2019. Courtesy of Ewa Opałka.
[13] Ibid.
[14] See also in this publication the text by David Crowley, who analyses the polyptych *Black Frieze* from the perspective of Stanisław Lem's writings and the social fascination with space conquest in the 1950s and 1960s.
[15] David Tong, *Quantum Fields: The Real Building Blocks of the Universe*, lecture, The Royal Institution https://www.youtube.com/watch?v=zNVQfWC_evg&t=16s
[16] It was exhibited by the gallery Q Contemporary from Budapest.

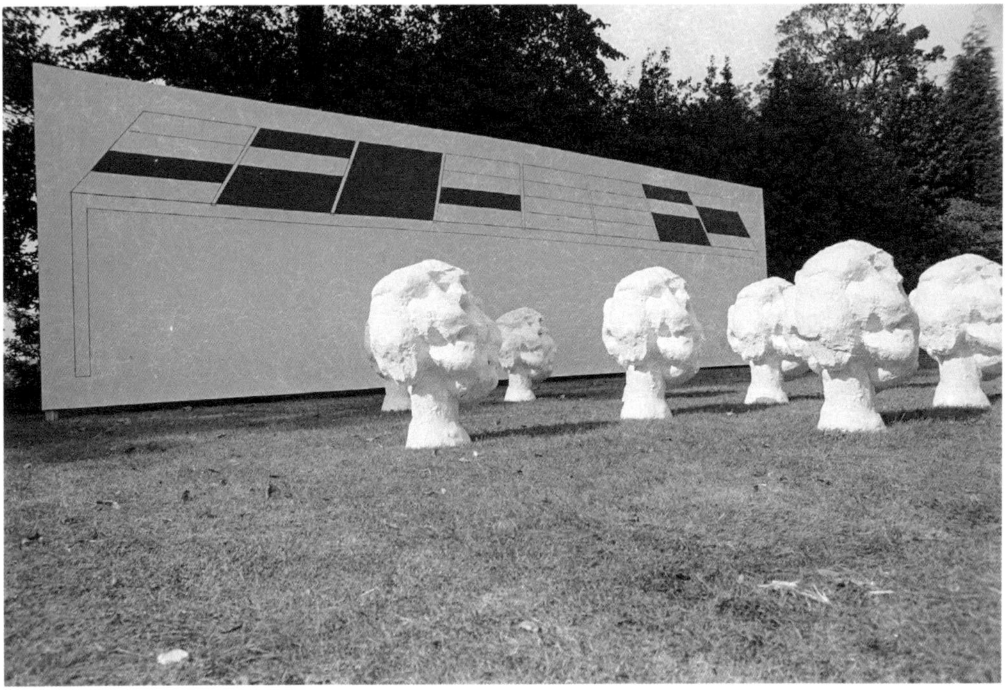

A Conversation with Wanda[1]

Richard Demarco

Wanda Czelowska's[2] sculptural creation, *The Table,* is a revolutionary work, both for sculpture and for the artist herself. Richard Demarco spoke with her in Cracow, in preparation for her appearance – and *The Table*'s – in Edinburgh, for the Festival's Exhibition of Contemporary Art.

Richard Demarco: Your latest work, "The Table", is undoubtedly a piece of sculpture. I'd like to know when you first wanted to say something in sculptural terms about the reality of "The Table", or the idea of a table.
Wanda Czełkowska: It is a long story. There was a time in my life when I created sculpture which I called "Instead Of." There are certain times when we have to act simply to document one's self-existence.

RD: I wonder if you meant "instead of" what you knew you should have really been doing, that is, feeling you had to be doing something even if it was only other people's ideas of sculpture, but nothing to do with your own creative impulses.
WC: I made sculpture at that time which was well received, and from that experience I was recognised in Cracow as a sculptor. At the same time I was angry. I walked about angry in my studio. I felt I wanted society to know clearly that this was my way of earning a living – not in terms of money, but in a moral sense. Suddenly I realised I had sufficient right to continue. I decided to break with any ideas I might be forming of myself as a sculptor, and so I came up with the idea of the Table about three years ago. I realised that the revaluation of my concepts of sculpture would meet with great difficulties – not material difficulties, but to do with the way with which it would be received.

1. *Conceptual Information about "The Table" (Informacja pojęciowa o "Stole")*, 1972, Scottish National Gallery of Modern Art, Inverleith House, Edinburgh. Demarco Digital Archive, University of Dundee & Richard Demarco Archive Photo: George Oliver

RD: At this point did you decide to make the dimensions 8 x 6 metres and to make the Table of steel?

WC: Yes. The scale is also an important means of expression for me. I do not think that if we do something on a small scale it could be received as it can be on a large scale. It is not true that something very small can have a big meaning. When I decided to realise the idea of a table, I was content to carry the idea in my mind for three years. I stopped considering my "Instead Of" activity, which had up to that point classified me as a sculptor, and I kept waiting for the point when I would make my ideas real.

RD: Explain 'instead of' in your own words.
WC: It is quite simple. It is a matter of using talent and experience, skill and craftsmanship. We are not always in a position to realise our own ideas, but are obliged to express those of others.

RD: When did you first exhibit "The Table"?
WC: On the 18th of last December, in the Cracow Exhibition Pavilion – with the goodwill of the committee. I was invited to the Exhibition as the sculptor of the "Instead Of" sculptures. I was expected to exhibit a sculpture of the kind I was known to produce. My fellow sculptors were offended by The Table. They did not see it as sculpture, whereas for me it was pure sculpture. This is my short history of The Table. After three years of contemplating it, I wrote this explanation for The Table:
"'The Table' : dimensions, 8 x 4 metres. It can be situated anywhere you can imagine a table being placed. There are several sculptures of one head placed on the Table: it's a sculpture of contemporary man, met by chance. It can be a head sculptured by tools which transfer precisely all the points of an existing model, and it can also be made as a sculpture entitled 'Head'. The most important thing is the table and the activity of its dimensions, on which the multiples of the head are placed. It is multiplied only 18 times, and the arrangement is made by chance, but once it is made it cannot be changed. The heads are placed on two sides of the Table facing each other. I still have 2 concepts of the Table which I would like to develop. I don't know when I will be able to realise them, because unfortunately the language of art depends on the possibilities offered. I don't know when it will happen within the space of time. I am not impatient to wait for favourable conditions.

The only thing that matters is the conception, and that will be realised some day. I may have to spend 20 years on it because it is my problem and it will last as long as I do."

I have tried to write about my concepts but they have no literary form. My writings serve only as notes.

RD: Why 18 heads?

WC: The Table was realised and thought out with all the dimensions and lines on it having their own meaning. If I were to explain it now it would loose all meaning. It would stop being the language of art. I can't logically explain it. It is one of the elements of the language of art, and its logic as well. The moment

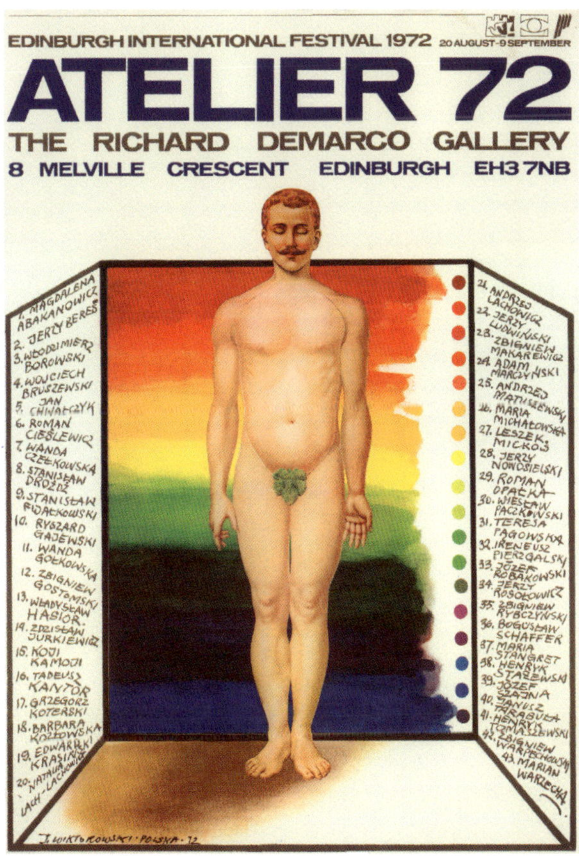

2. Poster of *Atelier '72* exhibition in the framework of the Edinburgh Festival in 1972. Demarco Digital Archive, University of Dundee & Richard Demarco Archive

you make it one way you realise you cannot make it another. When the Table was being erected for the Exhibition someone said that perhaps there were too many heads, but when it was erected they all agreed the number was right, and fitting. I did not set about creating 18 heads. It just came to be. The most important thing is the precise realisation of the Table because it is not a biological expression, but the exact realisation of a situation.

RD: Did you study sculpture?
WC: Yes, in Cracow, but from the very beginning I was not involved in the problem of form but in the expression of my thoughts and ideas.

RD: Do you think your work could change, through the experience of Scotland? Will your work become a different thing under the skies of Scotland?
WC: I can't say how I would react.

RD: Do you mind if I have the Table in the Gallery, or must it be outside?
WC: No, it can be anywhere where it can stand. It will not change as a human being might. It remains a table, whether on a hillside, on the Moon, or in a gallery.

RD: The heads face each other, nine against nine, divided by an empty space, but I can see it is not to be confused with a game of chess.
WC: Absolutely not. It is mere chance it looks like a chess game. The head is of "every man" – it doesn't matter what the material is. I chose gypsum because it was the only material available. I would have preferred clear plastic. I don't like stone or wood; I prefer materials which are essentially contemporary.

RD: Maybe the British Steel Corporation can make it possible for a second version of the Table, in steel. After all, you're expressing a universal truth in terms which are pure sculpture, and stressing the fact that still is a 20th Century material.
WC: The problem of the Table is still very much part of me; I still have to work on it. I feel certain that in Edinburgh I could see it in a much more

perfect form. I am surprised you should give me such attention to what is my own special problem.

RD: It is simply because that problem typifies the problem of any creative person who wishes to go beyond himself, and certainly beyond the accepted definitions of art. You are the kind of artist I want to help. It makes my own work most worthwhile.

Reprinted from the magazine *Umbrella* (June 1972), published by Richard Demarco Gallery. Courtesy of Scottish National Gallery of Modern Art Archive and the artist's estate.

[1] Too often women artists are still mentioned by their first name only. This interview published by Richard Demarco in 1972 is no exception.
[2] Transcription by Antonina Gugała.
Original spelling and punctuation. Correct spelling: "Czełkowska's".

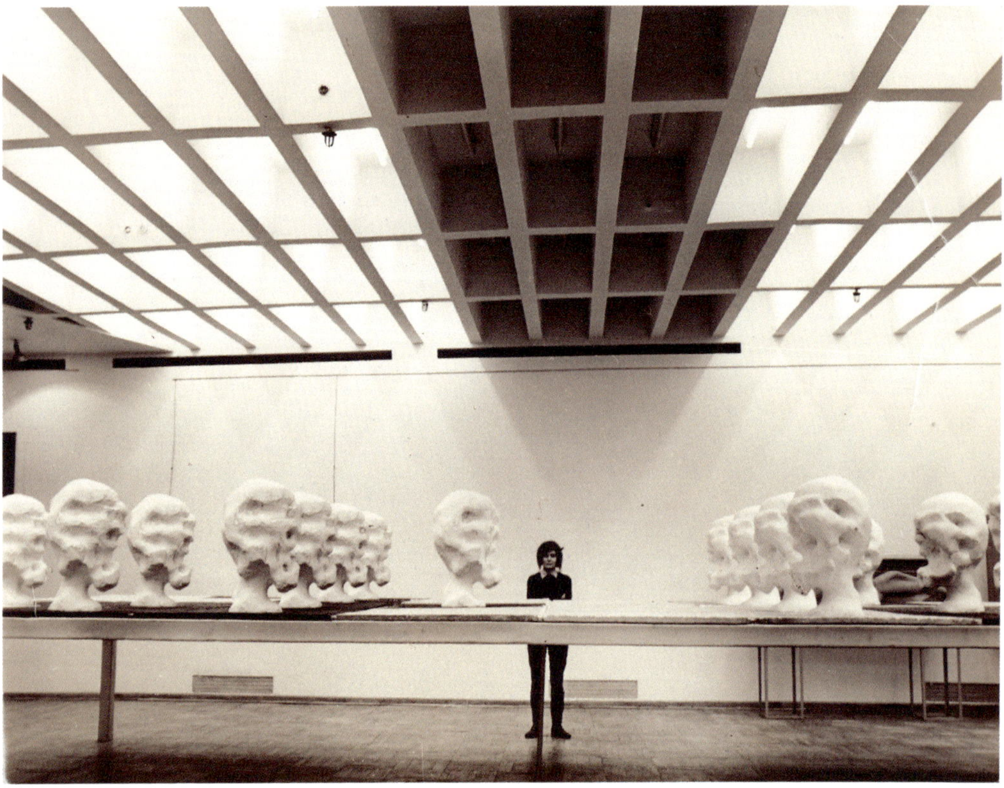

Heads that Cannot See: The "Eliminated" Sculpture of Wanda Czełkowska

Amelia Jones

Wanda Czełkowska produced a large number of heads that cannot see. Shaped vaguely or specifically like portrait busts, with disturbingly gouged surfaces and often featureless, her sculptural works in the 1960s and early 1970s perform few of the other functions portrait busts are generally meant to perform in the Western art tradition. They are not recognizable as individual people; they are often distorted, hacked apart, only remotely resembling the form of human heads. Those few that have "eyes" seem nonetheless to be unseeing. Their function hovers between representation and abstraction, or even between object and narrative. They have stories to tell, stories that are narrated not in words but through bodily experience in space and time. These heads, to which I will return at the end of this brief set of ruminations on Czełkowska's practice, epitomize the way in which the artist refused to follow conventional ideas about what sculpture *is*, what it should *do*, and how it will come to have meaning in her time and ours.

—

Wanda Czełkowska studied in Kraków in the 1950s and emerged as a mature artist onto the Polish scene later that decade. Viewed from the eyes of one trained in US-dominant histories of contemporary art, Czełkowska's practice from around 1960 into the 1970s can be seen as having translated the modernism being taken apart by younger generations of artists in Western Europe and North America, which Polish art schools were engaging after the "thaw" of 1956 opening Poland more to the West (with continuing echoes of the preference within the communist regime for a focus on realism), into a particular and powerful cross-cultural idiom.[1]

1. Wanda Czełkowska beside her installation *Stół* (*Table*), 1968–1971, 4th Kraków Meetings, BWA pavilion in Kraków, 1971. Courtesy of Szarota Nowak Photo: Wacław Nowak

In New York discourses on sculpture (New York having declared itself the centre of contemporary art and art criticism starting in the post WWII period) an all-out war was being staged. On the one side was the dominant formalist understanding of the artwork (in the case of sculpture, its "ability to defeat theatre" and its "wholly manifest" assertion of itself as sculpture "at every moment", as Michael Fried famously put it), and, on the other, the practices described by feminist critic Lucy Lippard as "dematerialized" manifestations of works in space and time, conceptually driven and often involving materials not formerly considered artistic (such as industrial metals and felt) and the direct activation of bodies.[2] With critics such as Fried claiming that sculptors were obligated to produce objects that acknowledged their instantaneous "presentness [as] … grace", younger New York artists, such as Hannah Wilke, Eva Hesse, Lynda Benglis, Scott Burton, or Robert Morris, often explicitly feminist or queer in approach, took the challenge and presented the art gallery with flaps or pours of latex (Wilke, Hesse, Benglis), his own theatrically performing body (Burton), or, in the case of Morris, large-scale "minimal" objects, such as his plywood *L-Beams* of 1965.[3] These young American artists were quite directly provoking the conservative formalist critics such as Michael Fried and his mentor Clement Greenberg, refusing such prescriptions of what art or sculpture in particular "must" do. Morris's giant *L-Beams*, for example, required that the spectator navigate around these huge geometric forms, re-establishing, in Morris's words, "a bond between the artist and the environment", and, reciprocally, between spectator and artwork; as well, Morris extended a phenomenological and psychological model of what sculpture could do, noting a new emphasis on the body's interaction with materials, which in turn foregrounded and exploited complex and rich "'tendencies' inherent in a materials/process interaction".[4] Wilke, Hesse, and Burton (along with others), in turn, were bent on destroying the heteronormative white male certainties of these formalist critics, introducing materials and bodies that refused to obey their rules.[5]

Czełkowska, indeed, side stepped these New York-centric battles between titanic white male egos (Fried and Morris), producing her own particular and dynamic work that mined the psychological and phenomenological power of thinking and making spatially. The apotheosis of such explorations at this fairly early point of her career might be her 1968–1971 work *Table* (*Stół*), a giant platform (too big to be a human-sized table, but nonetheless echoing its forms) marked on its surface by a large grid of black-and-white squares, with a series of the mysterious bulbous head-forms seemingly randomly placed on squares throughout – their only order being chess-like as they (blindly) "stare" each other down from across the two sides of the "table" (or is it a chessboard? Or a massive pedestal?)[6] (fig. 1). Even here, however, the situation is not static; sculpture is not still or passive, remaining only one thing: these heads or similar ones, in turn, found their way into Czełkowska's living space (she used four of them at one point to prop up a dining table) and into later installations such as *Ellipse* (*Elipsa*), 2016, where different "head" busts are arranged around the gallery on simply hewn wooden or metal pedestals, facing in contradictory directions (fig. pp. 86–87).

The heads thus have multiple lives. In images of her hosting dinner at the head-supported table, the heads are themselves made into pedestals (deployed directly as supports for social engagement; fig. p. 51); she also staged the heads in an ominous crowd-like cluster in the courtyard of her studio (fig. 2). In *Ellipse*, these singularly alienated busts, rather than "representing" individual people, seem to evoke atavistic and even totemic ideas of the power of a vertical head-like shape to evoke humanness; and the spatial experience of the installation is both interrupted and to some degree unified by a massive aluminium hoop, which dynamically springs from floor diagonally to ceiling, wrapping the disparate heads into one loop of visual and kinetic energy. Czełkowska shows a sculptor's understanding of the radical elasticity and psychological power of space and material to change our experience.

In two other related projects from this extremely fertile period of Wanda Czełkowska's career – *Absolute Elimination of Sculpture as a Notion of Shape* (*Bezwzględne wyeliminowanie rzeźby jako pojęcia kształtu*; fig. 3), an investigation started in 1972 and realized in 1995, and *Wall* (*Ściana*), 1975–1976 (fig. p. 150) – shed further light on what she was doing with *Table* and her blinded heads. With these installations Czełkowska expanded on this radical intervention in sculpture as a medium, anticipating the genre of multimedia installation that emerged in the 1990s in Western Europe and North America. In *Absolute Elimination*, as it was documented and displayed via an enlarged photographic print mounted across the gallery wall in 2016, the idea of sculpture following a set of rules pinning it down as "shapes" in material form is radically undermined – sculpture, she is telling us, can be much more than shapes or objects situated on pedestals. Sculpture is a philosophical premise, a means of conceptualizing bodies in relation to things, bodies, spaces.[7] In the 2016 version of *Absolute Elimination*, simple planes and squares of darker colour lie across the flat expanse in the photograph, which is mounted human-height above the floor.

With this later display of *Absolute Elimination*, Czełkowska moves beyond the brash explorations of New York minimalist sculptor Carl Andre, whose grids of metal plates hugging the surface of the floor, made around 1970, fought the closures of formalism noted above. She rather brings the floor up to the height of human eyes, forcing the dematerialization of three-dimensional space into another state of negation, as Ewa Opałka has compellingly argued.[8] Sculpture is no longer a thing – it is a concept, "devoid of space, tension, relationality or life".[9] It is representational as well as material, expanding into conceptual arenas while definitively leaving the "system of authority [in Poland under communism], which imposed a certain political and ideological paradigm", especially relating to the social realism trends of Czełkowska's early sculpture training in Kraków.[10] As Opałka points out, while in Western Europe and the United States such resistance to objecthood resisted the commodification in, say, the New York art world which threatened to swallow up all artist-made objects, in Poland this situation was bound to be very different. Czełkowska, then, pioneered in her own way by finding a way to resist national trends of representational art while adopting conceptually-driven and highly sophisticated strategies that were being played out in the West in materially and politically different ways.

In a similar fashion, Czełkowska's *Wall*, conceived in 1975–1976, was built and installed later in relation to *Edinburgh Head* (*Głowa edynburska*), 1972. Here, one has access to seeing/experiencing the beautifully constructed wooden back of the wall structure, held together by metal beams screwed into place through metal plates (fig. p. 152). The front side of the wall also clearly shows its constructedness – large bolts or screws are visible from the other side (in neat patterns of two or four), metal plates keep parts of the structure stable, and the panels, canvas stretched over wood frames, are painted in white oil paint with some of them covered with black sketches of head-like forms on necks, mirroring the object in front of the wall (the *Edinburgh Head*). On the floor sits a larger-than life human head-like form covered in fabric that is bound with string, especially tightly around its pedestal-like neck. This head is not only blinded, it is suffocated, controlled, with the vague approximations of jutting features fully contained. This object starts to seem distinctly like metaphor for traditional sculpture itself – more precisely, the portrait bust, situated (in Western art) on its pedestal, even as in this case the head, balancing on its neck/pedestal, stares blindly into space, a dumb object attempting to "represent" the actuality of a human visage wrapped over a skull.

—

Returning to and ending with Czełkowska's exploration of the expressive power of sculptures of heads (or head-like sculptures), it is interesting to note

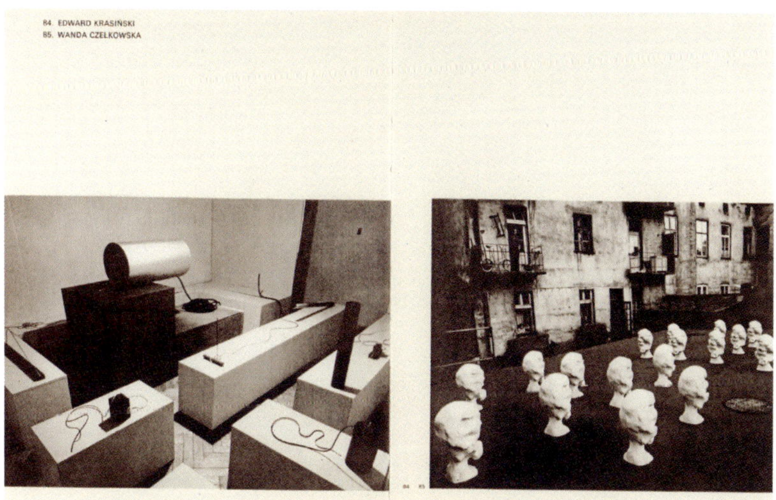

2. Spread from Andrzej Osęka, Wojciech Skrodzki, *Współczesna rzeźba polska* (Warsaw: Arkady, 1977). Courtesy of Arkady

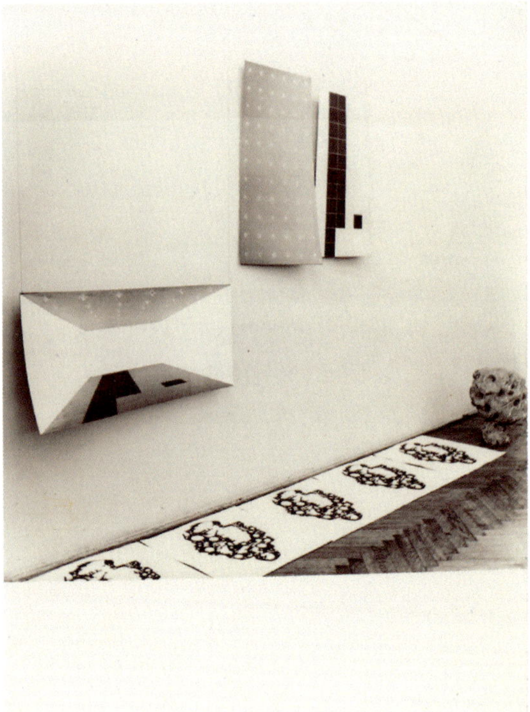

3. Exhibition at Galeria ZPAP Pryzmat, Kraków, January 1973. On the wall: Wanda Czełkowska's model of *Absolute Elimination of Sculpture as a Notion of Shape* (*Bezwzględne wyeliminowanie rzeźby jako pojęcia kształtu*), 1972; on the floor: *Fryz* (*Frieze*), 1973, and *Green Head* (*Zielona głowa*), 1973

that it began early. The works move fairly quickly from decorous realist busts and standing figures from around 1950 (fig. 4) to fascinating explorations of the evocative potential of art brut-like bulbous shapes, scratched and gouged with facial "features", in the mid 1950s, as with *Man's Head* (*Głowa mężczyzny*), 1957 (fig. 5), to a harrowingly expressive abstracted set of lumps emerging from a lower form – as with *Head* (*Głowa*), 1964 (fig. p. 59), where what appears to be its face is sliced almost in two, forming a gaping "mouth". At this point, Czełkowska's interests and materials – producing objects in space that compel human attention, with both phenomenological and psychological effects, most often with cast and painted plaster – have emerged and matured. By this latter piece (*Head*, 1964) she has, with muscularity and a seeming lack of fear, produced a piece that seems the materialization of the kinds of existentialist yearnings and energies that were so dominant in Western thought and art making after WWII, but again in her own terms. There is no sense that this is "expanding on" the by-then canonical existentialist works of, say, Alberto Giacometti. Czełkowska's heads, and her move into complex installations including these mute and blind forms, are something entirely different.

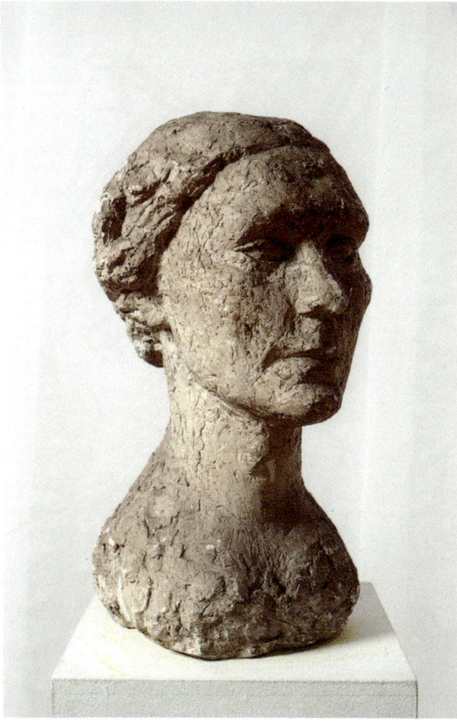

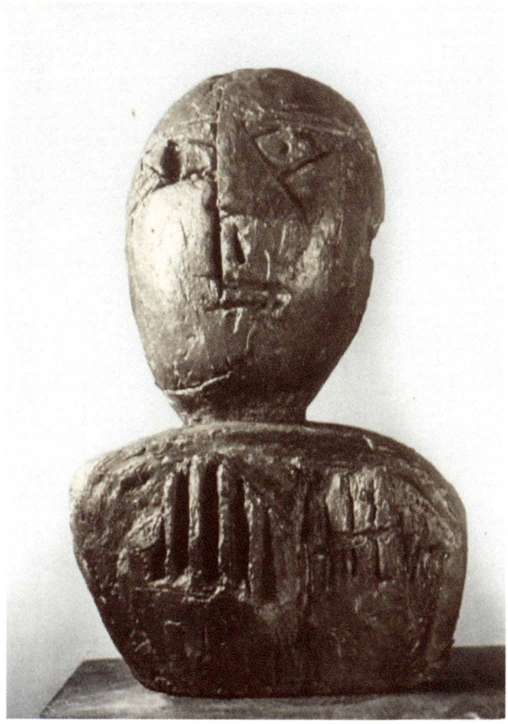

4. Wanda Czełkowska, *Untitled*, 1950, sculpture, cast in plaster, 61 × 34 × 30 cm. Courtesy of National Museum in Warsaw Photo: Szymon Rogiński

5. Wanda Czełkowska, *Man's Head* (*Głowa mężczyzny*), 1957, sculpture, cast iron Photo: Krzysztof Malski

This is clear in Czełkowska's *Table*, wherein rows of 18 seemingly identical cast gypsum heads are clearly set up in a game of chess that likely cannot be "won" by one side or the other. Riddled with holes, porous, they are (in the original installation, where photographs show Czełkowska standing on the opposite side of the gargantuan giant's "table") at least four times the size of a normal human noggin. If traditional sculptural busts are intended to "represent" a person who lives or lived in ways that can be easily recognized as a "portrait" by later viewers, Czełkowska produces heads that are monstrous, creepy in their muteness and with their plaster surfaces violated. Her anger towards conventional ideas of sculpture, expressed in an interview about the piece, is palpable.[11] (This feeling of violation, driven by creative anger, echoes the effect of the very powerful, earlier *Head* of 1968: also cast in plaster, it stands on a metal and wooden stand such that its hollow back and metal armature are exposed; it is literally sliced open, precariously supported by one metal rod connecting it to a misshapen set of "neck" and "shoulders"; fig. p. 136)

Theorizing with space and materialities, Czełkowska produces work that both resonates with Western European and North American conceptually-driven responses to modernism, and at the same time proposes a radically alternative – one is tempted to say "Polish" and "feminist" – proposition. Aside from the fact that she did not even want to be thought of as a woman artist, much less a feminist.[12] But in her courage and originality, Czełkowska's case parallels that of Alina Szapocznikow, one of the most brilliant feminist artists and sculptors of the post WWII period, from Poland but also Jewish, and an artist who made the move to Paris and became more aligned with Western feminism (the two in fact met in 1957 in Warsaw). While Szapocznikow, surely due to her experience having been persecuted in Nazi concentration camps during WWII, could hardly avoid making art driven by content, Czełkowska's work organized profound philosophical concepts into abstracted material forms. Both artists confront us with disturbing and moving human avatars, inviting us to think about what sculpture can do. Both reflect on human complexity and failure through sculptural form.

Czełkowska's complex sculptural works, such as *Table*, are both modernist and anti-modernist, both formalist and conceptual, both "Polish" and something transnational. And ultimately, they are psychologically charged objects – which remind us of the inevitable blindness of existing in the human condition – that can function as art or as furniture or as philosophy, lived and living in our spaces with us. This is their power.

[1] On Czełkowska's resistance to the social realism being taught in Polish art schools in the 1950s, see Louise Benson, "Land of the Lads: Celebrating the Female Avant-Garde", *Elephant*, 28 June 2018, https://elephant.art/where-are-all-the-women-artists/
[2] Michael Fried, "Art and Objecthood", *Artforum*, June 1967, reprinted in *Art and Objecthood: Essays and Reviews* (Chicago: University of Chicago Press, 1998), 148–172. On "dematerialization", see Lucy Lippard, *Six Years: The Dematerialization of the Art Object from 1966 to 1972* (New York: Praeger, 1973).
[3] Fried, "Art and Objecthood", 147.
[4] Robert Morris, "Some Notes on the Phenomenology of Making: The Search for the Motivated", *Artforum*, April 1970, reprinted in Robert Morris, *Continuous Project Altered Daily* (Cambridge, MA: MIT Press, 1993), see 75, 77.
[5] On these points, see my essay "Art History/Art Criticism: Performing Meaning", in Amelia Jones and Andrew Stephenson (eds.), *Performing the Body/Performing the Text* (New York–London: Routledge, 1999), 39–55.
[6] On this work, see the short interview between Czełkowska and Richard Demarco regarding her plan to display *Table* at the Edinburgh Festival, "A Conversation with Wanda", in *Umbrella* (June 1972), n.p. Here, Czełkowska asserts that the heads, of which there are 18 (nine facing nine), are arranged on the table "by chance, but once [the arrangement…] is made it cannot be changed". Reprinted in this book pages 111–115.
[7] Czełkowska wanted to study philosophy before shifting her attention to sculpture in her schooling in the 1950s. See Maria Hussakowska, "Wanda Czełkowska: The Mechanism of the Disappearance of the Artist and the Disappearance of the Sculpture", in Ewa Opałka, Jennifer Moore-Tymowska (eds.), *Wanda Czełkowska: Retrospection*, exhibition catalogue (Warsaw: National Museum, 2016), 73.
[8] See Ewa Opałka, "Why the Ruthless Absolute? Between dematerialisation and the flesh — the phenomenon of Wanda Czełkowska's sculptures", in *Wanda Czełkowska: Retrospection*, 47.
[9] Ibid.
[10] This history is outlined by Hussakowska in "Wanda Czełkowska" and in "Wanda Czełkowska Artistic Timeline", both in *Wanda Czełkowska: Retrospection*, 70–92 and 92–135.
[11] See Demarco "A Conversation with Wanda". Czełkowska makes it clear, as well, that "it is mere chance that it looks like a chess game," and "the head is of 'every man'".
[12] Czełkowska asserted that she was a "sculptor", not a "sculptress, noting that "a sculptress is this chick who makes sculptures, whereas this is about something entirely different"; cited in Opałka, "Why the Ruthless Absolute?", 41.

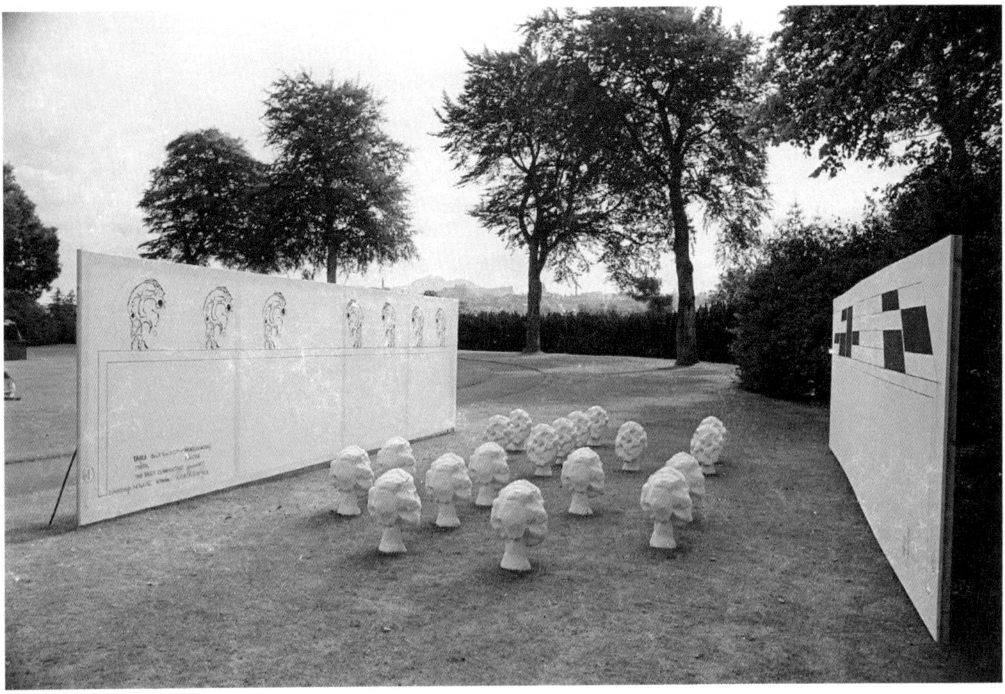

Conceptual Information about "The Table", 1972

June Geddes

From the very beginning I was not involved in the problem of form but in the expression of my thoughts and ideas.[1]
Wanda Czełkowska, January 1972

Wanda Czełkowska travelled to Scotland in August 1972 as part of Richard Demarco's Edinburgh Festival exhibition *Atelier '72*, Britain's first major exhibition of contemporary Polish art. Demarco's 1972 Festival programme is often remembered for Tadeusz Kantor's, now recognized as historic, introduction to English-speaking theatre audiences with his Cricot 2 production of *The Water Hen*, described by *The Daily Telegraph* theatre critic John Barber as "the least-publicised, most talked-about event at Edinburgh" (fig. 2).[2] However, *Atelier '72*, which was presented in collaboration with the Museum of Art in Łódź and showed the work of over forty artists, was equally important. It featured artists that, in retrospect, are understood as key figures of 1970's Polish avant-garde, such as Jerzy Bereś, Edward Krasiński, Roman Opałka, Józef Robakowski, and Zbigniew Warpechowski; but particularly women artists, including Magdalena Abakanowicz, Natalia LL, Barbara Kozłowska, Wanda Gołkowska, Maria Michałowska, and Wanda Czełkowska.

1. *Conceptual Information about "The Table" (Informacja pojęciowa o "Stole")*, 1972, Scottish National Gallery of Modern Art, Inverleith House, Edinburgh. Demarco Digital Archive, University of Dundee & Richard Demarco Archive Photo: George Oliver

Czełkowska's contribution was a sculptural installation, *Conceptual Information about "The Table" (Informacja pojęciowa o "Stole")*. Too large for Demarco's gallery, it was dramatically situated in the grounds of the Scottish National Gallery of Modern Art's Inverleith House, within Edinburgh's Royal Botanic Garden (fig. 1). The Scottish work was based on *Table (Stół)*, 1968–1971, the concept for which Demarco had seen during his May 1971 visit to Poland, when he readily accepted Czełkowska's suggestion to construct the work in Edinburgh for *Atelier '72*. Czełkowska developed the original *Table* concept over three years before presenting it at the Kraków

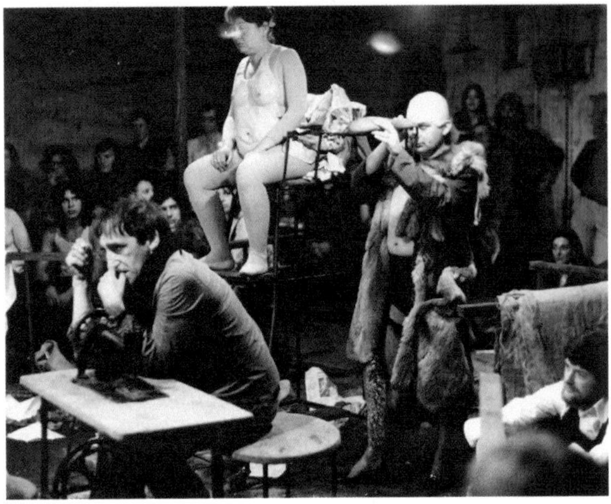

2. Scene from Cricot 2, *The Water Hen*, performed in the Poorhouse, Forrest Hill, Edinburgh, August 1972. From the left: Tadeusz Kantor, Maria Stangret, Zbigniew Bednarczyk. Demarco Digital Archive, University of Dundee & Richard Demarco Archive Photo: Richard Demarco

3. Page dedicated to Wanda Czełkowska in the exhibition catalogue *Atelier '72*, Richard Demarco Gallery, Edinburgh, 1972

Group exhibition in December 1970, where Kantor offered to help organize funds for its construction, having originally invited Czełkowska to join the Second Kraków Group in 1968. The completed work was first shown at the 4th Kraków Meetings in December 1971. In an interview with Demarco published in his gallery's magazine *Umbrella*, Czełkowska recalled that her fellow sculptors "were offended ... They did not see it as sculpture, whereas for me it was pure sculpture". She spoke of her increasing frustration with the kind of sculpture that she had previously been making, which she referred to as "Instead Of" sculpture, where she was not "in a position to realise [her] own ideas, but ... obliged to express those of others".[3]

The *Table* consists of eighteen plaster casts of one sculptured head arranged facing each other on two sides of an 8 x 4 x 1.2 metres steel table. This enormous scale was, Czełkowska maintained, the essence of the sculpture. Divided into thirty-two square metal plates, any simple comparisons to a chess board are negated by the uneven fourteen black and eighteen white squares. In 2016, Czełkowska described her *Head* (*Głowa*) as having a "third gender", but in 1972 she gave it a humanist context, quoting from her original concept text describing it as "a sculpture of contemporary man, met by chance".[4] She resisted, however, having an explanation for the number of *Heads* or the *Table*'s dimensions: "If I were to explain it now, it would lose all meaning. It would stop being the language of art ... The moment you make it one way you realise you cannot make it another".[5] Czełkowska made two new *Edinburgh Heads* (*Głowy edynburskie*), one of which she brought with

CZEŁKOWSKA

Wanda Czełkowska

Studied at the Academy of Fine Arts, Cracow.

Participated in exhibitions in Poland and abroad:
Art Festival, Cracow, 1959
Polish Sculpture 1945-60, Warsaw 1960
Creative Artistic Work during the 15 years of the Polish People's Republic, Warsaw 1961
'Planty'/Park, Cracow 1962
Exhibition of Drawings, Sculptures, Warsaw 1966
'II Salon Lutowy'/Second February Salon/,Zakopane 1968
Participation in exhibitions of the Cracow Group 'Krzysztofory' Gallery, Cracow since 1968
Cracow meetings, Cracow 1971

Exhibitions abroad:
Norway 1963, The Hague 1963, Paris 1963, Nancy 1966, Vienna 1967, Hungary 1970.
One-man Shows:
'Krzysztofory' Gallery, Cracow 1963/sculpture, drawings/
'Wspolczesna'/Contemporary/Gallery, Warsaw 1969/drawings/

EDINBURGH FESTIVAL 1972 AUG-SEP „ATELIER 72"

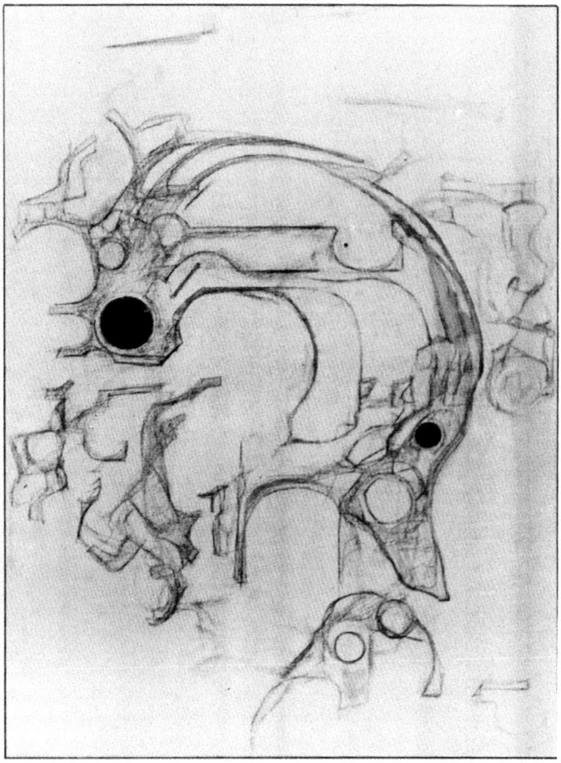

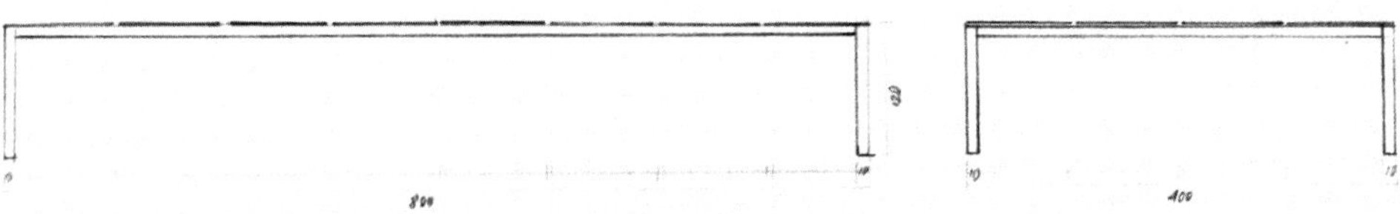

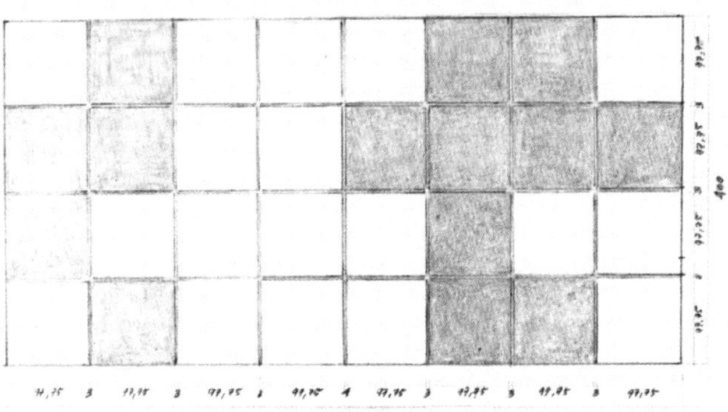

her to Scotland intending to reconstruct the *Table* on site, with her original concept drawings forming her *Atelier '72* catalogue page.[6] This followed the Demarco Gallery's traditional catalogue format, whereby each artist selected images, text, and often layout for their page (fig. 3).

However, despite the involvement of British Steel, the *Table* proved unrealizable: Czełkowska rejected British Steel's original version, which had been constructed with incorrect dimensions and there was not enough time to construct a second.[7] Instead, the project became *Conceptual Information*, where the enormous table was replaced by two large screens facing each other, described by art critic Edward Gage as "long canvases pointedly pegged to the ground beneath a transparent sheet": both with graphic depictions of the *Table*'s original concept.[8] Between them stood eighteen plaster casts of the *Edinburgh Head* facing each other in the same configuration as the 1971 original, referencing Czełkowska's concept that "the arrangement is made by chance, but once it is made it cannot be changed".[9] Described by *The Guardian*'s art critic Cordelia Oliver as "a canvas and sculpture environment", Czełkowska later recalled how the screens' conceptual information enabled visitors to imagine the *Table*'s original proportions and layout, envisaging black and white modules overlaid onto the green grass even though, physically, they did not exist.[10]

Like the steel table construction, the *Heads* were also problematic. As late as 2 August, the apparently unforeseen need to cast eighteen *Edinburgh Heads* was eventually resolved, with their delivery to the Demarco Gallery offering the opportunity to take an equally playful photograph of the *Heads* in relation to the human form as Czełkowska's Kraków photograph had done (fig. 4).[11] Demarco later likened the *Heads* to chess figures, but also something less prescriptive, suggesting that "the prehistoric sculptors who built the standing stones of Callanish would have understood" – a comparison made all the more relatable with the *Heads* standing on grass rather than a metal table, although Czełkowska may have rejected it having stated earlier that she "would have preferred clear plastic [to plaster]", adding: "I don't like stone or wood; I prefer materials which are essentially contemporary".[12]

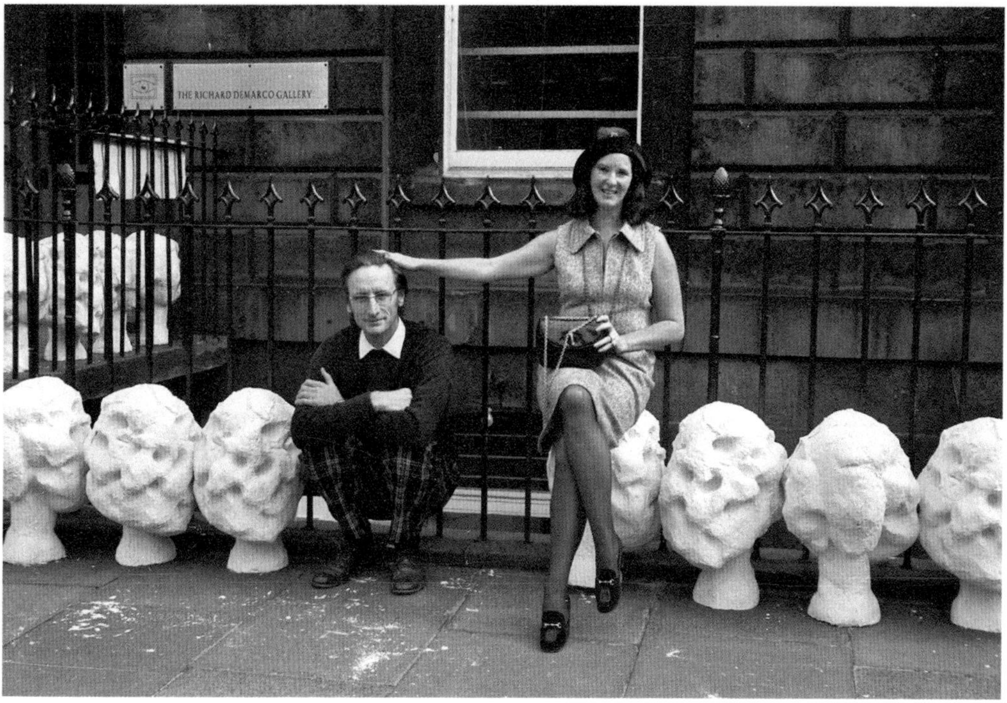

4. Pamela and James Currie outside the Richard Demarco Gallery, Edinburgh, with Wanda Czełkowska's *Edinburgh Heads* (*Głowy edynburskie*), August 1972. Demarco Digital Archive, University of Dundee & Richard Demarco Archive Photo: Richard Demarco

Maria Hussakowska quotes Janusz Tarabuła (shown at, but not invited to, Edinburgh) recalling that Czełkowska thought the Edinburgh installation was "a failure", adding her own criticism that only within the framework of "something to the effect of a white cube" did the spatial set-ups between gallery walls, the *Table*, and viewer work.[13] And whilst Czełkowska's own view was that the *Table* could be located anywhere – "It will not change ... It remains a table whether on a hillside, on the Moon, or in a gallery" – the drama of the original project's scale would certainly have been lost in Edinburgh, creating a different relationship between the *Heads* and the viewer.[14] Instead of Czełkowska's seemingly tiny figure in relation to the Kraków installation, the *Heads* were knee-high. However, the outdoor setting provided another perspective, with the viewer being able to wander amongst them and walk behind the screens providing a relationship to the installation's structural support that she reiterated in *Wall* (*Ściana*), 1975–1976, suggesting that she was happy that, like the 1968 *Head* that revealed its innards, a work's support structure as well as its concept should be revealed. And for Ewa Opałka, *Conceptual Information* offered a further (subversive) dematerialization from representational sculpture with the table "replaced by a concept-information" enabling "a much more radical spatial work".[15]

The potentially more performative nature of *Conceptual Information* was echoed by other *Atelier '72* works. Not just the performances embodied in Józef Szajna's *Replika*, Kantor's *The Water Hen*, or Warpechowski's series of actions that included *Water-Fire-Life*, *Drawing in the corner*, and *Nothing*, but also Edward Krasiński's essentially performative blue line which crept from room to room, round corners and over obstacles in the Demarco Gallery (fig. 5). Or Andrzej Matuszewski's installation in the grounds of St Mary's Cathedral, *Parallel Action-Synapsis* – a line of seven chairs, each sunk lower into the grass than the one before, with the last "almost completely sunk in the ground" – where Matuszewski imagined a passer-by sitting on a chair, perhaps looking at the sky, or reading a paper, whilst "maybe two persons ... talk or remain silent".[16] Surpassing these was the performativity of Abakanowicz's red ropes. While one snaked in and out of the windows of the Demarco Gallery alongside her *Abakan* sculptures, another was marched two minutes along the road and onto the roof of St Mary's. The performative element was provided by those, including Abakanowicz, who carried the rope along the street and dragged it over the roofs of the large Gothic revival cathedral (fig. 6).

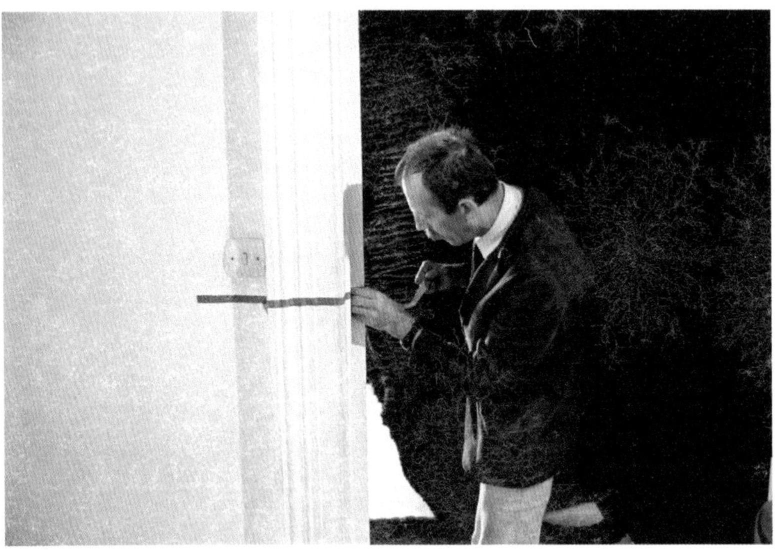

5. Edward Krasiński installing *Blue Line* in Melville Crescent for *Atelier '72*. Demarco Digital Archive, University of Dundee & Richard Demarco Archive Photo: George Oliver

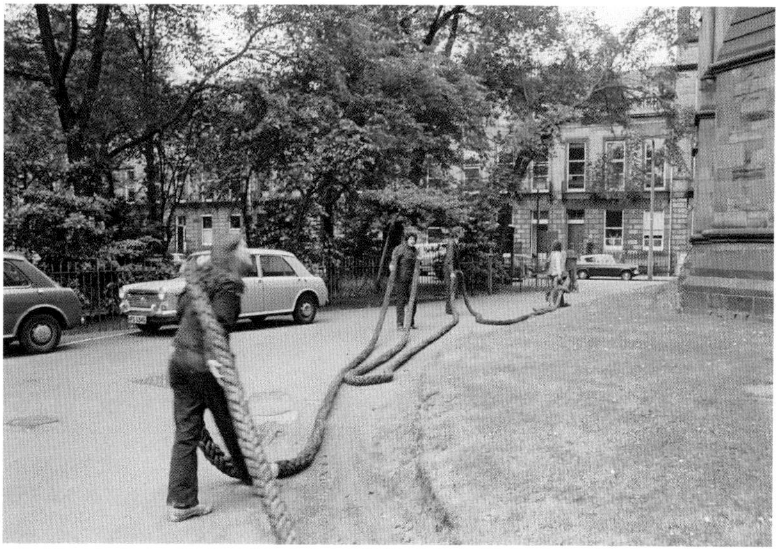

6. Installation of Magdalena Abakanowicz's red rope at St Mary's Cathedral, Edinburgh for *Atelier '72*. Demarco Digital Archive, University of Dundee & Richard Demarco Archive Photo: George Oliver

For Czełkowska, Edinburgh's "beautiful" surroundings not only enabled her to create a "huge" work, but also offered different perspectives of it, both in relation to the view of Arthur's Seat beyond and, as Inverleith House stood on a hill, the views of the work from below, reinforcing Czełkowska's statement in *Umbrella* that "the language of art depends on the possibilities offered".[17] The artist told Demarco in 1972 that she did not regard the *Table* as a finished work: "The problem of the Table is still very much part of me; I still have to work on it. I feel certain that in Edinburgh I could see it in a much more perfect form".[18] Whether *Conceptual Information* was as perfect as hoped is unknown, however, it can be seen as a transitional work, especially if one considers Czełkowska's 1972 statement that she still had two concepts of the table that she hoped to develop.[19] Seeing it outdoors, with its infinite spatial qualities, one can imagine why it might have been the inspiration for Czełkowska's dematerialized *Absolute Elimination of the Sculpture as a Notion of Shape*, 1972 [1995],[20] where the gallery walls, 66 concrete slabs on the floor and 66 electric light points in the ceiling shaped a void, empty of any other sculptural forms. The aborted *Edinburgh Table* structure and the possibility of placing a legless tabletop on the ground may also have contributed to Czełkowska's emerging ideas.

According to Opałka, *Conceptual Information* was "what forced Czełkowska back to Poland, to Kraków, to Karmelicka street, to 'her place', where the idea could find its crystallisation in the *Absolute Elimination of Sculpture as a Notion of Shape* (*Bezwzględne wyeliminowanie rzeźby jako pojęcia kształtu*)".[21] Demarco had hoped that Czełkowska would remain in and be inspired by Scotland to prepare for a solo exhibition in 1973, however it was not to be.[22] Although the Edinburgh installation was never repeated, the *Edinburgh Head*, covered in cloth and bound with rope, became part of Czełkowska's *Wall* (it is unknown what happened to the other *Heads* and screens from the Edinburgh installation). The connection to the Edinburgh installation is unmissable – once more the head is placed on the ground, with multiple drawings of the same on a freestanding screen, echoing, albeit on a smaller scale, *Conceptual Information*. However, the bound head suggests something more contained, possibly sinister; at the very least a loss of the freedom that Edinburgh's "beautiful surroundings" had offered.

Wall and *Absolute Elimination of the Sculpture* suggest that *Conceptual Information* may not have been Czełkowska's "perfect" realization of her "problem of the Table", but it demonstrated both her belief in the importance of the idea and her patience, or struggle, with its implementation, which she had outlined in her concept text and explained to Demarco: "I am not impatient to wait for favourable conditions. The only thing that matters is the conception, and that will be realised some day. I may have to spend twenty years on it because it is my problem and it will last as long as I do".[23]

[1] Richard Demarco, "A Conversation with Wanda", *Umbrella*, June 1972, n.p. Reprinted in this book pages 111–115.
[2] John Barber, "An inchoate vision of the world", *The Daily Telegraph*, 17 August 1972, 9.
[3] Richard Demarco, "A Conversation with Wanda".
[4] Anke Kempkes, "The Third Gender: Wanda Czełkowska and Rosemarie Castoro – Life in the Studio", in Ewa Opałka, Jennifer Moore-Tymowska (eds.), *Wanda Czełkowska: Retrospection*, exhibition catalogue (Warsaw: National Museum in Warsaw, 2017), 55; Czełkowska's statement in "A Conversation with Wanda".
[5] Demarco, "A Conversation with Wanda".
[6] A single plaster *Head* was included in the list of works sent to the Demarco Gallery by Museum of Art in Łódź, it was valued at £180, the equivalent of around £2,000 in January 2023 (Richard Demarco Archives, Scottish National Gallery of Modern Art, GMA A37/2/37/7). Czełkowska explained her decision to make the second *Head* in an [undated] interview with Ewa Opałka, *Eliminacje. Rozmowy z Wandą Czełkowską* (Eliminations. Conversations with Wanda Czełkowska), Warsaw, 2016, unpublished, 234–241.
[7] Opałka, *Eliminacje*, 241–242.
[8] Edward Gage, "A gallimaufry of Polish invention", *The Scotsman*, 24 August 1972.
[9] Demarco, "A Conversation with Wanda".
[10] Cordelia Oliver, untitled, *The Guardian*, 21 August 1972, 8; Dorota Grubba-Thiede, "Wanda Czełkowska i Tadeusz Sieklucki w poszukiwaniu nowoczesności", *Pamiętnik Sztuk Pięknych/Fine Arts Diary*, vol. 9 (2015), 171, https://journals.ub.uni-heidelberg.de/index.php/psp/article/view/61577
[11] "Polish Exhibition: state of work as of 2nd August", Richard Demarco Archives, Scottish National Gallery of Modern Art, GMA A37/2/38.
[12] Richard Demarco, "The Road to Meikle Seggie leads to the Galeria Krzysztofory: Richard Demarco's visit to Poland, 4-8 May 1973", 5. Richard Demarco Archives, Scottish National Gallery of Modern Art, GMA A37/2/72/1; Demarco, "A Conversation with Wanda".
[13] Maria Hussakowska, "Wanda Czełkowska: The mechanism of the disappearance of the artist and the disappearance of the sculpture", in *Wanda Czełkowska: Retrospection*, 82.
[14] Demarco, "A Conversation with Wanda".
[15] Ewa Opałka, "Why the Ruthless Absolute? Between dematerialisation and the flesh — the phenomenon of Wanda Czełkowska's sculptures", in *Wanda Czełkowska: Retrospection*, 46.
[16] Matuszewski page in *Atelier '72* catalogue, n.p.
[17] Wanda Czełkowska, quoted in Dorota Grubba-Thiede, "Wanda Czełkowska. *You are in art.* Selected elements of the artistic calendar", unpublished, 2017/2021, emailed to the author on 22 February 2021.
[18] Demarco, "A Conversation with Wanda".
[19] Ibid.
[20] See fig. pp. 64–65 in the *Life in Images* section.
[21] Opałka, "Why the Ruthless Absolute?", 46.
[22] Richard Demarco, interview with June Geddes 13 November 2018.
[23] Demarco, "A Conversation with Wanda".

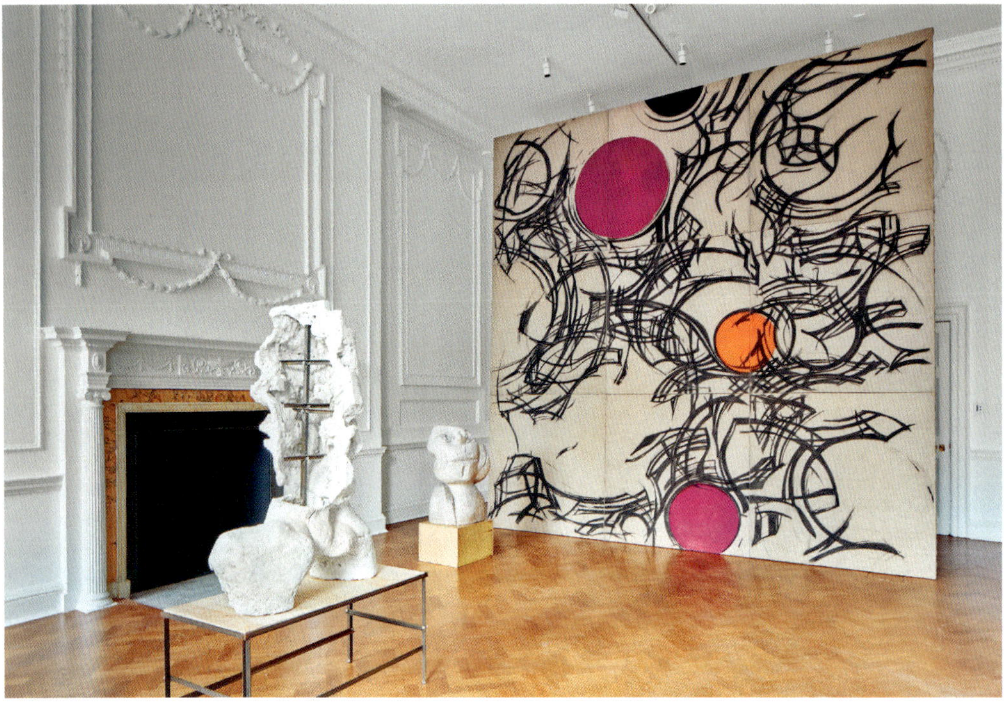

Afterword: Wanda Czełkowska's *Heads* in London, 2018

Sarah Wilson

Wanda Czełkowska's plaster *Heads* (*Głowy*) first appeared in London in 2018.[1] They were installed individually on small tables of different heights in conjunction with the huge propped canvas *Elegy* (*Elegia*), 1990, whose energetic black curved lines were punctuated by half a black circle and three large discs, one orange and two of a dark, crimson pink. Floating in space, they gave a perceptual uplift to an installation of heavy pieces otherwise drawn gravitationally to the ground; their colour animated a room in the Thaddeus Ropac gallery whose walls, with their decorative plaster mouldings, had been painted white (fig. 1).

I knew of Wanda's Edinburgh installation of 1972 thanks to the research work of June Geddes.[2] My growing fascination was related to the collision between the *Heads* of the *Table* (*Stół*) installation – a typical expression of the *informel* in Poland (not merely "neo-primitivism" as her exegetes would have it) and nascent conceptual art, so splendidly rehearsed with the other artists in Edinburgh.

Czełkowska's *Heads* have a breathtaking yet silent presence, above all as regards the relationship between evocation, perception – the essence of a glimpse – and matter falling into itself as brute material or re-emerging into representation. The anti-erotic heaviness of Picasso's *Bust of a Woman (Marie-Thérèse)* of 1931, with its lumpy excrescences and huge phallic nose might also be a memory (fig. 7 p. 156). Surely the most striking and disconcerting aspect of *Table*, as it was first conceived and shown at the 4th Kraków Meetings, is the almost wanton collision between an *informel* heritage – the great, lumpy heads with bored holes for eyes – and the quasi-conceptual *Table*. Together with its aleatoric chequered surface decoration – a symbolic chess game gone awry – the *Table* renounces the concept of pedestal. Disconcertingly domestic, it is outrageously outsized: see the small, exultant artist with her feet raised to rest upon it in

1. *Land of Lads, Land of Lashes: Rosemarie Castoro, Wanda Czełkowska and Lydia Okumura*, exhibition view, Thaddeus Ropac gallery, London, 2018. Featured artworks (from the left): *Head* (*Głowa*), 1968; *Head* (*Głowa*), 1964; *Elegy* (*Elegia*), 1990. Courtesy of Thaddeus Ropac gallery, London–Paris–Salzburg Photo: Tom Carter

1971 in Wacław Nowak's photograph taken at such an effervescent moment for the expanding art scene in Poland (1971; fig. pp. 44–45). I recall Dorota Koczanowicz's brilliant paper on political violence in relation to "muscle memory" in the case of Eliżbieta Jabłońska's outsize table at the Wrocław conference of 2014 on *Democracy, Dialogue, Memory.*[3]

The uniform array of speechless, lumpen plaster heads and Czełkowska's table is indeed violent. They do violence to figurative sculpture, and the portrait bust in particular. I think back to Zofia Kulik's ferocious and humorous "attacks" on Michelangelo's plaster *Moses*, from the Warsaw Academy of Fine Arts, and her films with the model's head which attack the very origin of the bust in the live pose (*Instead of Sculpture*, 1968–1971; fig. 2). The multiplication and alignment of Czełkowska's *Heads* on the *Table* deconstruct the reverent placing and commemorative function of the portrait bust. Their uniformity and the lack of personality suggest moronic brainwashing, consensus in stupidity and mutual non-communication – memory perhaps, but certainly not democracy or dialogue.

For *Table* is certainly a political work. The European *informel* was generated in part by Jean Fautrier's *Hostage Heads* (*Otages*; fig. 3), created in a context

2. Zofia Kulik, *Instead of Sculpture Copying Moses (3 stages)*, 1968–1971, from the series *Sequences*, three photographs, 31.8 × 22 cm each. © Zofia Kulik, courtesy of Kulik-Kwiekulik Foundation

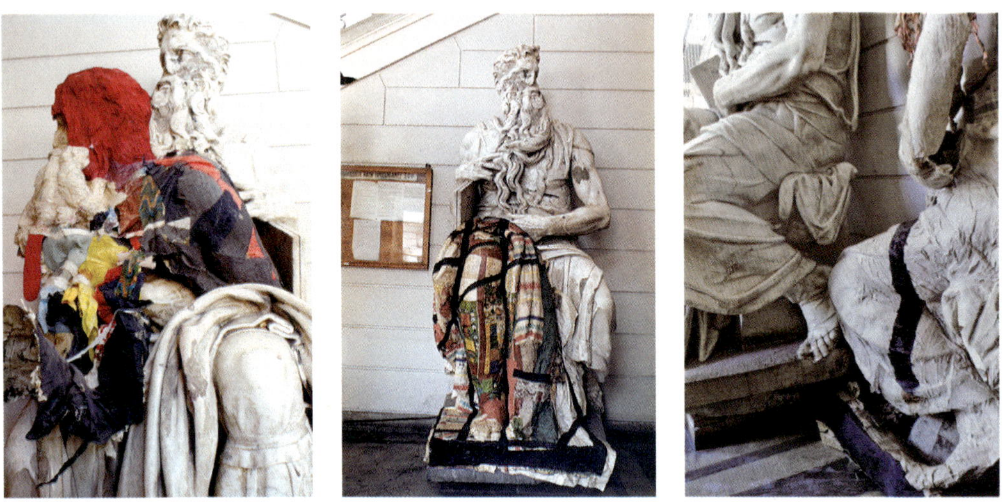

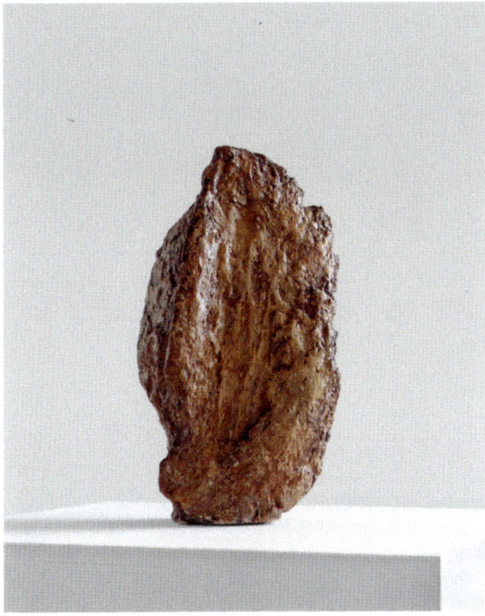

3. Jean Fautrier, *Head of a Hostage* (*Tête d'Otage or Otage*), 1943, plaster, height 48 cm. Courtesy of Stiftung Insel Hombroich, Neuss Photo: Achim Kukulies, Düsseldorf

of Nazi atrocity in France.[4] Taking the stance of the artist as witness, Fautrier added an aura of horror to his formless heads, like that made first in plaster (Neuss, Insel Hombroich collection) which generated the impasted *Otages* – called "hieroglyphs of pain" by his friend André Malraux.[5] It was Fautrier who was acknowledged as pioneer of postwar *informel* painting, thanks to his great triumph at the Venice Biennale in 1960. *Passeurs* between East and West, such as Tadeusz Kantor, so important for Czełkowska as part of the Second Kraków Group, would be supremely aware of his influence on Polish contemporaries.[6]

Wall (*Ściana*), 1975–1976, evolving from the *Table* via the experience of *Conceptual Information about "The Table"* (*Informacja pojęciowa o "Stole"*) (Edinburgh, 1972; fig. p. 126), maintains a political sense: the *Edinburgh Head* (*Głowa edynburska*), bound and blinded in wrapped cloth and rope, is placed before a white wall of riveted panels whose ascending black head-shapes, rising vertically upwards, emanate a desire to traverse or escape. The Edinburgh experience – a conceptual interlude where screen-like canvases flanked eighteen heads placed out of doors (with descriptions of the original *Table* installation) – seems retrospectively a transitional moment of passage. *Absolute Elimination of Sculpture as a Notion of Shape* (*Bezwzględne wyeliminowanie rzeźby jako pojęcia kształtu*, 1972; fig. pp. 64–65), with its 66 lights in the ceiling, signifies complete dematerialisation, anticipating Martin

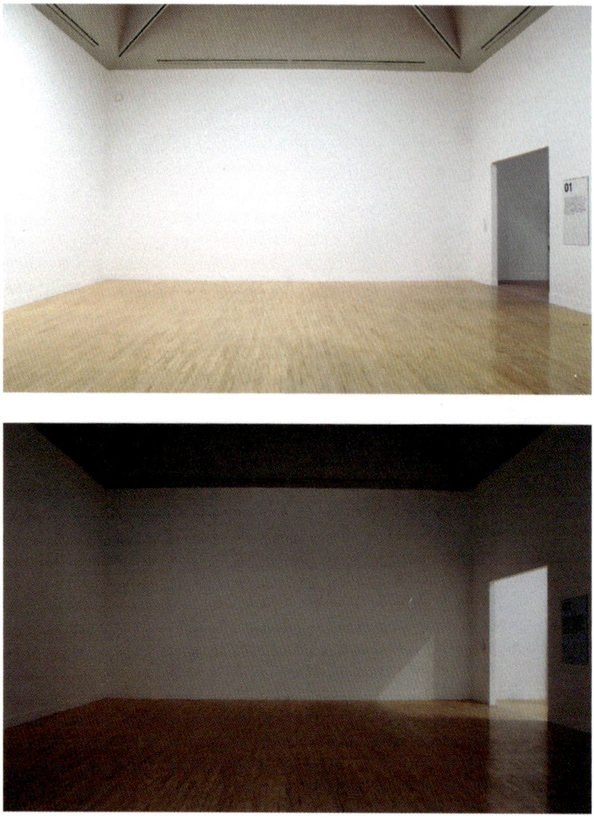

4. Martin Creed, *Work No. 227: The lights going on and off*, 2000, installation at Tate Britain, London, 5 seconds on / 5 seconds off, Edition 2/Tate, London Photo © Tate

Creed's *Work No. 227: The lights going on and off* (Tate, 2000; fig. 4), though far more intellectually daring. But why? Surely in Poland this dematerialisation was as significant as – or an equivalent to – Czełkowska's previous trope of obliteration (the obliteration of facial features).[7] One thinks forward to the eloquent, profoundly political silence – Holocaust-ridden – of black space within the dark chamber of Mirosław Bałka's *How it is*, installed in the Turbine Hall at Tate Modern in 2009.[8]

Czełkowska was such a substantial, brave and challenging artist, despite her small and fragile figure. I was privileged to meet her in London in 2018: the power of this brief encounter lingers in my imagination.

[1] *Land of Lads, Land of Lashes, Rosemarie Castoro, Wanda Czełkowska, Lydia Okumura*, curated by Anke Kempkes, Thaddeus Ropac gallery, London, 25 June – 10 August 2018. See https://www.galleriesnow.net/shows/land-of-lads-land-of-lashes/

[2] Sincere thanks to June Geddes for her catalogue contribution, which relates to her PhD, "Richard Demarco, Networking Scotland to the international avant-garde", University of London, 2022, which I had the pleasure and privilege of supervising.

[3] See Idit Alphandary, Leszek Koczanowicz (eds.), *Democracy, Dialogue, Memory. Expression and Affect beyond Consensus* (London: Routledge, 2020). Dorota Koczanowicz's paper was first published under the title "In the gallery and in the Kitchen. Somaesthetics and social critique in Eliżbieta Jablońska's works", in Marianna Papastephanou, Torill Strand and Anne Pirrie (eds.), *Philosophy as Lived Experience: Navigating the Dichotomies between Thought and Action* (Berlin: LIT Verlag, 2014), 77–91.

[4] Sarah Wilson, "Medardo Rosso, Jean Fautrier and the *informel*", for "Medardo Rosso: Sight Unseen", study day, Courtauld Institute of Art with Thaddeus Ropac gallery, 2 February 2018, in the context of their exhibition.

[5] See André Malraux's preface in cat. exh. *Les Otages, peintures et sculptures de Jean Fautrier*, Galerie René Drouin, Paris, 26 October – 17 November 1945.

[6] Sarah Wilson, "Kantor's art from *informel* to installation", in Katarzyna Murawska-Muthesius (ed.), *Kantor was here* (London: Black Dog Publishing, 2011), 129–139.

[7] For the artist's previous figurative heads and bold female nudes, see https://contemporarylynx.co.uk/art-is-intelligence-on-the-works-by-wanda-czelkowska

[8] The historical and political depth of conceptual art in Central East Europe may be compared to the American situation outlined in Lucy Lippard's classic *Six Years. The Dematerialisation of the Art Object from 1966 to 1972* (New York: Praeger, 1972).

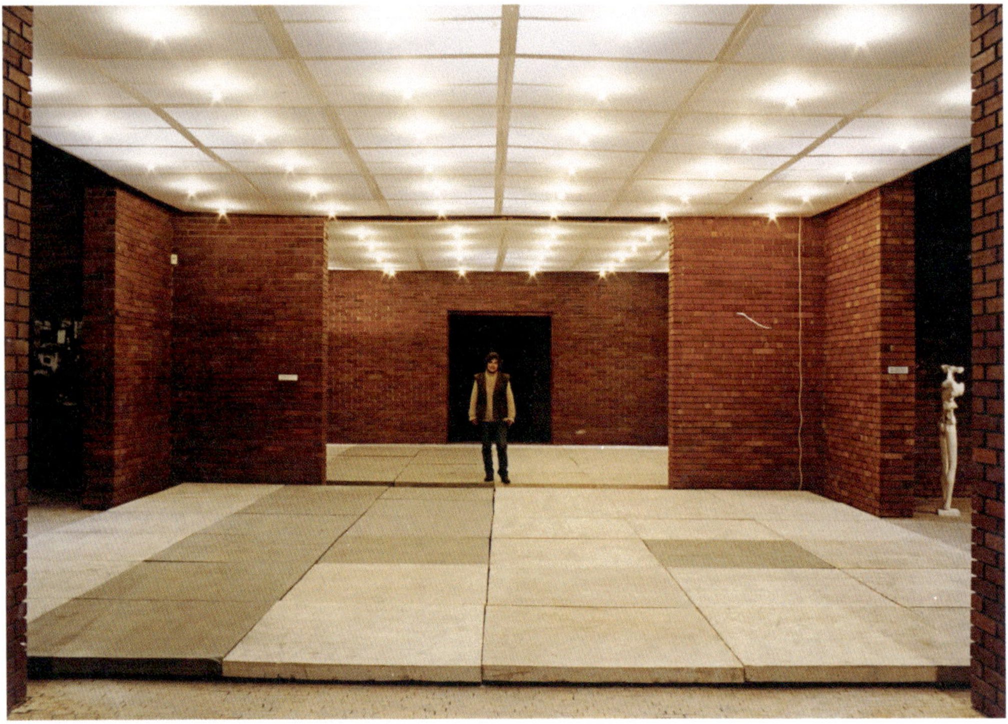

The Time Travel of an Anti-Concept

Wanda Czełkowska, *Absolute Elimination of Sculpture as a Notion of Shape*, 1972 – (Re)constructed in 1995

Mathieu Copeland

Wanda Czełkowska's *Absolute Elimination of Sculpture as a Notion of Shape* (*Bezwzględne wyeliminowanie rzeźby jako pojęcia kształtu*; fig. 1) is an immersive work of art existing simultaneously in two different times. The first time is when the piece was conceived and the second when the work was originally realized. It took the artist 23 years to construct the piece, claiming that "its production exceeded the material possibilities of Communist Poland of the 1970s and 1980s".[1] It will thus forever be a work from 1972,[2] when it was first envisaged during Czełkowska's stay in Scotland, where she was participating in the Edinburgh Festival at Richard Demarco's invitation, and from 1995, when she finally produced the work on a 1:1 scale and exhibited it in the show *Wokół rzeźby polskiej lat 70-tych i lat 80-tych XX wieku* (Polish sculpture of the 1970s and 1980s)", curated by Jan Stanisław Wojciechowski, at the Centre of Polish Sculpture in Orońsko.

In art historical terms, these two years are highly significant, as both present us with two essential theoretical tools to apprehend Wanda Czełkowska's *Absolute Elimination of Sculpture as a Notion of Shape*:

- 1972 is the sixth year chosen by Lucy Lippard in her influential volume *Six Years: The Dematerialization of the Art Object from 1966 to 1972*... Even though it will not be published until 1973 by Praeger (New York) and thus it is unlikely that Wanda Czełkowska was aware of it until its release, the Zeitgeist and the serendipity of time makes this piece a protagonist of the conceptual art adventure as defined by Lippard;
- 1995 is right within the booming of a renewed Relational Aesthetics, as defined by Nicolas Bourriaud. Of all the occurrence of the mid-1990s, this one seems so potent and so apt to cast a definitive light on Czełkowska's finally realized work. Again, we will not speculate whether or not Czełkowska was aware of this theoretical current or the oeuvre of these artists; however, once again, the Zeitgeist and the serendipity of time inscribe Czełkowska's work right within this intellectual framework.

1. *Wokół polskiej rzeźby lat 70-tych i lat 80-tych XX wieku* (Polish Sculpture of the 1970s and 1980s), exhibition view, Centre for Polish Sculpture in Orońsko, 1995. Showing Wanda Czełkowska in the space of *Absolute Elimination of Sculpture as a Notion of Shape* (*Bezwzględne wyeliminowanie rzeźby jako pojęcia kształtu*), 1972 [1995]

The title itself is rooted within a conceptual framework. Indeed, what is left if we eliminate "shape", or at least its notion, out of sculpture? In the original Polish, *bezwzględny* means both "absolute" and "cruel". The word *absolutny* exists in the vocabulary so one could therefore reflect on why Czełkowska chose the other term.[3] Matylda Taszycka suggests that it could relate both to the lexical field of mathematics and to human behaviour.[4] According to the Cambridge Dictionary, a sculpture is "the art of forming solid objects that represent a thing, person, idea, etc. out of a material such as wood, clay, metal, or stone, or an object made in this way". The word comes from the Middle English, from Latin *sculptura*, from *sculptus*, past participle of *sculpere*, to carve, alteration of *scalpere*, to scratch, carve. A definition that insists on physical materiality. By extension, shape is a necessary adjective to the substantive "sculpture". Regardless of whether we interpret Czełkowska's title as the deprivation of the concept of sculpture to the notion of shape or the prevalence of shape over sculpture, to seek for an "absolute elimination" presents us with a radical and clear break within the concept of "sculpture", and to strip it of a notion of shape is to seek a complete redefinition of the idea of sculpture itself.

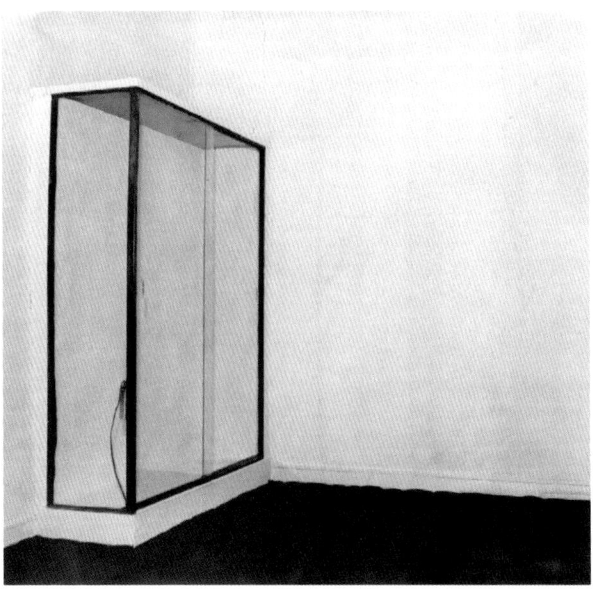

2. Yves Klein, *La sensibilité picturale a l'état matière première, spécialisée en sensibilité picturale stabilisée* (The Specialization of Sensibility in the Raw Material State of Stabilized Sensibility), exhibition view, Galerie Iris Clert, Paris, 28 April – 12 May 1958 © The Estate of Yves Klein c/o ADAGP, Paris

3. Shunk-Kender, Arman exhibition opening, *Le Plein* (The Full-Up), Galerie Iris Clert, Paris Shunk-Kender © J.Paul Getty Trust. Getty Research Institute, Los Angeles

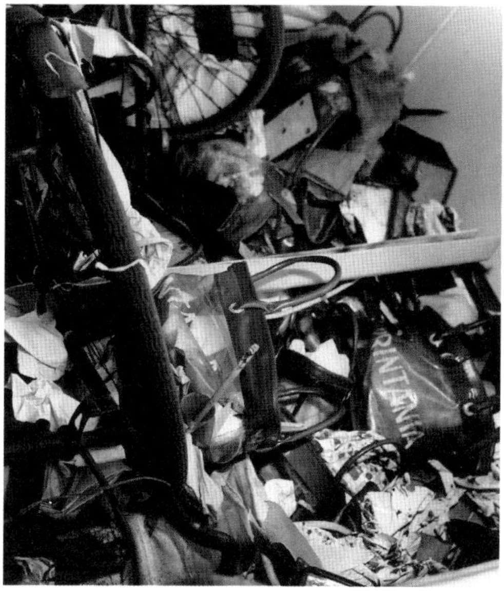

Devoid of shape, emptied of its representational quality, the question we ask is what remains within the concept "Sculpture"? To return to this simplistic definition that seems to overlook the developments of the concept of sculpture during the past century and a half, Czełkowska's statement would propose the art of forming a solid object without a formed surface or, in other words, the making of a form devoid of outer reality, of epidermis. Two opposite possibilities arise from this conceptual understanding, the whole and nothing, the full and the void. To absolutely eliminate the notion of shape entails the impossibility to grasp its textural, physical surface. To consider everything, us included, negates the possibility of appreciating its outer limits. To consider nothing, us excluded, denies any possibility of appreciating its sensory reality (the visual, the tactile…). In other words, to separate the notion of form and sculpture is either the result of it being too monumental to be grasped (it encompasses the world), or too minute to be seized (it excludes the world). These two diametrically opposed understandings replay one of the infamous conflicts in modern art history: Yves Klein's Void and Arman's Full Up.

Most often referred to as *The Void*, Yves Klein's *La spécialisation de la sensibilité à l'état matière première en sensibilité picturale stabilisée* (The Specialization of Sensibility in the Raw Material State of Stabilized Pictorial Sensibility; fig. 2) was held between 28 April and 12 May 1958 at Galerie Iris Clert, Paris. Having repainted the inside of the gallery white, the artist left it entirely empty.

A little over two years later, in the same gallery, Arman's *Le Plein* (Full Up; fig. 3) exhibition was held from 25 October to 5 November 1960. Inaccessible, the exhibition space, overflowing with objects, relegated spectators to the position of outsiders. For the gallerist Iris Clert, this opposition was for her a way to seek revenge. Klein had recently left the gallerist roster. Arman proposed: "If you want to make Yves furious… after 'The Void' we will do 'Full Up'". Iris Clert further recalled: "The idea of dirtying a space imbued with the sensitivity of one of them with the waste of the other was music to my ears".[5] Wanda Czełkowska's *Absolute Elimination of Sculpture as a Notion of Shape* is an attempt at resolving this historical duality, in convoking emptiness through saturation. So to say, to further Clert's explanation, Czełkowska reconciles the sensitivity of disappearance embedded in her title-statement with over-production as realized in her monumental sculptural intervention.

In filling up the gallery with 66 concrete plates (black and white) and 66 electric light points (bare light bulbs), Wanda Czełkowska reveals a void. The sculptural gesture was undeniable, as Maria Hussakowska reminds us: "The floor was covered by an orderly geometrical basis, or rather form made up of 66 flat, concrete, prefab plates in the same size but two different shades. The lights in linen coffers installed in the ceiling were distributed in a geometrical pattern matching that on the floor". Hussakowska continues: "What was most important, however, was the space in between – empty, contained by the walls, the ceiling, and the plates, a metaphorical pedestal for this void space. It is unique, because it can be walked on".[6]

Alistair Rider wrote: "Carl Andre has always felt that viewers should be perfectly entitled to walk across his metal floor metal-based works".[7] Rider further analyzed: "Consciously stepping on to an Andre floor-based sculpture can sometimes feel peculiarly transgressive, as though a threshold of some great significance is being crossed. Then again, whatever significance is ascribed to the gesture will depend largely on the power of the viewer's imagination, since standing on flat pieces of metal can hardly be said to 'transport' anyone to an altogether different aesthetic zone. Yet if, for instance, you deliberately walk towards a sculpture such as Andre's 1967 *Monchengladbach*

Square and self-consciously traverse its surface, then it is hard to imagine yourself passing – ghostlike – through the place where sculptural substance usually resides. In that sense, his works achieve a peculiarly pronounced sense of emptiness, in spite of their substantial and obdurate physicality".[8]

As Wanda Czełkowska told Ewa Opałka in an unpublished interview, even though it is not clearly stated in the original protocol from 1972, in 1995 the public was invited to move freely on the work and that delighted the artist. To walk on the piece is to experience the full space of the gallery as defined by the tiled floor and the lit ceiling. All emphasize the viewer's experience of the present, the now of a situation. The catalogue accompanying the exhibition *Nowoczesna rzeźba polska 1955-1992* (Modern Polish Sculpture 1955–1992) reads: "Wanda Czełkowska is among the unquestionable achievements of new art, consistently evolving towards the limits of the traditional notion of the sculpture, and sometimes even crossing them; it is an original and, to a significant effect, a pioneer phenomenon in contemporary art".[9] This challenge for the New anchors Czełkowska's in the present of the work's realization, namely, 1995. The mid-nineties can be characterized as a time when many artists were producing an aesthetic of the inter-human and the encounter or, as Nicolas Bourriaud would qualify it in 1998, a Relational Aesthetics. One of its key protagonists, Liam Gillick, has been producing screens and platforms as discussion islands, spaces for conversations (fig. 4). Despite their formal and material differences, these two works share a fascinating parallel in how both define and delineate a space. If we are to believe Czełkowska's title for the piece, and for that matter, Gillick's desire to define areas of discussion, we are drawn to dismiss the cumbersome sculptural elements at stake to entirely focus to what is not there. Gillick tells us that his platforms "designate a space for something to take place". He continues: "You need platforms in order to designate a space until a better context appears. This is why my works has always been semi-autonomous. It needs something to hang on, or hang off".[10] Wanda Czełkowska requires a similar level of engagement for her piece to be completed. The relational quality of the work relies on the unequivocal necessity for the public to engage not so much with a consideration of the material surfaces, but with the artist's desire as mediated by the work.

4. Liam Gillick, *Big Conference Platform Platform*, 1998, aluminium and plexiglas, 240 × 360 × 0,6 cm, Tate, London
Photo © Tate

With his *Anti-Civilisation Exhibition*, Matsuzawa Yutaka mentally voided the second All-Japan Independent Exhibition in 1965 in simply distributing a leaflet that acted as both an instruction and a manifesto. Dr Reiko Tomii described this radical and influential piece. In the flyer Matsuzawa Yutaka commanded the visitor to "first, completely vanish the All-Japan Independent Exhibition unfolded in front of you, with your eyes closed or open" and "replace it entirely with my, no, your *Anti-Civilisation Exhibition*", in which only "Nil [that is, nothingness] is brimming". Tomii summed up Matsuzawa Yutaka proposition: "Plainly put, he ordered the viewers to visualize a completely empty gallery cleared of the clutter of a group exhibition in order to comprehend a new possibility that he named 'Anti-Civilisation'".[11] In the same way that Matsuzawa Yutaka wants to come to terms with the reality of what constitutes an exhibition and thus reassess the organizational system of art, Czełkowska seeks with a title to propose a new acceptation of a whole practice of art. Both do so whilst still proposing a work of art. Dr Reiko Tomi wrote on "contemporaneity" of artistic practices across the world: "More than a compendium of local/national histories, 'world art history' in my definition is a networked whole of local/national histories linked through resonances and connections. The connectedness in both explicit and implicit, underscored by the idea of 'international contemporaneity'".[12] The Zeitgeist that informs Czełkowska's art reflects these notions of shared time platforms and this web of present and historical interconnected art trends. Czełkowska, very much like Yutaka, harvests the ripped present conception of art and infuses it with timeless referents. With *Absolute Elimination of Sculpture as a Notion of Shape*, Wanda Czełkowska literally calls for an anti-aesthetic. Stripped of its defining qualities as characterized by its shape, the sculptural element at stake in this piece is the concept of sculpture itself – nothing else, nothing more, just everything. An anti-sculpture as the epitome of what a sculpture must now be in Czełkowska's revised paradigm. To discard what it represents, alludes to or its physical appearances, and to only consider its inner core, its constitutive reality. Ultimately, the tiles and the ceiling are nothing but the foundation for the conceptual appreciation of a newly and redefined notion of "sculpture". As the public stands on the concrete floor and underneath the lights, we are within the designated

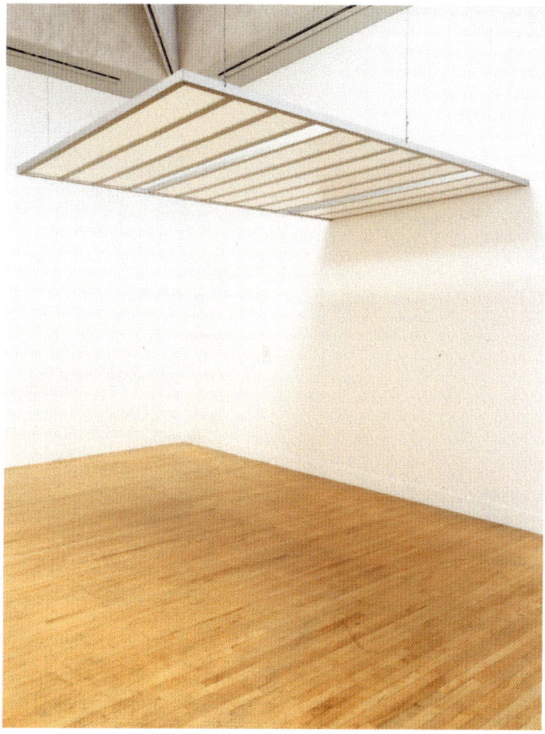

surface. We are not only within a Temporary Autonomous Zone – to use the late Hakim Bey's 1991 definition – but within the constitutive material of sculpture itself. Amorphous, shapeless and formless, but not devoid of materiality, the empty space defined by Wanda Czełkowska's proposition is nothing short of a complete overhaul of an in-formed, secular art.

[1] Ewa Opałka, "Why the Ruthless Absolute? Between dematerialisation and the flesh – the phenomenon of Wanda Czełkowska's sculptures", in Ewa Opałka, Jennifer Moore-Tymowska (eds.), *Wanda Czełkowska. Retrospection*, exhibition catalogue (Warsaw: National Museum, 2017), 48.
[2] It is worth noting that Czełkowska showed the concept of the installation in 1973 at the Pryzmat Gallery in Kraków, and later in Sopot during the exhibition *Porównania* (Comparisons), curated by Ryszard Stanisławski. In Opałka, "Why the Ruthless Absolute?", 48.
[3] I thank Matylda Taszycka for pointing this out.
[4] In an email conversation with Matylda Taszycka, 16 January 2023.
[5] Iris Clert, in *Iris-time l'artventure* (Paris: Denoel, 1978), 210.
[6] Maria Hussakowska, "Wanda Czełkowska. The mechanism of the disappearance of the artist and the disappearance of the sculpture", in *Wanda Czełkowska. Retrospection*, 86.
[7] Alistair Rider, Carl Andre, *Things In Their Elements* (London: Phaidon Press, 2011), 36.
[8] Ibid.
[9] Romuald K. Bochyński, "Wanda Czełkowska", in *Nowoczesna rzeźba polska 1955-1992*, exhibition catalogue (Orońsko: Centrum Rzeźby Polskiej, 1995), quoted in Dr Dorota Grubba-Thiede, "Wanda Czełkowska. Artistic Timeline", in *Wanda Czełkowska. Retrospection*, 125.[10] *The Exhibition of a Film*, Liam Gillick in conversation with Mathieu Copeland (Dijon: Les Presses du réel, 2015), 166.
[11] Reiko Tomii, "Voiding the Exhibition: Hi Red Center and Matsuzawa Yutaka", in *VOIDS* (Zurich: JRP-Ringier, 2009), 430.
[12] Reiko Tomii, "'International Contemporaneity' in the 1960s: Discoursing on Art in Japan and Beyond", *Japan Review* 21, 2009, 125. I thank Matylda Taszycka for reminding of me of this quote.

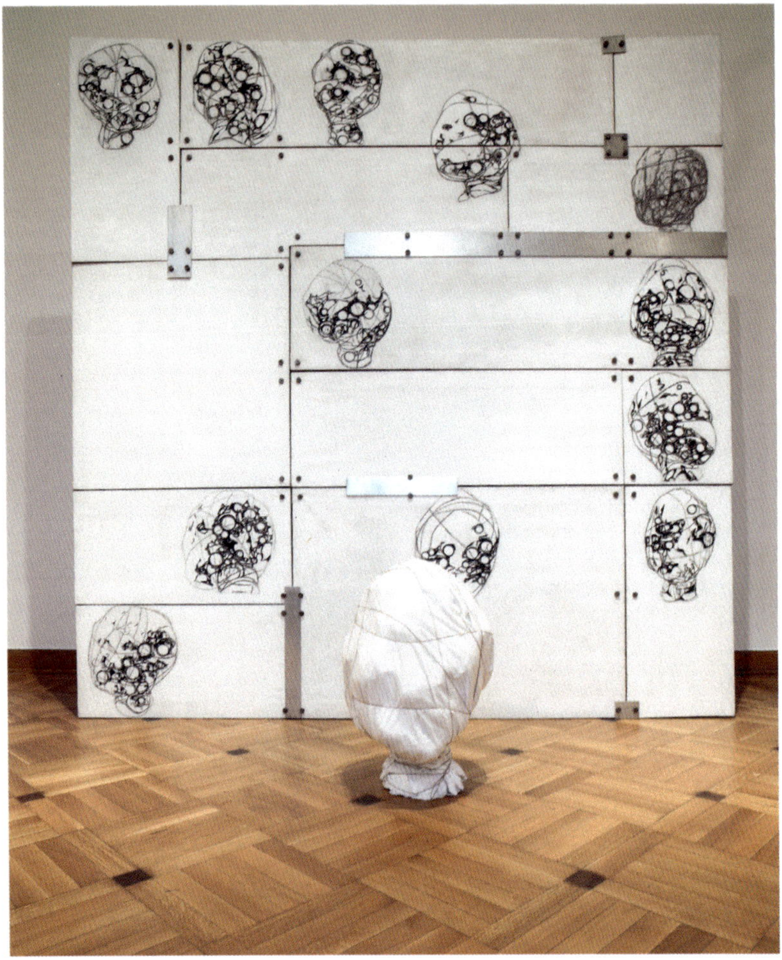

The Head and the Frame

Émilie Bouvard

"I was angry ... I felt I wanted society to know clearly that this [making sculptures] was my way of earning a living – not in terms of money, but in a moral sense."

Wanda Czełkowska in an interview with Richard Demarco, 1972

In the mid-1970s, certainly after having created *Table* (*Stół*) and *Absolute Elimination of Sculpture as a Notion of Shape* (*Bezwzględne wyeliminowanie rzeźby jako pojęcia kształtu*), Wanda Czełkowska produced another monumental installation: *Wall* (*Ściana*, 1975, National Museum, Kraków; figs. 1–2). This large sculpture was to be shown at an exhibition dedicated to Xawery Dunikowski at CBWA Zachęta.[1] It was also photographed in the artist's studio. Czełkowska poses in front of the work, which is a rarity in the relatively abundant collection of photographs kept in her studio, an indication of its importance to her.

1. *Wanda Czełkowska. Retrospekcja* (Wanda Czełkowska: Retrospection), exhibition view, Królikarnia – Xawery Dunikowski Museum of Sculpture (National Museum in Warsaw), 2017. Featured artworks: *Wall* (*Ściana*), front, 1975–1976, and part of the installation *Edinburgh Head* (*Głowa edynburska*), 1972 (from the collection of National Museum in Kraków). Courtesy of National Museum in Warsaw Photo: Szymon Rogiński

Wall consists of two parts. Thirteen primed canvasses of different sizes with strange 'head' drawings in ink and graphite pencil are hung on a steel-framed structure. The mounting screws are clearly visible. Longitudinal plates of polished steel cover the interstices between the canvasses here and there, slicing into the drawings. The back of the structure has three protruding steel supports with several crossbars running through them. Czełkowska had opted in 1990 to have the public first see this reverse side before discovering the front, confirming its significance. The simultaneous effect is that of a frame or a table that been tipped over onto its side, so creating a canvas wall that gives the appearance of being a backdrop. A sculpture is placed on the ground in front of the wall. It's a head, in the same vein as those found on *Table*, though there is some uncertainty around this, as it is covered with a cloth that is secured with rope. We can only guess at its shape.

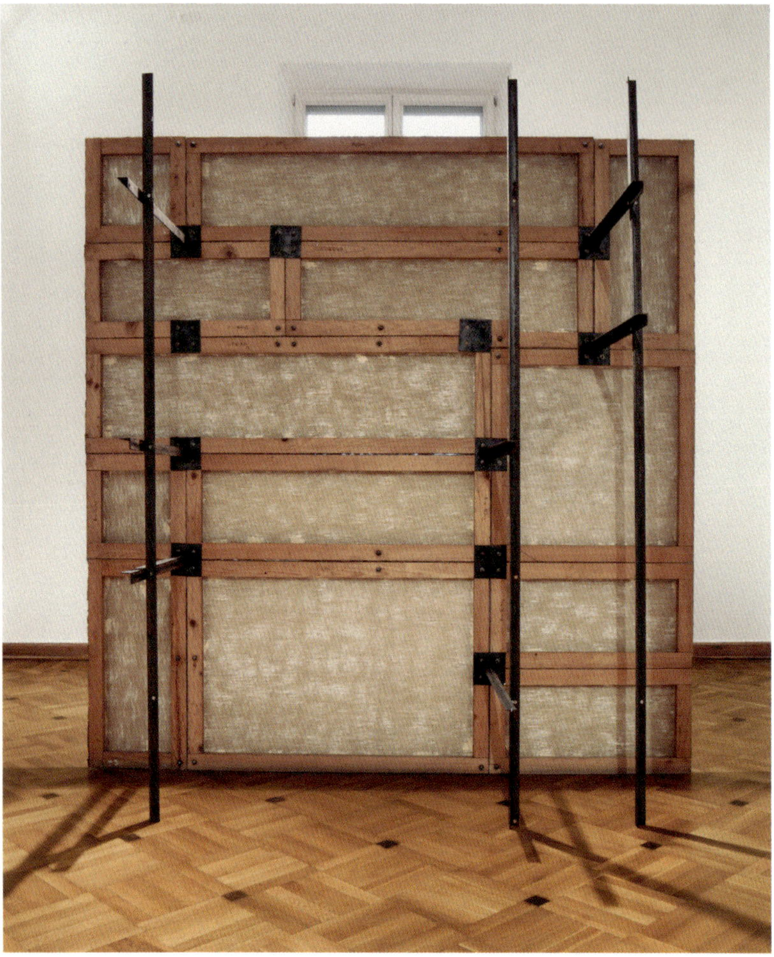

2. *Wanda Czełkowska. Retrospekcja* (Wanda Czełkowska: Retrospection), exhibition view, Królikarnia – Xawery Dunikowski Museum of Sculpture (National Museum in Warsaw), 2017. Featured artworks: *Wall* (*Ściana*), back, 1975–1976. Courtesy of National Museum in Warsaw
Photo: Szymon Rogiński

In 1972, Czełkowska gave an interview[2] to Richard Demarco about *Table* while preparing to attend the *Atelier '72* exhibition (as part of the Edinburgh Festival). This interview was essential for understanding the concept behind *Wall*. The two works are clearly linked: created in the same "cycle", they are two installations that mirror each other. The upturned *Table* becomes the *Wall*, the *Table*'s frame becomes the vertical support and even a "canvas", a transparent allusion to the practice of painting on the part of the artist. In Edinburgh, according to the photographic archive, *Table* is exhibited as two wall screens set on either side of a series of heads placed directly on the floor (*Conceptual Information about "The Table"* [*Informacja pojęciowa o "Stole"*]). One screen shows a long table in profile with drawings of head sculptures similar to those on the floor. On the other, a perspective drawing of the draught board that will become *Table* is drawn. This reflection is about the transition from the plan, from the drawing, to the space. The brochure announcing the event reproduces these motifs. Czełkowska explains very precisely to Richard Demarco what motivates her at that moment, as can be read in the foreword to this essay. She also states: "I prefer materials which are essentially contemporary … From the beginning, I was not interested by the problem of forms but in the expression of my thoughts and ideas."[3]

After *Table*, *Wall* is a conceptual installation affirming what sculpture work is for Czełkowska. It is "the expression of [her] ideas and [her] thoughts"

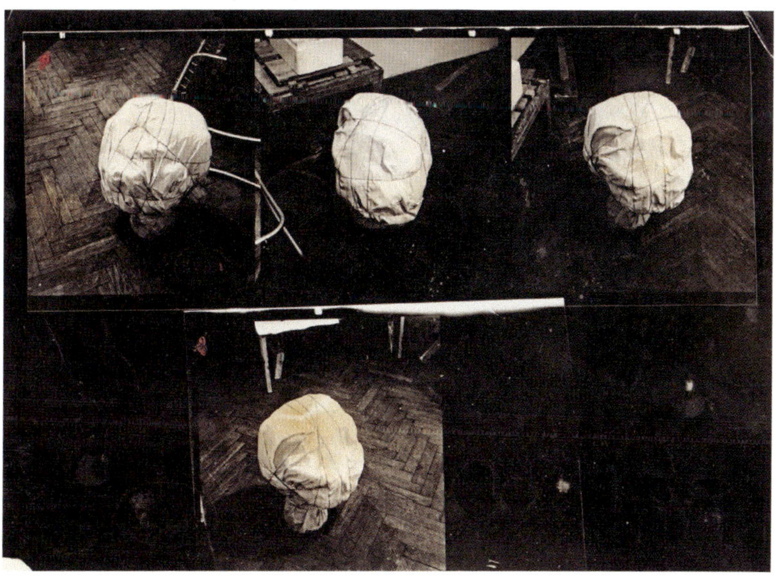

3. Wanda Czełkowska, *Untitled* (*Wrapped Head* [*Zawinięta głowa*]), c. 1975, black-and-white photograph. Courtesy of the artist's estate

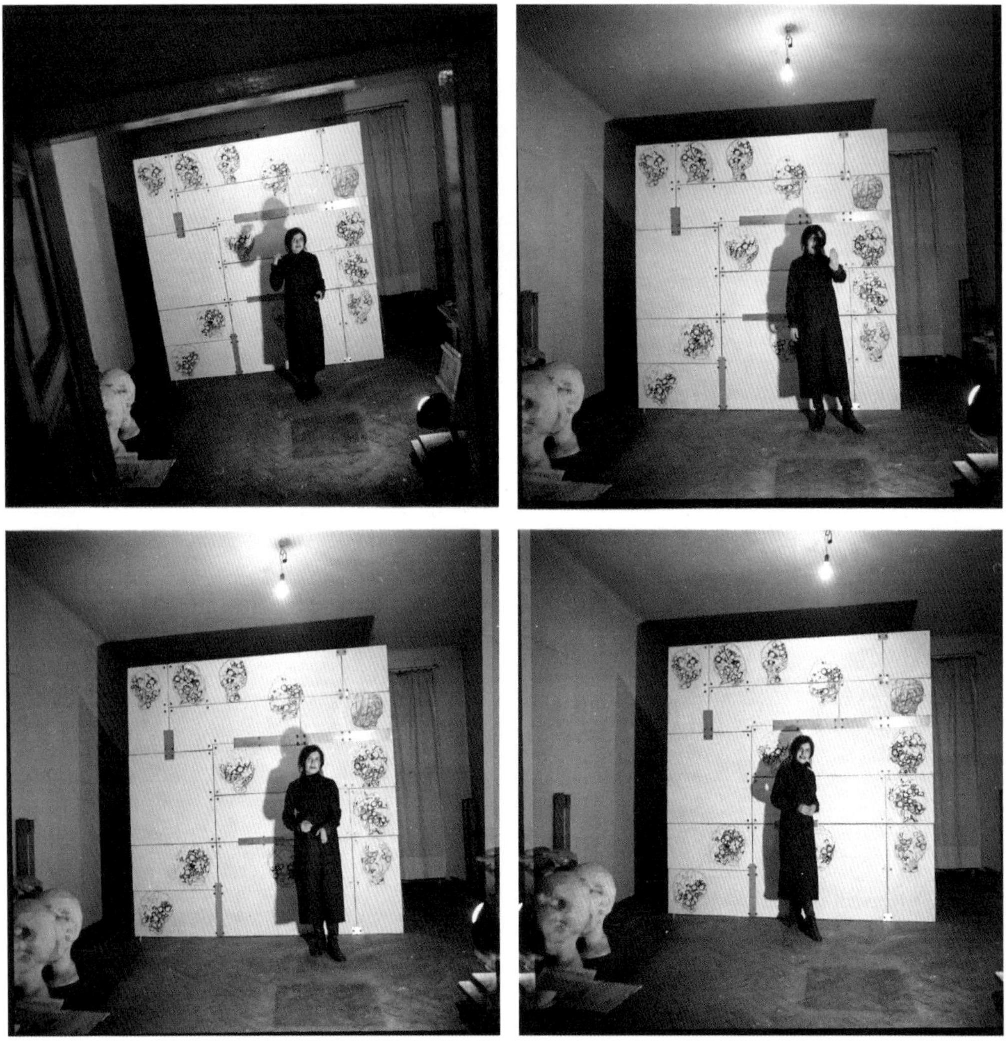

4. Wanda Czełkowska with *Wall* (*Ściana*), 1975–1976, installation, mixed technique. Courtesy of the artist's estate

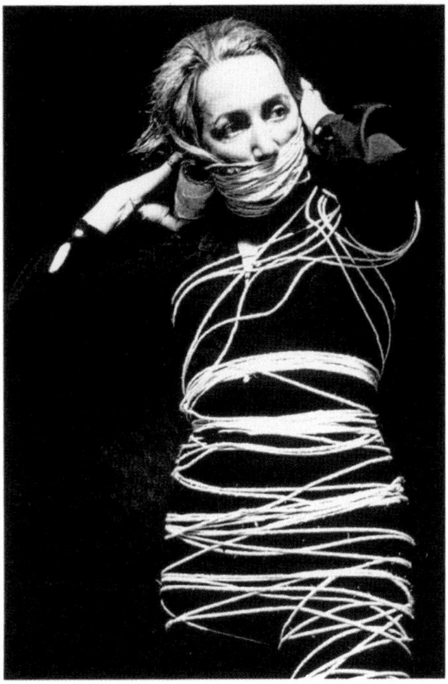

5. Françoise Janicot, *Encoconnage*, 1972, from the series *FNAC 95191*, Centre national des arts plastiques, Paris.

about sculpture. The first point is the relationship between the plan and the figure. The upturning of *Table* creates the transition from the second to the third dimension. The drawings on the flat canvasses are representative of the sculptures set out in front of the canvas, from all possible perspectives: Czełkowska shows the ropes that tether the cloth, which are transformed into key elements that make it possible to compose a volumetric drawing.[4] Facing *Wall*, the eye experiences, in turn, a representation of a figure drawn from several aspects, and the perception of a sculpture in space. The layout of the installation should make it possible to move between the canvasses and the sculpture, in order to be able to enjoy all the perspectives of the latter.

The question of perspective lies in the relationship between the sculpture and the screen: the distance between the two elements of the work has to be right. The search for the right scale, for the right distance between the onlooker and the work,[5] was already questioned by the drawing of the chequerboard for *Table* in Edinburgh. This matter is addressed here by the distance between the sculpture and the grid of drawings. *Head* (*Głowa*) has to be "at the right distance" from the screen, creating a vanishing point. Czełkowska realizes with *Wall* the idea, which was essential, for example, for Alberto Giacometti, that a sculpture is a representation, and not a simple object placed in the space. The

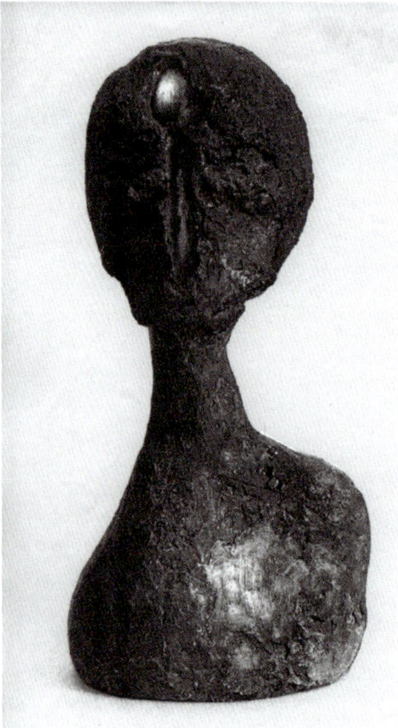 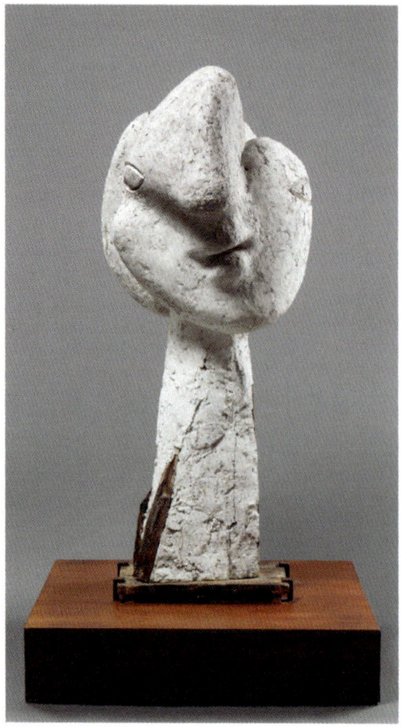

work entails one or more perspectives to orient the form. *Wall* embodies this reflection, deploying in the drawing the different possible views of a sculpture, itself situated at an appropriate distance in front of this screen. In 1979, in her painting *Le milieu du tableau* about Artemisia Gentileschi, Lea Lublin created a perspective from the "female gaze" and reintroduced the body – an abused body in this case – into the perspective of the painting. It opens us up, as we shall see instantly, to the way in which a minimal and conceptual approach can be influenced by the female experience.

Finally, the sculpture under the cloth is a direct reference to the practice that every sculptor knows: clay is left under a wet cloth overnight so that it can be reworked and remain soft, the following day, for modelling. A photograph of Czełkowska's studio shows that she did this, as did everyone else (fig. 3). Czełkowska does not forget her taste for traditional sculpting; she also asserts her mastery of industrial steel. The latter responds to her preference for "contemporary materials"; it says: "I am of my time", and it slices into the drawings. *Wall* is, therefore, a complex piece that brings together traditional sculpture, industrial trends and conceptual approaches.

6. Alina Szapocznikow, *Head with Spoon* (*Głowa z łyżką*), 1966, assemblage, cement, iron filings, metal spoon © Piotr Stanislawski. All right reserved

7. Pablo Picassso, *Head of Marie-Thérèse* (*Tête de femme*), 1931–1932, original in plaster and wood, 128.5 × 54.5 × 62.5 cm, Musée National Picasso, Paris © 2023. RMN-Grand Palais /Dist. Foto SCALA, Firenze

In the interview with Demarco, Czełkowska also refers to her "anger". A series of photographs adds a more subjective dimension to the way *Wall* can be understood. In the photographs showing *Wall* in the studio, the sculpture is in fact replaced[6] by Czełkowska herself in various poses in front of the screen of canvasses (fig. 4).[7] The studio is in darkness, and a projector is used to project the shadow of the artist's body onto *Wall*. She uses her hands for shadow play. Certainly, directed by Czełkowska, this series confirms the desire for affirmation that is linked to the conception of this installation. In this series, the artist participates in the installation, enters the space of the sculpture. Later, it is a sculpture that will 'take' her place in the final installation, a veiled sculpture, with a concealed form. I am struck by the obvious echo between this linen-covered sculpture and another series of photographs[8] that show Czełkowska with her head covered in a dark, semi-transparent scarf, sometimes bare-chested. In some of them she holds her neck as if she were suffocating, spreads her arms or shadow plays with her hands in a similar way as she did, fully dressed, in front of *Wall*. And there, in my opinion, lies the desire and the anger; there, in the shadows, where she joins Lea Lublin. The desire to think sculpture, and also to show that she is thinking it, is etched into an entire body. One also thinks of *Encoconnage* by Françoise Janicot (1972–1974; fig. 5). During this series of performances, Janicot covered her whole body with cord, over her clothes, to the rhythm of a recording of sound poetry by Bernard Heidsieck. The work goes as far as suffocation, by cutting the string. Janicot literally shows herself to be 'speechless', prevented from speaking. Janicot said to Esther Ferrer, who interviewed her in 1989, that she felt "the need for a strong image to get out of the difficult situation of being an artist, mother and wife at the same time, at that time."[9] To Fabienne Dumont, she declared: "*L'Encoconnage* was an observation of the state I was in, that is to say, tied up in my work as an artist by the impossibility of being able to communicate. I had to show that I was tied up, completely trapped by existence, that it was not possible."[10] Czełkowska, for her part, expresses both her search for sculpture, for the perhaps impossible, hidden form, and her situation as a sculptor, hidden, but wanting to be visible, heard, and looked at.

The sculpture is obscured by cloths, of course. But, the drawings themselves are very visible. In her exhibitions, other heads similar to the hidden one are often exhibited not far from *Wall*, as was the case again in 2016 at the National Museum in Warsaw. "Creating a head" is the basis of sculpture, as Alberto Giacometti would opine in his day. A subject that was also, for example, evident in Alina Szapocznikow's approach several years earlier (fig. 6).

In a certain way, and particularly because of the strong links between *Wall* and *Table*, we know what kind of head is under the cloths. In the case of these sculptures and similarly for the drawings on the canvasses, the heads are abstract, but their non-geometric form, evoking organic tissue, cells, or nodose matter, borders on biomorphism. The flatness of the screen is dented by the volumetric drawings of the heads, and in particular by the circles that pepper them, a recurring theme in Czełkowska's work, which create "holes" in the motif. There is something of the emergence of the body in the frame, of a tension between the *Tetris* of canvasses and the steel framework which supports them at the back and which is clearly visible, and these heads bordering on shapelessness, hidden but transparent, open, and with proliferating nodules. In the past, Czełkowska had made figurative heads[11] clearly evoking the rotundity inspired by the shapes of the prehistoric female figures in Pablo Picasso's *Head of Marie-Thérèse* (1931–1932; fig. 7). The reference to modern art has disappeared; she has kept its metamorphic potentiality, and the organic character that she juxtaposes with the frame. Czełkowska thus refuses to make a choice between forms considered as incompatible in the history of art in her time. She adopts a position mirroring that of Louise Bourgeois, from the 1960s, or Eva Hesse, of the affirmation of a sculpture that is both abstract, but refers to the body, rigorous in its definition, integrating a conceptual dimension, but also sensitive and human.[12]

Recent art history is constantly re-qualifying the way in which we understand the movements of the 1970s, thanks to the view of women artists who are often described as marginal – even though Czełkowska enjoyed a degree of recognition during her lifetime. Czełkowska's work was thus exhibited in 2018 at the Thaddeus Ropac gallery (London) alongside that of Rosemarie Castoro and Lydia Okumura. *Land of Lads, Land of Lashes* revisited, amongst many other projects, post-minimalism in the light of the artistic experiments of these women, who were always described as drawing a parallel "organic" current, an "eccentric abstraction", to employ the beautiful expression coined by Lucy Lippard in 1966. Recently, at the Venice Biennale and the Tate Modern, Maria Bartuszová (1936–1996) prompted similar (re)readings. It is time to consider, as Czełkowska forcefully and angrily asserts with *Wall*, that these practices, that her practices, have a central position in the history of art, composing, collectively and without consultation with many male and female artists, a chorus of minimal, conceptual voices, but for whom the body was not to be supressed.[13]

[1] VI Festiwal Sztuk Pięknych. Hommage Xaweremu Dunikowskiemu. W setną rocznicę urodzin (VI Fine Arts Festival. Hommage to Xawery Dunikowski. 100th anniversary of the year of the artist's birth), CBWA Zachęta, Warsaw, 9–19 March, 1973.

[2] Richard Demarco, "A Conversation with Wanda", in *Umbrella*, 1972, n.p. Reprinted in this book pages 111–115.

[3] Ibid.

[4] This technique is the basis for academic drawing from a model.

[5] I don't know whether Czełkowska was aware of Alberto Giacometti's thoughts on the matter, because it is at the heart of his work as a sculptor. She may have read Jean-Paul Sartre's 1948 essay "The quest for the Absolute", which has been reprinted many times, and which takes up the Swiss artist's reflections on the subject, particularly the central idea that perspective must also be taken into account by the sculptor.

[6] It is also possible that the decision to place a sculpture in front of *Wall* came after this series of shots.

[7] Other photographs of Czełkowska, nude from the waist up and preserved in the studio collection, visibly seek a similar confrontation between her body and the pieces in the surrounding space, in particular an earthenware stove whose tiled, grid-like pattern is repeated in pen on the photograph, covering the artist's body.

[8] *Theme* (*Temat*, 1970–1971) and other untitled photographs by the artist taken during the same session or at the same time. I am grateful to Matylda Taszycka for bringing these photographs to my attention.

[9] Esther Ferrer, "Entrevista con Françoise Janicot – Ver para comprender", *Lapiz* 63, December 1989, 39.

[10] Fabienne Dumont, *Des sorcières comme les autres*, 385, https://www.icigrandsboulevards.fr/product/93115/dumont-fabienne-des-sorcieres-comme-les-autres-artistes-et-feministes-dans-la-france-des-annees-1970. Fabienne Dumont highlights that this performance is also concurrently called "Cache-bibi", hiding oneself.

[11] Examples: *Untitled*, 1950, plaster; *Man's Head* (*Głowa mężczyzny*), 1957, cast iron; *Self-Portrait* (*Autoportret*), 1959, plaster (also exists in bronze); *Pink Head* (*Różowa głowa*), 1962, plaster; *Blue Head* (*Niebieska głowa*), 1967, plaster.

[12] See Émilie Bouvard, *Violentes !* (Paris: Gallimard, forthcoming).

[13] Asked by Ewa Opałka on the haptic character of the sculpture *Self-Portrait* (*Autoportret*, 1959), the artist replied: "There is no body!". In the twilight years of her life, her attitude towards the presence of the body in her own works was, to say the least, ambivalent, https://www.youtube.com/watch?v=89GZmIIkITY [conference in Polish].

I would like to extend my thanks to Matylda Taszycka for the translation.

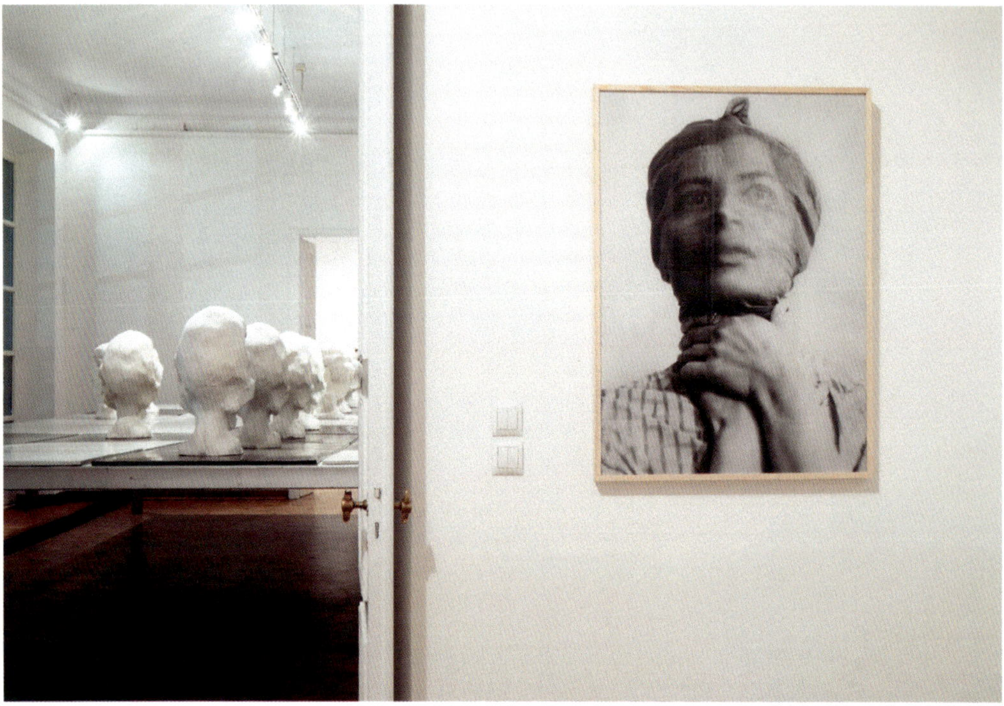

Theme and Variations: Wanda Czełkowska's Heads and Face

Abigail Solomon-Godeau

At the end of the 1960s and early 1970s, internationally there emerged what was called at the time the Women's Liberation Movement or the Women's Movement, as well as various articulations of feminist consciousness, activism, theory and philosophy. Within contemporary art worlds, especially in the global North, these had diverse ramifications. For women who were artists (in all media), this posed problems relating to identity, representation, identification and gender encompassing and sometimes radically transforming all aspects of cultural production. These ramifications included reckoning with the role of institutions in the practices of inclusion/exclusion, the omissions of the art historical record, and the continuing effects of sexism and misogyny on women's professional prospects. These in turn prompted the question of whether any given woman artist wished to align herself with a universalist, that is gender-blind notion of art, or, alternatively, whether to approach her work in a critical relation to the given terms of sexual and gender difference, femininity, or alterity. As with many women artists of her time and place, and notwithstanding the emancipated terms of her private life (*e.g.*, no children and a refusal of domesticity), Czełkowska rejected the label of "woman artist", much less that of feminist artist, even after the Women's Movement emerged in Poland. This reflected the *aporias* of gender identity for women artists; if they identified as such, they were often condemned to a gendered ghetto. If they didn't, defining themselves as artists *per se*, it was rarely the case that they were considered the equal of men.

1. *Wanda Czełkowska. Retrospekcja* (Wanda Czełkowska: Retrospection), exhibition view, Królikarnia – Xawery Dunikowski Museum of Sculpture (National Museum in Warsaw), 2017. Featured artworks (from the left): *Table* (*Stół*), 1968–1971 (from the collection of the National Museum in Kraków); *Theme* (*Temat*), 1970–1971 [2016] (from the artist's studio). Courtesy of National Museum in Warsaw Photo: Szymon Rogiński

As far as is known, Czełkowska made few if any photographs during her lengthy career. However, there exists a series, dated approximately 1970–1971,[1] for which she posed in various positions. They appear to have been shot in a single session, though the author of the photographs is uncertain: they could have been taken by her then partner Bohdan Prądzyński, a poet and graphic artist; or by Czełkowska herself (although there is no visible trace of a self-timer cable, this does not exclude that the exposure was done by her using a timed setting). In particular, one of the photographs that might have come from this series (or perhaps from a different session) might be considered a self-portrait – although this is not how I would characterize it.[2] Entitled *Theme* (*Temat*; fig. 1 and fig. p. 37), in a certain sense it could be perceived as a kind of icon of Czełkowska herself. Moreover, a recognizable reference to the photograph appears in at least one of her drawings (fig. 2). Once one starts looking for them, different kinds of self-representations can be found among her work. And while it is the case that all portraits are self-representations, not all self-representations are portraits.

Theme was first exhibited in her retrospective exhibition in Warsaw, *Wanda Czełkowska. Retrospekcja* (Wanda Czełkowska: Retrospection). Presumably,

2. Wanda Czełkowska, *Drawing – sculpture* (*Rysunek – rzeźba*), 1969, pencil. Courtesy of the artist's estate

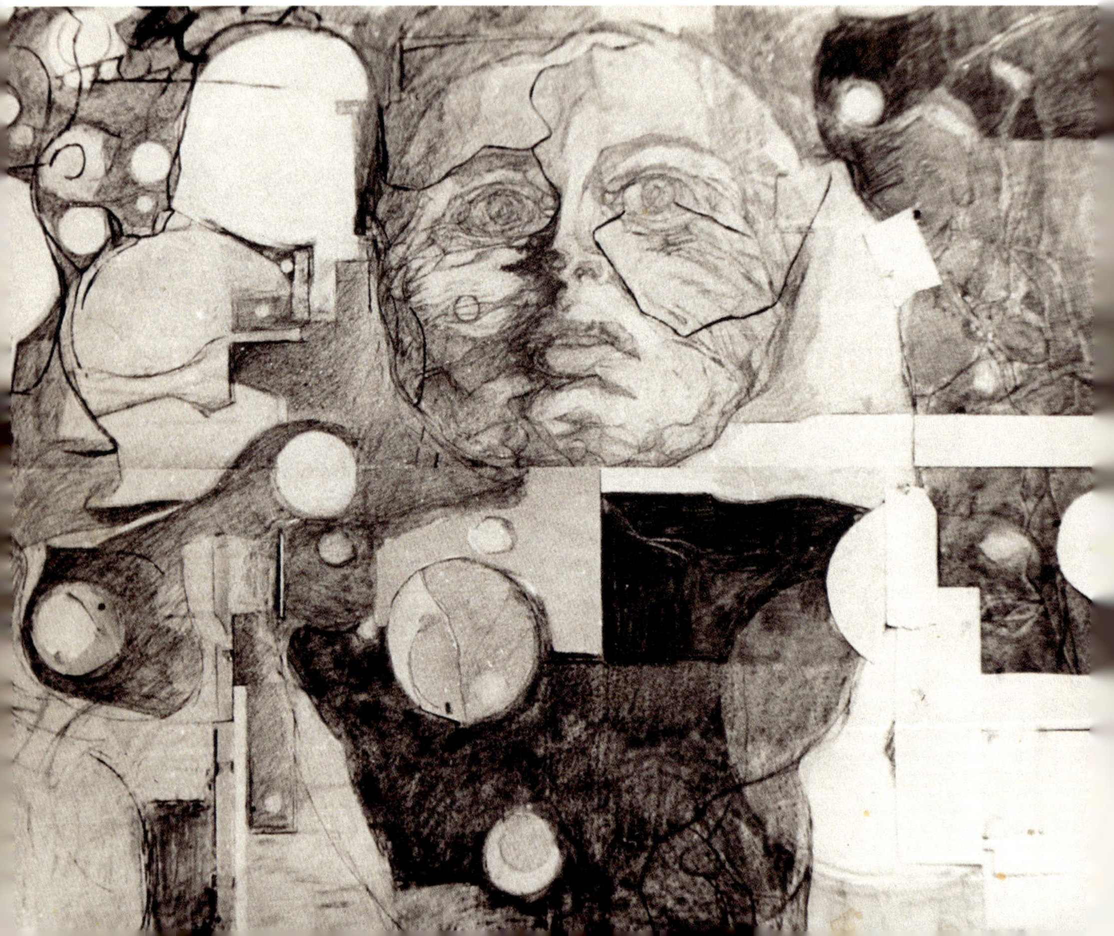

3. Wanda Czełkowska, *Untitled* (*Self-Portrait* [*Autoportret*]), c. 1971. Another version of the same photograph was published on the cover of leaflet catalogue for the 11th Kraków Group exhibition, 1971. Courtesy of the artist's estate

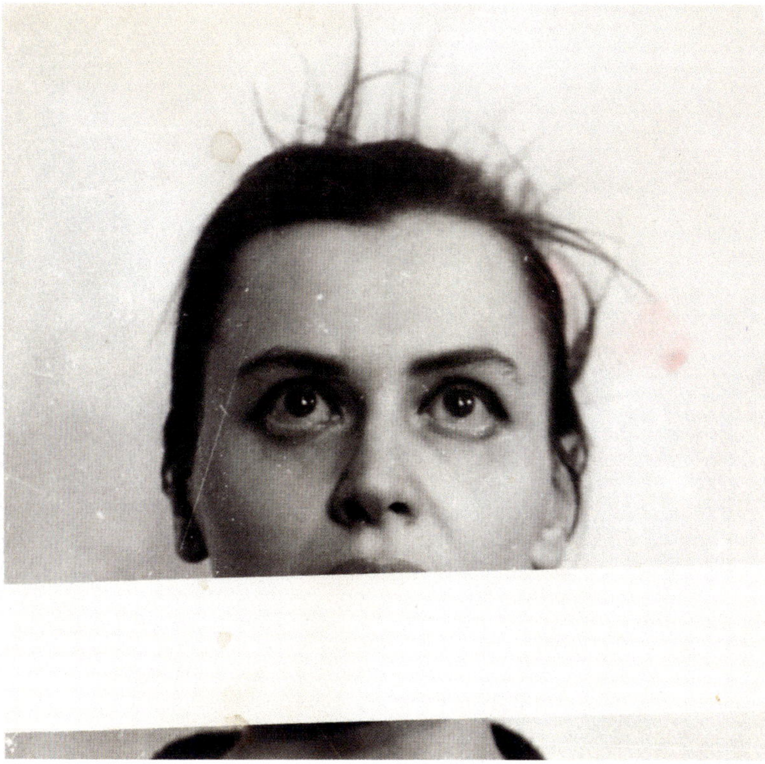

it was Czełkowska who determined the size of the enlargement, its frame, and its placement within the exhibition space. The same photograph was also used on the cover of the exhibition's catalogue, presumably also selected with her approval. There exist several prints, variously cropped or masked (fig. 3). In one striking instance, she cropped the image just below eyebrow-level, so it is only her forehead and the top of her head that are depicted. These cropped versions were reproduced in the exhibition brochure from 1971, establishing the elements for her 1968–1971 installation project *Table* (*Stół*). In the 2016 exhibition photograph she is posed frontally wearing a striped shirt, and the angle from which the exposure was made is slightly lower than her head. Face and head wrapped with a gauze-like material, her hands clasped at her neck, because of the camera's point of view, the viewer looks up at her. In her catalogue essay, Ewa Opałka suggested that the hands might be those of a man: "Thick-boned, with protruding veins, man-like, the hands are very much in contrast with the breath-taking beauty of the female face. Upon a closer look, the intention is more than clear – the viewer is bound to see the artist's hands as belonging to someone else".[3] To my mind, this

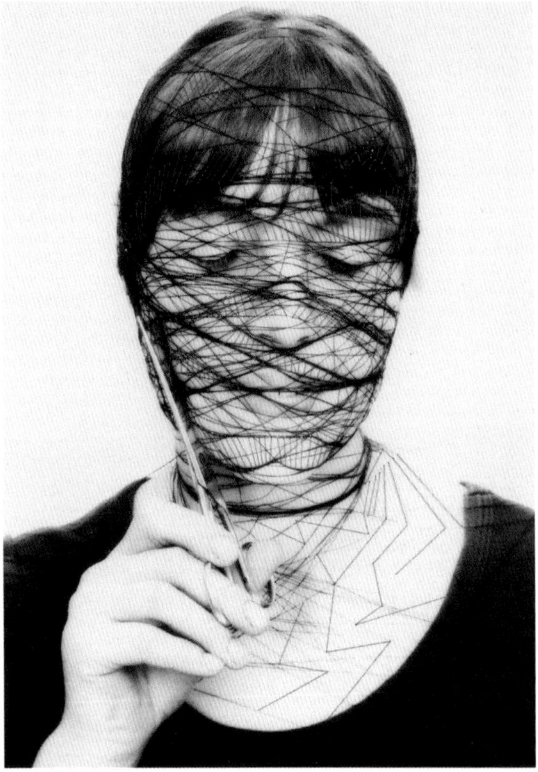

4. Annegret Soltau, *Self #29*, 1975, photo overstitching, 39 × 28 cm. Courtesy Annegret Soltau

claim is not wholly convincing. The delicate ring on the index finger as well as the shape of hands and wrist are surely those of the artist. For Opałka, the photograph implies a form of violence, indeed strangulation, but it could be read differently as suggesting a state of hypnotic fixity or immobilization. Perhaps a form of self-iconization? Whatever she intended by her facial expression, or the position of the hands, remains ambiguous and unknowable. More significantly, however, it was Czełkowska who gave the photograph its title, *Theme*. And while she did in fact give titles to certain of her works – sometimes rather mystifying ones – in much of her other work she employed generic identifications such as *Head* (*Głowa*). A Polish dictionary gives as its primary English translation of *temat* the following, that "which constitutes the basic thought, subject of a conversation, work, piece", best translated by the word *theme*. But what is the theme to which her title refers? Is the theme relevant exclusively to this single work or is it meant to link it to other aspects of her production then on view? Would that then connect it to the photographic series first mentioned above? This seems unlikely, since those photographs were never exhibited, and as far as known, neither enlarged, reprinted, or framed.

In this respect, it seems more useful to distinguish between the sculptural heads for which she was already well-known in her lifetime, and this two-dimensional photograph, which like all analogue photographs, is both an index and icon.[4] Here, it is not the head, but the face, notwithstanding its veiling, and the position of the hands that constitutes the photograph's actual content. Consequently, it is important to distinguish between the three-dimensionality of a head (however abstracted) and the illusory two-dimensionality of a face viewed frontally. Which, in the medium of photography and in the case of *Theme*, is quite literally a flat surface. Of course, Czełkowska worked in two as well as three dimensions; her drawings, paintings, and constructions attest to her ease in moving from one medium and dimension to another, though it should be noted that the latter works avoid figuration and after 1968 are generally abstract. There are some exceptions, notably the 1959 *Self-Portrait* (*Autoportret*), a bust-length sculpture with large eyes and exposed breasts that stirred controversy when first shown in the 1960 Spring Exhibition of the Kraków District of ZPAP at the Palace of Art in Kraków (fig. p. 77). But it is by no means a naturalistic representation, and already implies that self-portraiture was for Czełkowska something other than the depiction of her actual appearance. But what was it?

Before a certain date, Czełkowska's *Heads* manifested similarities to "primitivizing" sculptural practices, some evoking the stone effigies of Easter Island, some suggesting artistic genealogies with Etruscan or Cycladic sculpture, and others to the simplified forms of non-figurative twentieth-century sculpture. It was sometime around the 1960s that Czełkowska abolished most of the features that could stand for facial physiognomy. The plaster heads are far closer in appearance to discomposing forms, or to rock, lava or other mineral configurations shaped by the processes of time and nature. Their concavities, excrescences, and hollows suggest, as Opałka remarked, a kind of violence in their facture; they imply a material process of gouging, poking, and punching distinct from the more conventional processes of modelling, shaping, and smoothing the material. Iconographically, the face generally announces its gender – as well as other characteristics, including age and race – with far greater particularity than does the head, which, if viewed from the back, is unidentifiable. Interestingly, Czełkowska said of these works that "my heads are a 'Third Gender'", and perhaps this signals what can be seen as a structural contradiction between her disavowal of sexual difference as a concept with political implications, and an impulse, also disavowed, towards self-representation. The face, as opposed to the head, can also be fashioned as a complication, refusal or occlusion of identity, in the forms, for example, of the mask or the masquerade. By the early 1970s, many women artists were employing their faces, their bodies, or both in diverse media, seeking to destabilize, parody, subvert or otherwise counter stereotypes and ideologies of femininity (fig. 4). Unlike these practices, Czełkowska's *Heads* appear, and were surely intended to appear, genderless, or as she stated, constituting an alternative third incarnation. But her *Theme*, by virtue of its medium reveals the artist's identity unavoidably as a sexed subject, as an immobilized young and lovely woman, that has been long understood to prompt a particular, essentially masculine form of spectatorial gaze. So how then should we think about Czełkowska's *Theme*, in which she offers the viewer an image of the seemingly immobilized artist who happens to be a beautiful woman? As it happens, all of Czełkowska's sculptural work is permeated with references to self-portraiture, and to the face, even in their most abstracted versions such as *Self-Portrait* and the 1964 *Blue Head – Self-Portrait* (*Niebieska głowa – Autoportret*).[5] In the exhibition of *Wall* (*Ściana*), for example, a cloth-wrapped and twine-bound plaster head was strategically positioned on the floor between the constructed wall bearing her painted head-like forms and its facing structure of bolted multiple stretchers. If the identical multiple plaster heads, as in *Table* (*Stół*), bespeak anonymity, repetition, seriality, or mass production, perhaps the wrapped head implies a willed and wilful effacement, a shrouded or hidden identity that is unavailable to an Other's regard. In which case, the theme, or *a* theme in Czełkowska's work, might be interpreted as a dialectic movement between the particularities of subjective identity – of which the assignment of gender is a fundamental element – and an aesthetic ambition to surmount or sublimate this in the material and objective substance of art, an art that positions itself outside the bonds of the social, the sexual, and the political.

[1] An echo of this image is present in the work titled ***Drawing – Sculpture*** (***Rysunek – rzeźba***) from 1969, suggestive of the idea that the artist used the black and white image as reference for her drawing. It is therefore possible that the photograph was made a couple of years earlier (1968 or 1969).

[2] In much of my work on women artists, I maintain a general distinction between the art historical genre of the self-portrait and the more flexible and open-ended category of self-representation. Where the former definition pivots on the notion of an individual and unique identity, the latter notion may describe either a subversion of identity (for example, the deployment of masquerade) or a subversion of gender identity as contingent, fictitious, collective, or performative. See for example, Abigail Solomon-Godeau, "The Woman Who Never Was: Self-Representation, Photography and First Wave Feminist Art", in Cornelia Butler and Lisa Gabrielle Mark (eds.), ***WACK!: Art and the Feminist Revolution*** (Cambridge, Mass.: MIT Press, 2007).

[3] Ewa Opałka, "Why the Ruthless Absolute? Between Dematerialisation and the Flesh — the phenomenon of Wanda Czełkowska's sculptures", in Ewa Opałka, Jennifer Moore-Tymowska (eds.), ***Wanda Czełkowska. Retrospection***, exhibition catalogue (Warsaw: National Museum, 2017), 41.

[4] This distinction was first formulated by the American philosopher Charles Sanders Peirce in 1867. With a third entity he called the symbol, he defined each term according to its relation to what it represented. The icon (for instance, a portrait or a diagram) ***resembles or imitates*** its object, but an index is made by the object itself. Thus, a footprint is the material imprint of a foot, a fingerprint the imprint of the finger. Because an analogue photograph is produced by the automatic action of light on a light-sensitive surface, its semiotic status is that of ***both*** icon (any image) ***and*** index (a trace).

[5] The reference comes from Grubba-Thiede's reconstruction of Czełkowska's exhibition history, in this case, a painting and sculpture show mounted in 2001 in Kraków at the Krypta Gallery entitled ***Face***.

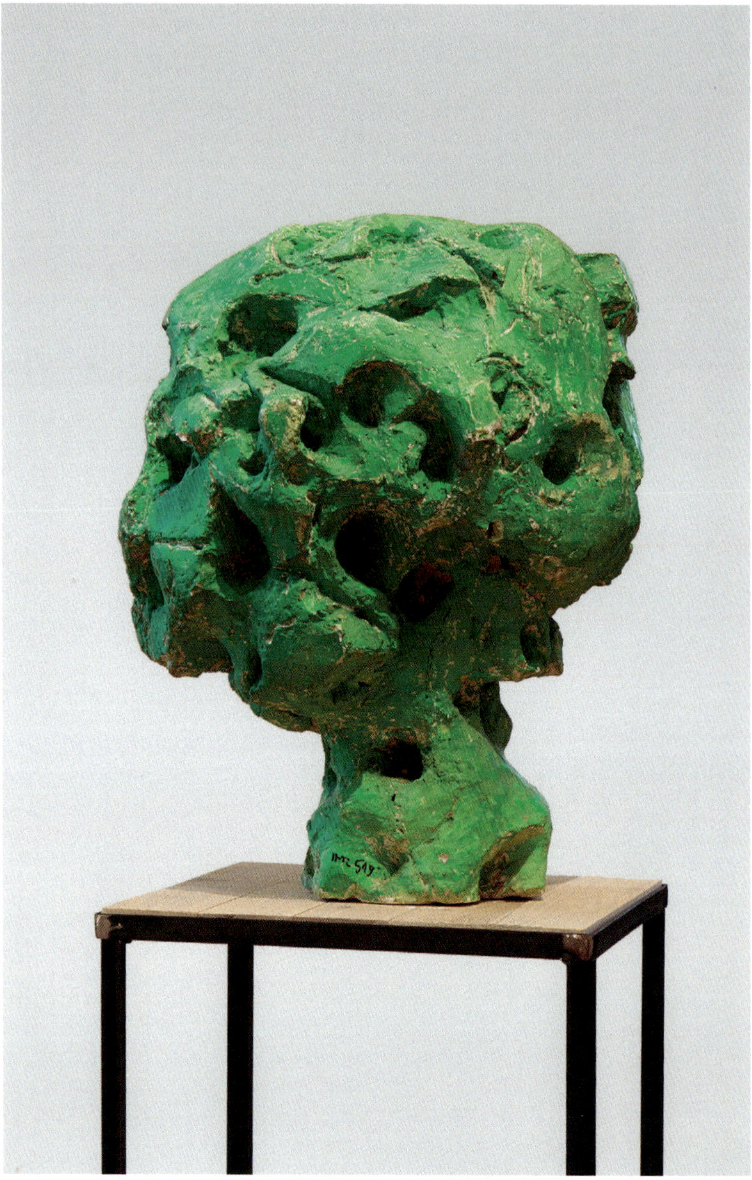

Sculptural Heads and Feminist Minds

Charlotte Matter

In the late 1960s and early 1970s, Wanda Czełkowska created a series of enigmatic head sculptures. Their shapes and surfaces are cluttered all over with bumps, cavities, and holes, leading the spectator's gaze to wander restlessly over them in search of something that might pass for an eye, a nose, or a mouth; something recognizable to hold on. But the explanation-seeking gaze is given no relief as any hint of familiarity dissolves upon closer inspection. These heads are elusive yet not formless – they are just defying any hasty categorization. Czełkowska made her head sculptures from plaster, an inexpensive material easy to work with that she had been using since the 1950s. She would often paint over the plaster, giving her works the appearance of a different materiality. The earthy *Pink Head* (*Różowa głowa*, 1962), for example, evokes fired clay, while the dark *Blue Head* (*Niebieska głowa*, 1967) is reminiscent of iron. *Green Head* (*Zielona głowa*, 1973), on the other hand, does not sit comfortably within such material associations (fig. 1). It is most akin to raw malachite, a mineral formerly used as a pigment in decoration and occasionally in sculpture, though not one of the traditional materials of European sculpture to which Czełkowska mostly referred. This green head – as well as a second one created towards the end of her life – somehow stands out as an "alien".[1] Above all, however, it ties in with Czełkowska's ongoing engagement with heads, which runs throughout her entire oeuvre, whether in her sculptures, drawings, and even her photographic works. Due the scarcity of sources and in the absence of a conclusive statement by the artist, one can only speculate about the meaning of all these heads, but it is well worth considering them against the background of a concurrent feminist preoccupation with heads, and in relation to the works of other artists of her time.

1. Wanda Czełkowska, *Green Head* (*Zielona głowa*), 1973, plaster and paint, 57 × 43 × 46 cm. Courtesy of National Museum in Kraków

Czełkowska's early heads, such as the plaster cast of a woman with sharp features and braided hair (*Untitled*, 1950; fig. 4 p. 123), evoked idealized figurations in the spirit of socialist realism. Yet, her emphasis on materiality and manufacturing, manifested in her choice to leave visible the traces of the modelling process instead of smoothing out the skin surface, already suggested a conceptual approach beyond a mere conventional interest in the classical genre of the bust. Over time, her sculptures became increasingly expressive, leading to the abstracted heads with their hollows and bumps from the late 1960s onwards. Because of their massive dimensions, there is something monstrous and rather threatening about them, but they also appear like wounded and abused figures into which something or someone has penetrated and left gaping holes. Czełkowska's pierced and hollowed heads might be read as joining the ranks of the violent depictions of disfigured or severed heads that abound in European art and cultural history, many of whom can – or indeed must – be questioned in terms of gendered power dynamics. The myth of Medusa is quite exemplary of this: as punishment for her own rape, she was cursed and transformed into a snake-haired creature whose gaze could turn anyone to stone. Medusa was then beheaded in her sleep by the half-god Perseus, who proceeded to use her severed head as a weapon, thus empowering himself from the power of the woman he had slain. As feminist scholars have shown, the serpentine head of Medusa remains one of the most frequently invoked images when it comes to perpetuating misogynistic ideas and undermining powerful women.[2] On the other hand, it is precisely her strength that has made Medusa a felicitous figure for queer/feminist reappropriations. Already in the 1970s, philosopher Hélène Cixous suggested that the recasting of Medusa as a monstrous creature was related to the fear of female desire: if (cis) men would only dare to look Medusa in the eye, they would realize that she was not deadly, but indeed beautiful and laughing.[3] Perhaps Czełkowska's heads are also laughing in defiance. For what it's worth, a gorgeous photograph is preserved of the artist herself smiling radiantly beside her heads installed on *Table* (*Stół*, 1968–1971; fig. pp. 44–45), when it was first exhibited on the occasion of the 4th Kraków Meetings. Whether Czełkowska was aware of it or not, heads – especially severed ones – were very much on feminist minds at the time. While Cixous was musing about Medusa, the work of Italian painter Artemisia Gentileschi was in the process of being rediscovered; her depiction of Judith beheading Holofernes (c. 1620) might as well have been the poster child of the 1970s women's liberation movement, as a caption that accompanied Linda Nochlin's famous essay "Why Have There Been No Great Women Artists?" read.[4]

2–3. Nancy Grossman, *Untitled (Head)*, 1968, leather, wood, metal, 43.8 × 18.7 × 22.2 cm. Dallas Museum of Art, Dallas Art Association Purchase. Courtesy Dallas Museum of Art

Unlike the heads in the stories of Medusa or Judith, however, Czełkowska's heads are not readily ascribed within a gendered binary logic as either female or male. While she once described them as depicting "contemporary man, met

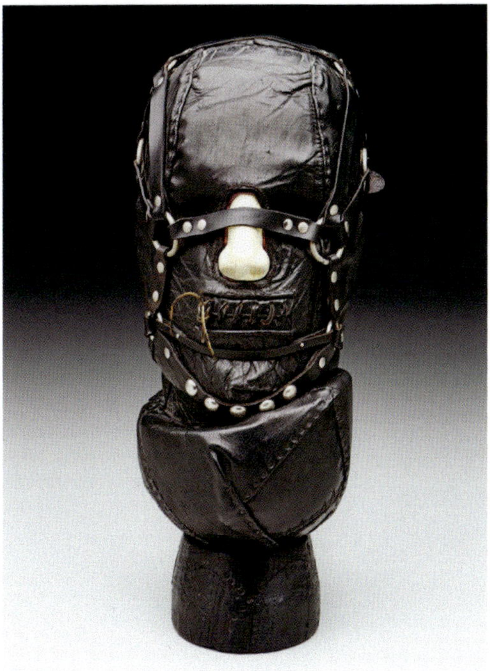 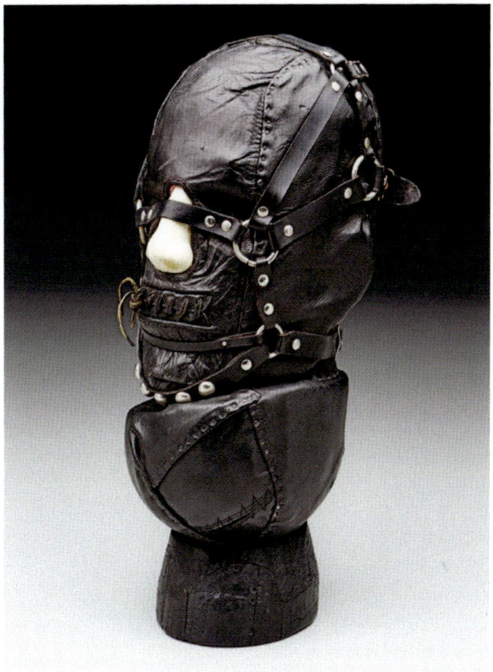

by chance", she later claimed they were a "Third Gender".[5] In this regard, they bring to mind the work of Nancy Grossman, another artist who was equally concerned with the figure of the head at around the same time, albeit on the other side of the Iron Curtain. Grossman created a series of evocative head sculptures from the late 1960s through to the 1980s which she carved from wood and covered almost entirely in black leather, often leaving only their nose exposed (figs. 2–4).[6] Due to their sizes and features, these heads are often read as masculine, but Grossman herself insisted on the fluidity of gender and in fact claimed they were self-portraits.[7] This, in turn, makes them all the more interesting in relation not only to Czełkowska's sculptural heads (raising the question of whether they, too, should be understood as inquiries into self-portraiture), but also to the startling photographic self-portrait in which Czełkowska has her head wrapped in cloth and her hands clasped around her neck, as if on the brink of (self) asphyxiation (fig. p. 37). The notion of sensory deprivation, similarly implied by Grossman's leather-clad heads, whose eyes are covered and whose mouths are sealed shut with straps, zippers, or laces, as in *Untitled* (1968; figs. 2–3), has led to them often being associated with kink. While Grossman did not discount sexual connotations, she also asserted that she was only made aware later of the affinities between her sculptures and erotic practices of domination and submission.[8] Grossman actually drew on a wide array of references, including Mexican Lucha Libre wrestlers, but also medical prostheses and protective masks, as photographs of her studio show.[9]

A similar dynamic is at play with the heads of Czełkowska. Depending on one's perspective, and just as crucially on their mode of display, they can be read as aggressive or vulnerable, dominant or submissive. But why confine them to an either/or? Take her large plaster cast heads: when positioned on an elevated plane and strictly arranged as a group of eighteen, as in *Table*, they appear massive and mighty. An entirely different impression unfolds on a series of photographs taken in the artist's studio. From main protagonists on top of the table, the heads have literally become subordinates and are relegated underneath. Apparently, they occasionally served as table legs when Czełkowska hosted dinner parties in her studio, until they were acquired by the National Museum in Kraków in 1983.[10] In the photographs showing the remnants of such a party, a square tabletop is precariously positioned on top of four sculptures, the corners barely resting on the tip of their foreheads (fig. p. 51). Scattered on the white tablecloth are numerous used glasses, a few plates, a hefty, half-eaten cake, a vase of pale roses, an overflowing ashtray, and empty bottles of red wine and vodka. Candles are still burning, as if the guests had only just left the table. And yet, the pictures seem strangely staged. Did the

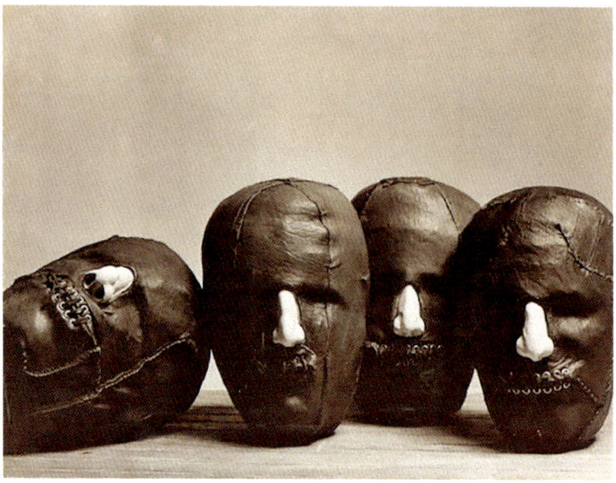

4. Nancy Grossman, sculpture, Cordier and Ekstom, photograph by Richard Avedon

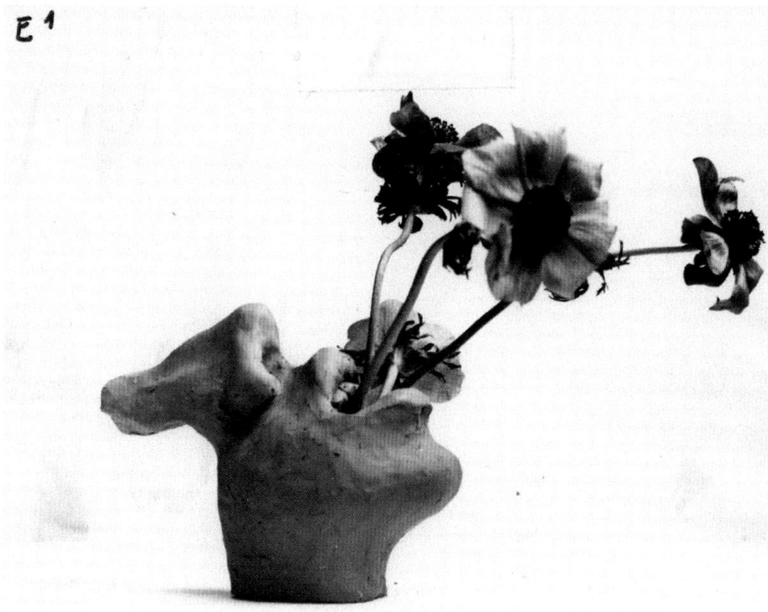

5. Alina Szapocznikow, *Ceramika I*, 1965, terracotta and flowers

party take place at all? Without visible guests nor any chairs where they would have sat on, the question arises as to whom the meal was set out for in the first place – and whether it is not the heads themselves who are celebrating a feast. At any rate, the four of them are facing each other, as if mischievously defying their subordination in a secret congregation under the table. Such is the case with all of Czełkowska's heads: they resist being pinned down and seem to lead a mysterious life of their own. They are odd, vulnerable, and intimidating at once, and thus uncomfortable, but there is also something exhilarating about them. Czełkowska's nonchalance in dealing with these sculptures, which she converted from artwork to utility object (and back again), somehow resonates with the works of other artists who were simultaneously exploring the frictions between art and commodity in relation to the body. Alina Szapocznikow, for example, whom Czełkowska incidentally knew, conceived a series of lamp sculptures in the mid-1960s from polyester casts of body parts, such as lips, breasts, and phalli, that are uncanny, sensuous, and funny. Szapocznikow called these objects "awkward", which may just as well apply to Czełkowska's cumbersome plaster heads.[11] In terms of motif and materiality, the latter also share affinities with further works by Szapocznikow. In a ceramic series from 1965, fragments of figurative yet slightly distorted heads serve as vases, once again hovering in an ambiguous state between empowerment and abuse; the flowers that stick out of their gaping heads and mouths might imply either joy or an act of violation (fig. 5). "The head is where the power is", Grossman observed in 1975 in reference to her sculptures.[12] It is precisely for this reason that heads seem to have occupied the minds of so many feminist researchers and artists throughout the 1960s and 1970s. In a departure from essentialist representations of the body that were prevalent at the time, the head offered, in a crucial way, an opportunity to think about gendered power dynamics beyond binary constructs. In this and many other respects, the heads of Czełkowska, Grossman, and Szapocznikow are certainly worth staying on our minds.

[1] Green, as a skin colour, being commonly associated with representations of extraterrestrial beings in popular culture, this work might possibly be read in light of the widespread interest of artists in science fiction at the time and, more specifically, Czełkowska's acquaintance with the writings of Stanisław Lem. On the latter, see David Crowley's text in this book.

[2] See, among others, Mary Beard, W*omen & Power: A Manifesto. Updated* (London: London Review of Books, 2018).

[3] Hélène Cixous, "Le Rire de la Méduse" [1975], in *Le Rire de la Méduse et autres ironies* (Paris: Galilée, 2010), 54.

[4] Linda Nochlin, "Why Have There Been No Great Women Artists?", in Thomas B. Hess and Elizabeth C. Baker (eds.), *Art and Sexual Politics: Women's Liberation, Women Artists, and Art History* (New York: Collier Books, 1973), 11.

[5] Richard Demarco, "A Conversation with Wanda", *Umbrella*, June 1972, n.p. Reprinted in this book pages 111–115. See also Wanda Czełkowska in conversation with Anke Kempkes and Ewa Opałka, Warsaw, June 2016, quoted in Anke Kempkes, "The Third Gender: Wanda Czełkowska and Rosemarie Castoro – Life in the Studio", in Ewa Opałka, Jennifer Moore-Tymowska (eds.), *Wanda Czełkowska: Retrospection*, exhibition catalogue (Warsaw: National Museum, 2017), 55.

[6] As David Getsy thoughtfully observes, even these seemingly unveiled parts do not actually disclose the wooden core of the sculpture, since they are coated with a glossy layer of epoxy. David Getsy, *Abstract Bodies: Sixties Sculpture in the Expanded Field of Gender* (New Haven–London: Yale University Press, 2015), 181.

[7] Ibid., 147 and 202.

[8] Nancy Grossman in conversation with Cindy Nemser, in *Art Talk: Conversations with Twelve Women Artists* (New York: Charles Scribner's Sons, 1975), 342.

[9] The photographs, taken by Richard Avedon in late 1970, are reproduced in Getsy, *Abstract Bodies*, 190.

[10] I would like to thank Matylda Taszycka for providing me with this information.

[11] Alina Szapocznikow, "The roots of my work…" [April 1972], in *Alina Szapocznikow*, trans. Tim Nevill, exh. cat., Kunstparterre, Munich (Bielefeld: Kerber, 2011), 31. In the French original, first published in the catalogue of her posthumous retrospective organized by Pierre Restany, Szapocznikow uses the word "maladroit", which may also be translated as "clumsy" or "inexpert". *Alina Szapocznikow, 1926–1973: Tumeurs, herbier*, exh. cat., Musée d'art moderne de la Ville de Paris (Paris: Éditions du dialogue, 1973), n.p.

[12] Nancy Grossman in conversation with Cindy Nemser, in *Art Talk*, 346.

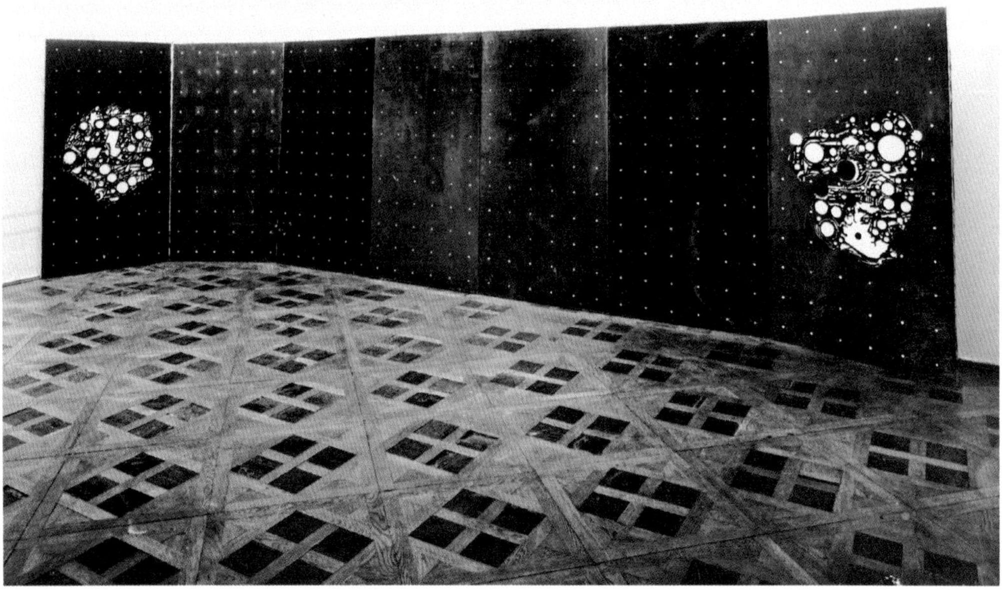

Black Frieze

David Crowley

In the version photographed here, Wanda Czełkowska's *Black Frieze* (*Czarny fryz*; fig. 1) takes the form of seven canvas panels organized in tessellated ranks. Pitch black, each screen is punctuated by dozens of regularly-placed white "pin-points". This is a grid; the archetypal form of "modern aesthetic production" according to Rosalind Krauss, one that "in the overall regularity of its organization, it is the result not of imitation, but of aesthetic decree".[1] In the twentieth century, modernist artists turned to grid to assert the autonomous and autotelic character of their art. And, in so doing, demonstrated their modernity. In the panels which form the flanks of this version of Czełkowska's *Black Frieze*, the regular grid of dots is overcome by a bubbling design. Lacking cues to scale, what these whorling patterns might depict is open to speculation. Perhaps they suggest the psychedelic appearance of liquid crystals under the microscope or are schematic representations of cloudy galaxies viewed through a telescope. Whether or not these patterns refer to vast macrocosms, the size of the work was important to the sculptor. Of her better-known installation *Table* (*Stół*, 1971), she said "scale is an important means of expression … it is not true that something very small can have big meaning".[2] More than five meters wide and almost as tall as the artist herself, this version of *Black Frieze* fills the sightline, with Czełkowska accentuating this effect by installing it in a corner. Standing on the floor, these canvases eschewed painting's conventional attachment to the wall.

1. Wanda Czełkowska, *Black Frieze* (*Czarny fryz*), 1968–1969–1971–1973, tempera, acrylic, drawing on canvas, 148 × 567 cm. Courtesy of the artist's estate

Black Frieze is little known. It was rarely exhibited and only occasionally reproduced.[3] First conceived in 1968, *Black Frieze* has been a "shape-shifter".[4] Exhibited in a Second Kraków Group show in the Krzysztofory Gallery in 1973, it was formed from just three panels. And more than forty years later, Czełkowska was still adapting the work in her studio, replacing the central panel for another that was white and supported a grid of tiny lights. When interviewed, Czełkowska offered few reflections on her intentions for it. In a wide-ranging conversation with Ewa Opałka held from 2014 to 2019, the artist was somewhat taciturn, accepting her interlocuter's suggestion that *Black Frieze* was a transitional work, one which anticipated Czełkowska's declarations – made in the early 1970s – about the "elimination of shape" in favour of a conception of sculpture as the organization of space or an event.[5] The bubbling patterns also resemble her drawings of "heads" made at the end of the 1960s (figs. 2–3), and so suggest a phase in the long "de-anthropomorphization" of her art that art historians have charted.[6] Heads which once were like fleshy plaster forms in Czełkowska's hands were now abstract lines and look more a section of a brain than a portrait. While the idea that *Black Frieze* was a switch in the artist's career is surely convincing, the question of what meanings might be attached to this enigmatic work remains unanswered. This short essay is a first throw of that dice.

Czełkowska associated geometry with affect, once declaring: "Sculpture is a structure of space, it's mathematics. Mathematics is a form of defined feeling".[7] This seems counter-intuitive. What kind of affect attaches to

2–3. Wanda Czełkowska, *Untitled*, c. 1968, charcoal, exhibited during the artist's solo show at Galeria Współczesna in Warsaw, January 1969. Courtesy of the artist's estate

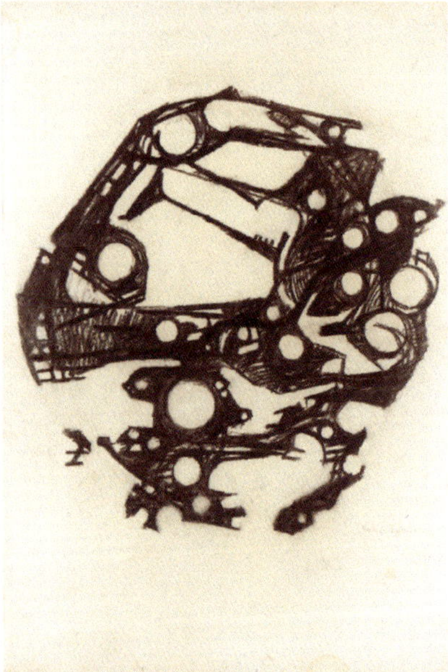

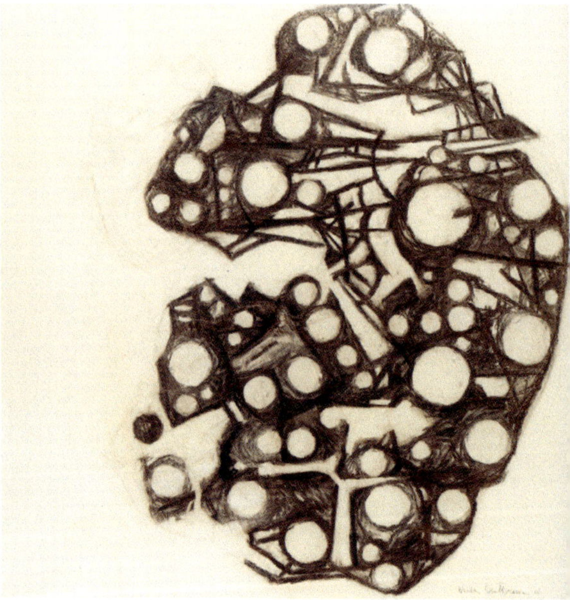

counting or measuring, describing the shapes or arrangements of objects or any other mathematical operation? But, Czełkowska was by no means alone in making this connection: after all, the pioneers of the modernist abstraction – Malevich and Mondrian – imagined geometry as entry points into ideas about being, spirit or the universe. And, of course, the grid suggests infinity, it regular order extending forever. Krauss calls this capacity to combine physics with metaphysics, the grid's "mythic power": "It makes us able to thing we are dealing with the concrete (or sometimes science, or logic) while at the same time it provides us with a release into belief (or illusion or fiction)".[8] Might *Black Frieze* be understood as search for what Czełkowska's called "feeling" in mathematics? It certainly reflects her long-standing interest in science and philosophy. In 1959, she conceived a scheme for an environment in which the effects of the Earth's gravity could be suspended. The viewer would enter into a large cube in which a spinning and hovering sphere would produce a sound much like breathing. Czełkowska sought out physicists in Kraków to establish the feasibility of her idea.[9] The idea of anti- and artificial-gravity had considerable appeal at the time, with sci-fi novels like Andrzej Ostoja's *Aspasia* (*Aspazja*, 1958; fig. 4) and popular science magazines in Poland – like elsewhere – speculating on the design of future space craft equipped with antigravity devices that would make rockets redundant or of rotating platforms which could generate their own gravitational forces in deep space. While Czełkowska's early project remains little more than a memory, it seems like a presentiment of some of the "impossible" techno-utopian schemes which were to form a branch of conceptual art in Poland in the late 1960s. Artist Jerzy Rosołowicz, for instance, conceived the *Neutrdrom* (1967), a 100m-high inverted cone, as an early expression of his concept of "neutral activity".[10] Travelling in an elevator at the core of the tower, visitors would rise through darkness into the dazzling luminosity of the circular platform on top of the structure. Standing on a mirror, they would be bathed in a cosmic symphony of light. Others could enter into a 35m diameter sphere rolling around the foot of the tower. Filled with light and sound, this was to be a closed universe of sensation. Both Czełkowska and Rosołowicz's fantastic projects were extrapolations of the promise of new "clean" technologies – cybernetics, artificial intelligence and computing,

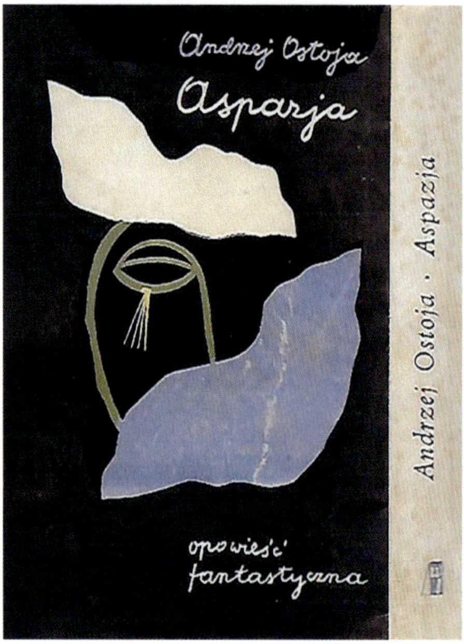

4. Andrzej Ostoja, *Aspazja*, Wydawnictwo Łódzkie, Łódź, 1958. Cover design and illustrations by Stanisław Fijałkowski

and electronics – that commentators on both sides of the East-West divide declared to be the stimulus for the "Scientific-Technological Revolution" then underway. For artists electrified by the new inventions of the 1960s, the challenge was not necessarily how to "apply" science to practical tasks but how to elicit feeling from it.

First conceived in 1968, *Black Frieze* was made at a time when much of the world seemed to be looking skyward to witness the exploration of the outer space by satellites and astronauts. Constellations of mythical animals and gods now formed a background for humanity's attempts to colonize space. With so many looking up, it is hard not to see *Black Frieze* as having some kind of cosmological aspect. In it, space – and the Earth's place in it – is unfamiliar. The stars have been ordered as a grid: is this the will of an omnipotent creator or perhaps the attempts by humankind to lay coordinates over the emptiness of space? And if this is a fantastic map, where is the Archimedean Point from which one might commence one's journey? Where is the pole star?

In this, *Black Frieze* seems less an engagement with the science and technologies then delivering astronauts and cosmonauts into space than with their mysteries. And perhaps particular affinities can be drawn between *Black Frieze* and the ideas of Stanisław Lem whose brilliant and philosophical articles and books were widely read in Poland in the 1960s (and counted Czełkowska among their readers). *Solaris* (1961), his most famous novel, describes a sentient planet, albeit one that appears to be indifferent or resistant to human attempts at communication or to read its "thoughts" (fig. 5). The data from automated machines scanning Solaris fails to cast light on the planet-being, and the scientists in their research station can do little more than observe the patterns which seem to form on its ocean surface. What they call "symmetriads" – fiery balls – emerge from the regular waves of the ocean to form massive baroque columns above the surface of Solaris; "mimoids" excrete dust to form massive facsimiles of anything in their vicinity. When, in Lem's words, a mimoid "starts an amazing hyper-production", an unforgettable spectacle develops "… to the delight of the abstract painter and the despair of the scholar who tries in vain to understand anything of the processes taking place".[11] Hypothesis after hypothesis offered by scientists to explain these perplexing phenomena fall short, not least because the symmetriads sometimes "illustrate" and sometimes contradict the laws of physics. "These hypotheses", Lem writes, "brought out from the grave and revived one of the oldest philosophical problems – the relationship of matter and spirit, consciousness."[12] This relationship might well be understood as

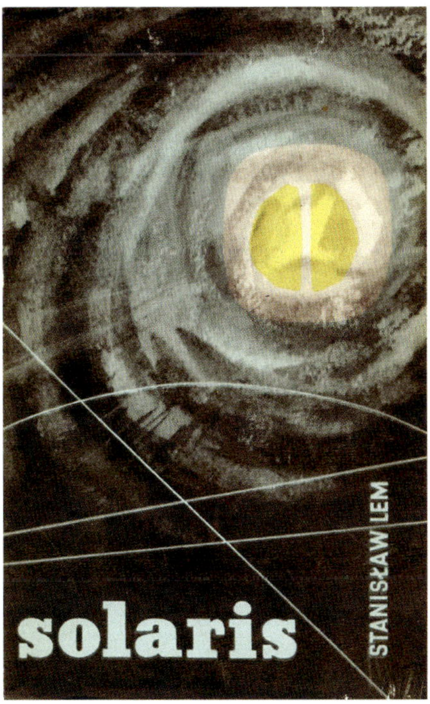

5. Stanisław Lem, *Solaris*, Wydawnictwo Ministerstwa Obrony Narodowej, Warsaw, 1961 (first edition). Cover design by Konstanty Maria Sopoćko

Czełkowska's concern, too. In *Black Frieze* she seems to be asking how might the mind conceive of the infinity of space, and perhaps even to know itself. *Solaris* expresses Lem's indictment of his own profession, namely, the hubris of science fiction writers and film-makers who imagine the cosmos populated with human-like beings and earth-like landscapes: "Thanks to time travel and FTL [faster than light – DC] the cosmos has acquired such qualities as domesticate it in an exemplary manner for story telling purposes", he wrote, "but at the same time it has lost its strange, icy sovereignty. SF doesn't know of the cosmos of colliding galaxies, the invisible stars sucked in by the curvature of space, the pulsating magnetic fields".[13] *Black Frieze* is by no means an illustration of *Solaris*, or any of Lem's other works (and one suspects that Czełkowska would have been offended by the suggestion). Nevertheless, she may well have been one of his delighted abstract artists, and the bubbling designs of the flanking panels of *Black Frieze* were her own symmetriads. As an invitation to scan the night sky, *Black Frieze* sought the sublime qualities of deep space. And the contrasting rhythms of the pulsing dots and the bubbling effervescence of the cosmic clouds seem to separate the known and the unknown, calculation and consciousness, or spirit and matter. Holding on to what Lem called the Cosmos's "strange, icy sovereignty", *Black Frieze* invited feeling, albeit of a perplexing kind.

[1] Rosalind Krauss, "Grids", *October* 9, Summer 1979, 50.
[2] Richard Demarco, "A Conversation with Wanda", in *Umbrella*, 1972, n.p. Reprinted in this book pages 111–115.
[3] It appears, for instance, alongside Jan Michalski's insightful catalogue essay "Rzeźby, idee Czełkowskiej" but is not discussed. See *Wanda Czełkowska. Elegia. Przypomnienie po latach* (Kraków: Galeria Zderzak, 1990), 3–4.
[4] It appears to have shifted names too. In the catalogue of the exhibition *Artyści z Krakowa* (Zachęta National Gallery, Warsaw, August–September 1993), Czełkowska's work is entitled *Nostalgia*. In later years she reverted back to calling it *Black Frieze*.
[5] Ewa Opałka prepared this material for publication in 2019 but it remains unpublished. I thank her for sharing this material with me.
[6] See Dorota Grubba-Thiede, *Nurt figuracji w powojennej rzeźbie polskiej* (Warsaw–Toruń: Tako, 2016), 216–222.
[7] Cited in Dorota Grubba-Thiede, *Medytacje Fibonacciego + sztruksowy zając wobec Katarzyny Kobro (1898-1951)* (Sopot: Państwowa Galeria Sztuki, 2018), 25.
[8] Krauss, "Grids", 54.
[9] Dorota Grubba-Thiede, "... prosta nieskończona ... Wanda Czełkowska, Krystian Jarnuszkiewicz, Andrzej Wojciechowski", *Sztuka i Dokumentacja* 6, 2012, 165.
[10] For Rosołowicz's own description of the project, see *Sympozjum Plastyczne Wrocław '70* (Wrocław: Ośrodek Teatru Otwartego "Kalambur", 1983), 123–129.
[11] Stanisław Lem, *Solaris* (Kraków: Wydawnictwo Literackie, 2002), 184–185.
[12] Ibid., 40.
[13] Stanisław Lem, "Cosmology and Science Fiction", *Science Fiction Studies* 4, no. 2, July 1977, 108.

Author Biographies

Émilie Bouvard

Émilie Bouvard is an art historian and curator of French art heritage. In 2017, she defended a thesis entitled *La Violence de l'art des femmes, 1958-1978. Surréalisme, psychanalyse et féminisme*, and published several articles on Louise Bourgeois, Niki de Saint-Phalle, Alina Szapocznikow, and more recently Ghada Amer (MUCEM, 2022). She is currently working on an essay based on her doctoral research, set to be published in 2024 by Éditions Gallimard, Paris. Presently, she is the Director of Collections and Scientific Programme at the Fondation Giacometti, after having worked for six years at the Musée National Picasso-Paris. She curated the exhibitions *Picasso Guernica* (2018), *Picasso. Chefs-d'œuvre !* (2019) at the Musée National Picasso-Paris, as well as *Alberto Giacometti. Le réel merveilleux* (Grimaldi Forum, 2021) and *Alberto Giacometti/Barbara Chase-Riboud* (Institut Giacometti, 2021; MoMA, 2023), and has edited several works on these two artists. She regularly curates contemporary art exhibitions.

Mathieu Copeland

Mathieu Copeland is a curator, lecturer and publisher. He develops a curatorial praxis that seeks to subvert the traditional role of exhibitions and renew our perceptions of them. Copeland co-curated the exhibition *VOIDS. A Retrospective* at the Centre Pompidou, Paris and the Kunsthalle, Bern (2009), and co-edited the celebrated anthology *VOIDS*. Among many others, he curated *A Choreographed Exhibition* at the Kunsthalle St Gallen (2007), *Soundtrack for an Exhibition* (2006), *Alan Vega* (2009) and *Gustav Metzger* (2013) at the Musée d'Art Contemporain, Lyon, and *A Mental Mandala* at MUAC, Mexico City (2013). He initiated and curated the series *EAC* (2004–2006), *A Spoken Word Exhibitions* (2007–ongoing), *Reprise* (2011–ongoing) and the *Exhibitions to Hear Read* (2010–on going, presented in 2013 at MoMA, New York.) His recent exhibitions include

Exhibition Cuttings at the Hermès Foundation in Tokyo (April–July 2021), and *A Staged Exhibition* at La Ferme du Buisson (September 2021), *The Exhibition of a Dream* at the Gulbenkian Foundation (2017), and *A Retrospective of Closed Exhibitions* at the Kunsthalle Fribourg (2016). Curator-at-Large at the Rockbund Art Museum, Shanghai (2020–2021).

David Crowley

David Crowley teaches at the National College of Art and Design, Dublin. He is a historian and curator with an interest in Eastern Europe under communist rule. He has curated various exhibitions including *Cold War Modern* at the Victoria and Albert Museum in 2008–9 (co-curated with Jane Pavitt); *Sounding the Body Electric. Experimental Art and Music in Eastern Europe* at Muzeum Sztuki, Łódź, 2012 and Calvert 22, London, 2013 and *Notes from the Underground. Music and Alternative Art in Eastern Europe, 1968-1994* at Muzeum Sztuki, Łódź, 2017 and Akademie Der Künste in Berlin in 2018 (both co-curated with Daniel Muzyczuk). His next exhibition will be *Henryk Stażewski: Late Style at* Muzeum Sztuki, Łódź in 2023.

June Geddes

June Geddes is an art historian based in London. After a career in information, research, and marketing, she returned to academia and received her PhD from The Courtauld Institute of Art in November 2022. Her PhD thesis, *Richard Demarco: networking Scotland to the international avant-garde*, was based on the Richard Demarco Archives in Edinburgh and focused on artists from Central and Eastern Europe from the late 1960s to the mid 1990s.

Antonina Gugała

Antonina Gugała is an artist, curator and researcher, living and working in Warsaw. Her practice revolves around the medium of photography. Professional photography is an important theme in her work. In 2022, she curated the exhibition *Celina Osiecka. Photography Services* (Praga Museum of Warsaw, 2022). As a researcher on demand she has collaborated with numerous cultural agents. Her works have been exhibited in Poland and abroad. She is assistant curator of *Wanda Czełkowska: Art Is Not Rest* exhibition at Muzeum Susch.

Amelia Jones

Amelia Jones is Robert A. Day Professor at Roski School of Art & Design, USC. Publications include *Seeing Differently: A History and Theory of Identification and the Visual Arts* (2012) and *Otherwise: Imagining Queer Feminist Art Histories,* co-edited with Erin Silver (2016). Her catalogue *Queer Communion: Ron Athey* (2020) was listed among the "Best Art Books 2020" in the *NY Times*, and the curated show was listed among Top Ten 2021 exhibitions in *Artforum* (December 2021). Her book entitled *In Between Subjects: A Critical Genealogy of Queer Performance* was published in 2021. Her current work addresses the structural racism and neoliberalism of the twenty-first century art world and university.

Charlotte Matter

Charlotte Matter is an art historian. She is a postdoc researcher at the University of Zurich, where she teaches and coordinates the Master's program in Art History in a Global Context. Her doctoral thesis explored the use of plastics in 1960s and 1970s art from a feminist perspective. She is currently investigating the notion of collectivity in art through the lens of intersectionality. She is a founding member of CARAH – Collective for Anti-Racist Art History and co-initiator of the research project "Rethinking Art History through Disability", which aims to rethink the intersections of disability theory and art history through the lens of the non-normative body.

Abigail Solomon-Godeau

Abigail Solomon-Godeau is a critic, curator, historian of photography, feminist. Professor Emerita in art history, University of California, lives and works in Paris. She is the author of *Photography at the Dock: Essays on Photographic Histories, Institutions, and Practices* (1991), *Male Trouble: A Crisis in Representation* (1997) and *Rosemary Laing* (2012). Her essays on photography, art history, contemporary art and feminism are widely anthologized.

Agnieszka Tarasiuk

Agnieszka Tarasiuk is culture manager, researcher, curator. Author of numerous exhibitions and performances as well as lectures and texts published in catalogues and academic publications. At the beginning of the century, after graduating from the Warsaw Academy of Fine Arts, she organized unconventional artistic ventures in the remote countryside of the Polish-Byelorussian border, creating the space for an avant-garde art very far from cultural centres. In the years 2008–2011, she worked as a director of The Art Residential Center in The Wigry National Park. From 2011 to 2021, she was the chief curator of the Xawery Dunikowski Museum of Sculpture, a division of the National Museum in Warsaw. While managing the biggest Polish collection of classical sculptures, she combined traditional museum practices with experimental curatorial strategies. From January 2022, she has been the head of the Collection Department of the Museum of Modern Art in Warsaw.

Matylda Taszycka

Matylda Taszycka is Head of Research Programmes at AWARE: Archives of Women Artists, Research and Exhibitions where she leads initiatives and directs research on women artists from the 19th and 20th centuries. Among other things, she is in charge of the planning of conferences in partnership with museums and universities, as well as the coordination of the AWARE Prize for women artists. A graduate from the École du Louvre in Paris, she worked at the Monnaie de Paris, before joining the Polish Institute of Paris as Head of Visual Arts. Taszycka is also an independent curator and art critic. She is the curator of *Wanda Czełkowska: Art Is Not Rest* exhibition at Muzeum Susch.

Sarah Wilson

Sarah Wilson is professor of Modern and Contemporary Art at The Courtauld Institute of Art, University of London. She is an art historian and curator whose interests extend from post-war and Cold War Europe and the USSR to contemporary global art. Her major publications include *Paris, Capital of the Arts, 1900-1968* (Royal Academy, 2002), *The Visual World of French Theory: Figurations, The Visual World of French Theory II: interventions* (in preparation).